THE PROBATION
AND
AFTER-CARE SERVICE

THIRD EDITION

Edited on behalf of
the National Association
of Probation Officers

by

JOAN F. S. KING, M.B.E., M.A.

Senior Assistant in Research,
Institute of Criminology, University of Cambridge

LONDON

BUTTERWORTHS

1969

ENGLAND: BUTTERWORTH & CO. (PUBLISHERS) LTD.
              LONDON: 88 Kingsway, W.C.2

AUSTRALIA: BUTTERWORTH & CO. (AUSTRALIA) LTD.
              SYDNEY: 20 Loftus Street
              MELBOURNE: 343 Little Collins Street
              BRISBANE: 240 Queen Street

CANADA: BUTTERWORTH & CO. (CANADA) LTD.
              TORONTO: 14 Curity Avenue, 374

NEW ZEALAND: BUTTERWORTH & CO. (NEW ZEALAND) LTD.
              WELLINGTON: 49/51 Ballance Street
              AUCKLAND: 35 High Street

SOUTH AFRICA: BUTTERWORTH & CO. (SOUTH AFRICA) LTD.
              DURBAN: 33/35 Beach Grove

©

Standard Book Number: 406 26461 9

Printed in Great Britain by
The Whitefriars Press Ltd., Tonbridge, Kent, England

DEDICATED
TO THE MEMORY OF
FRANK DAWTRY, O.B.E.

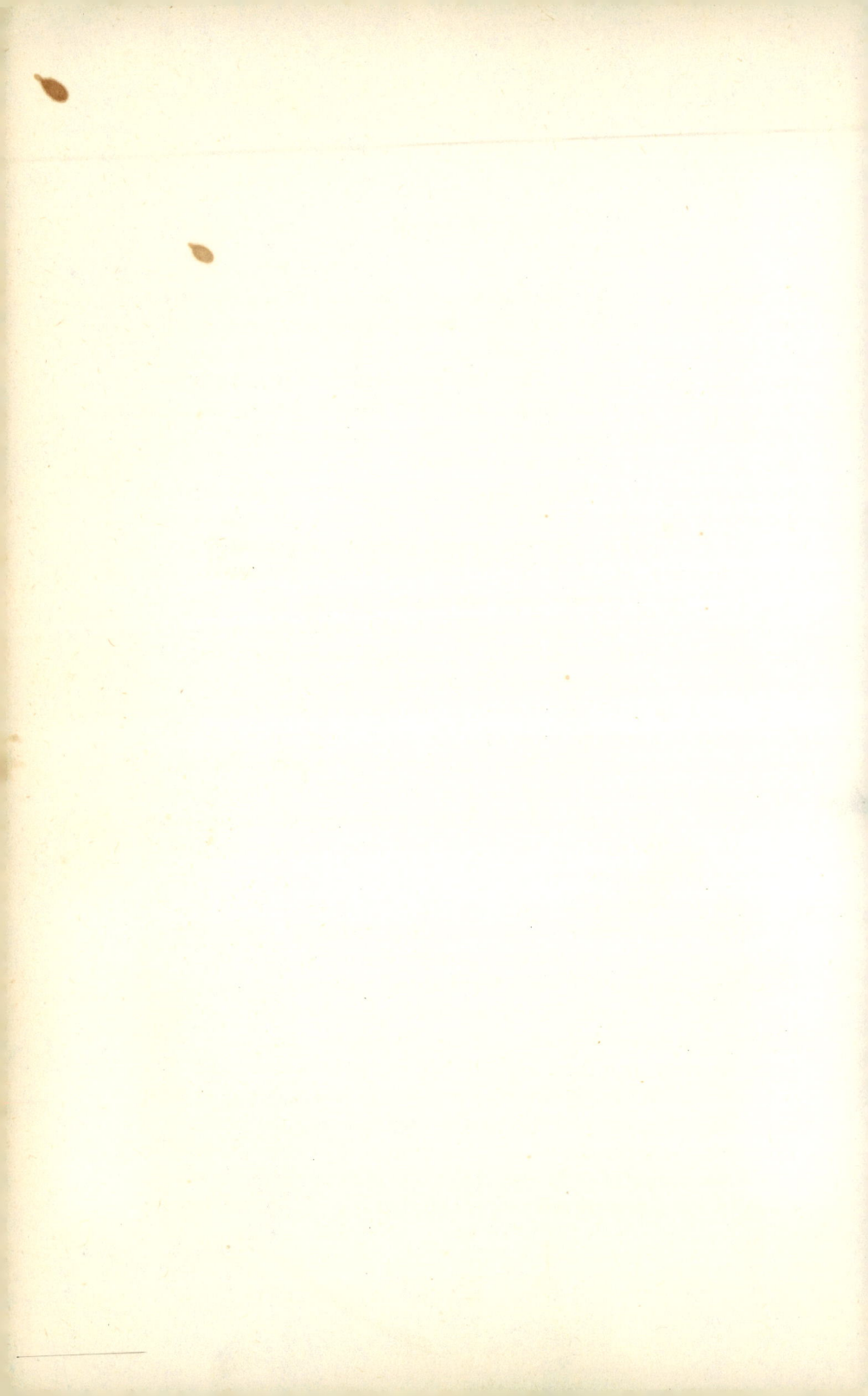

PREFACE

To attempt at this juncture to describe the role of the Probation and After-Care Service in England and Wales is very necessary but also very hazardous. It is necessary because during the past few years that role has been changing considerably. It is hazardous because in the next few years it may well change even more. New responsibilities are opening up, in the extension of reports to the Courts, of prison welfare and after-care. Old responsibilities are being handed on as the Children and Young Persons Bill prepares the way for Children's Departments to take over the care of most juvenile delinquents. For the future, there are the possibilities of more diversity in methods of working, with groups, hostels, volunteers and increased community co-operation reinforcing the traditional individual approach of casework. At the same time there are controversies about the future context of the service. Should it become part of comprehensive local authority social work departments such as those recommended by the Seebohm Committee? Or should it form the basis of a specialist, but expanded, social service of the courts, or of the penal system, or of both? Should its organization continue to be local or become regional or national? All aspects of the work and training of probation officers are being affected, and are likely to be affected still more, by changes and by questions such as these.

The first version of this book was published in 1958 under the title of *The Probation Service*. Even then it was recognized that, though the service had much learning and experience behind it, it had much new learning and experiment ahead, and that, at every turn, there were "new questions and new demands rather than traditional answers and rigid methods". The pace has become much hotter now. At every turn there are controversies and experiments in face of new demands and new ideas. For that very reason it is an exciting and challenging time for the service, calling for all the devotion of its founders combined with all the resources of modern knowledge.

It is not a time of consensus. On many matters there has not yet emerged any comprehensive survey of what is going on, still less any agreement on the way things should develop. This volume, like its forerunners, is based on the writings and opinions of serving probation officers. In a few cases it has been possible for one officer, with special experience, to deal with a topic single-handed. In many other cases, however, it has been necessary to combine, and sometimes contrast, the views and experience of several. It is hoped that this will at least provide a basis for looking at the service as it is now and for considering what it may become.

Thanks are due not only to the contributors listed on the next page but to many other members of the service, who have given their views in letters or discussion, or whose published articles and books have been referred to. In particular the editor would like to thank the prison welfare officers and other office and branch groups who went to so much trouble to help. Certainly the service does not lack those who are keenly and actively concerned to widen its experience and increase its usefulness.

JOAN F. S. KING

INSTITUTE OF CRIMINOLOGY,
UNIVERSITY OF CAMBRIDGE
August, 1969

ACKNOWLEDGEMENTS

The following are amongst the past and present members of the probation and after-care service who have contributed to this book:

Mr. R. S. Bailey

Mr. A. Bannerman

Mr. H. Barr

Mr. A. E. Bottons

Miss R. M. Braithwaite

Mr. J. P. Dunphy

Mr. S. R. Eshelby, M.B.E.

Miss D. M. Fletcher

Mr. W. A. Hallas

Mr. D. Haxby

Mr. W. L. Herbert

Mr. H. E. James, M.B.E.

Miss E. C. Murphy

Mr. D. S. Palmer

Mr. R. E. Piesse

Mr. D. J. Powell

Mr. S. Ratcliffe

Miss G. M. Stafford

Miss D. Sullivan

Miss J. Sullivan

Mr. C. Thomas

Mrs. B. E. Tunney

Mr. W. B. Utting

CONTENTS

CHAPTER   PAGE

1   THE BASIS OF THE SERVICE . . . 1

     1 Roots 1
     2 The Legal Basis of Probation 6
     3 The Legal Basis of Other Duties . . . 13
     4 The Social-Work Basis 20
     5 The Probation Officers 26
     6 Leadership 31
     7 Responses to Change 35

2   THE SERVICE AND PENAL INSTITUTIONS . 41

     1 Continuity 41
     2 Statutory After-Care of Young Offenders . . 44
     3 Parole 47
     4 Voluntary After-Care 53
     5 Social Work in Prisons 59
     6 Families of Offenders 70

3   THE SERVICE AND CIVIL CASES . . 72

     1 The Breaking Marriage 72
     2 The Children 77
     3 Who Else? 81

4   CASEWORK: PROBATION 83

     1 The Probation Officer as Caseworker . . 83
     2 The Probationers 84
     3 Principles of Casework 90
     4 The Casework Relationship 98
     5 The Processes of Casework 100
     6 The Tools of Casework 107

CHAPTER   PAGE

5 CASEWORK: OTHER SETTINGS   .   .   .   110
   1 Casework in Social Enquiries   .   .   .   110
   2 Casework in Prisons   113
   3 Casework in After-Care   119
   4 Casework with Prisoners' Families .   .   127
   5 Matrimonial Casework   131

6 WIDER INVOLVEMENT   .   .   .   136
   1 Voluntary Help   136
   2 Hostels   147
   3 Group Work   160

7 MEDICAL-SOCIAL PROBLEMS   .   .   168
   1 The Mentally Abnormal   .   .   .   168
   2 Alcoholics   175
   3 Drug Addicts   178

8 THE SERVICE AND THE COURTS   .   .   184
   1 A Continuing Relationship   .   .   .   184
   2 Social Enquiry Reports   .   .   .   185
   3 Supervision of Probationers   .   .   .   193

9 RELATIONS WITH THE COMMUNITY   .   200
   1 Relations with Other Social Services   .   200
   2 Conflicting Principles?   210
   3 Community Involvement   .   .   .   216

10 ADMINISTRATION   220
   1 The Administrators   220
   2 The Future   223
   3 Present Tasks   227
   4 The Grass-Roots   235

CHAPTER PAGE

11 THE MAKING OF PROBATION OFFICERS . 240

1 Is Training Necessary? 240
2 What Needs to be Taught? 241
3 Training and Recruitment 250
4 The Organization of Training . . . 254
5 Responsibility for Training 264
6 In-Service Training and Staff Development . 267

12 RESEARCH 274

13 THE NATIONAL ASSOCIATION OF PROBA-
TION OFFICERS 290

INDEX

CHAPTER I

THE BASIS OF THE SERVICE

THE probation and after-care service in this country has come to a time when it is having to look at itself anew, and to do so in a much wider context than in the past. It has to look at itself not only in terms of its own expanding duties but in terms of its changing relationship with other social services, with the penal system, with those engaged in research and in the planning of future policy, and with the community at large.

This preliminary chapter looks back over the past of the service, sometimes finding in its earliest days the seeds of some of its most modern pre-occupations. It traces, in broad outline, the way its functions, its methods and its structure have successfully responded to new knowledge and to social change. In later chapters the present situation, and its possible implications for the future, are examined in more detail. This chapter is by way of a preliminary survey of the whole in its historical perspective.

1   ROOTS

The Probation of Offenders Act 1907 contained all the basic provisions and principles of probation as we know it today, together with the germ of the probation service. It was both a culmination and a beginning. It marked the culmination of a series of experiments with informal devices for supervising offenders in the open as an alternative to imprisonment. It marked the beginning of a statutory responsibility for social work with offenders outside penal institutions, a responsibility which not only expanded to become, in itself, an important feature of the system of criminal justice but which in due course overflowed into other parts of that system: into the sentencing decisions of the courts and into the penal institutions.

Lord Samuel, who sponsored the original Bill, said half a century later that it had been envisaged not as a piece of machinery, but as a seed with a life of its own fed by its environment. Its roots have gone deep into its native soil, but from the first they have not gone in one direction alone. The plant owes its sturdiness and stability to the fact that it draws strength at once from the legal system and from social work. Each of these made its contribution to the original seed, and each has formed part of the environment in which it has grown. Provision for social work with offenders became embedded in the law, in the requirement that probation officers advise, assist and befriend their probationers. The use of legal authority and legal sanctions has become embedded in the probation officer's social work.

Amongst the most important strands in the legal ancestry of the probation order and the probation service is the recognizance. This device, present in the common law but increasingly included in statutes, enabled courts to release minor offenders without punishment, provided they entered into a recognizance to be of good behaviour and come up for judgment at a stated date or if called upon. The same device could be used in felony cases, in addition to punishment, as an extra deterrent against further crime. Not only might the offender himself be involved in recognizances, he might be called upon to find sureties who would go bail for his good behaviour, and thus also have an interest in seeing that he kept within the law. Thus the recognizance already contained in embryo four elements of probation: release instead of punishment; a responsibility laid upon the offender; a responsibility laid also upon others; and the possibility of return to court and of punishment if the undertaking was broken.

In the nineteenth century, growing concern about the effects of imprisonment upon children led a few magistrates and judges in different parts of the country to use the recognizance as a means of returning certain young offenders to the care of their parents or masters, with the stipulation that they should be better looked after in future. Such cases were sometimes followed up on behalf of the court, and good success was claimed for them.[1] But the device was limited by the fact that few of the young offenders most in need of

---

1. For a further account of this, see earlier editions of this book under the title *The Probation Service*, 1958 and 1964.

care and guidance had parents or masters fit to give it. Further advance had to await the development of a body of social workers on whom the courts could rely.

Philanthropists also had been experimenting during the nineteenth century, moving away from indiscriminate almsgiving towards organization, investigation, encouraging self-help, and devoting resources to the more deserving, or potentially responsive, of those in need. Alongside this general emphasis on the deserving, however, there were voluntary societies and social workers interested in some of the most degraded: prostitutes, ex-prisoners, drunkards.

In 1876 Frederick Rainer, a Hertfordshire printer, wrote to one such association, the Church of England Temperance Society, deploring the fact that once a person was convicted and imprisoned there seemed no hope for him, only "offence after offence, sentence after sentence". He sent five shillings to help start some practical work with drunks in the police courts to break this vicious circle. The Society at once took up the challenge, and the first police court missionary was appointed in London that same year. By 1900 the Police Court Mission employed over a hundred men and women at summary courts in London and elsewhere. They made enquiries about the background of offenders, they sometimes went bail for them, and they accepted responsibility for their care and supervision if the courts decided to release them. In all this they carried on the keynote of concern for the individual offender struck by Frederick Rainer. They were permitted to do so because a similar note had already been struck in some of the courts. And once they were in the courts they accelerated the process of humanization.

The work of the missionaries was facilitated by the Summary Jurisdiction Act of 1879, which expressly permitted discharge of offenders convicted of a summary offence, though it made no provision for their supervision. The Probation of First Offenders Bill, seven years later, originally included such provision, but it was taken out by the Lords before it became law. Fears were also expressed in the Commons about permitting "a lot of amateurs to say what persons who have been convicted should be allowed quietly to merge into the honest peaceful population and be heard of no more". The twenty-year delay before probation as we understand it today became law had, however, its advantages. The police court missionaries had time to develop their work and prove themselves, the courts and public opinion had time to come to know and trust them. When the Probation of Offenders Act was eventually passed, it was a far broader and more flexible measure than its forerunner.

Since then a lengthening series of official reports has commented upon, predicted and influenced the growth of the service. Each has been followed by legislation extending statutory recognition or establishing the framework for further expansion. First, within two years of the establishment of the service, there was the Report of the Departmental Committee on the Probation of Offenders Act 1907 (1909) followed by the Criminal Justice (Administration) Act 1914. Next, reflecting concern for the wider extension and better administration of the service, came the Report of the Departmental Committee on the Training, Appointment and Pay of Probation Officers (1922), followed by the Criminal Justice Act 1925, amended in 1926. Recognition of the fact that probation officers were serving the courts in many other ways besides supervising probationers led to the Departmental Committee on the Social Services in Courts of Summary Jurisdiction, which reported in 1936. It was followed very shortly by the Summary Procedure (Domestic Proceedings) Act 1937, recognizing the role of probation officers in matrimonial cases and, after the war, by the Criminal Justice Act 1948, restating the law on probation and bringing certain forms of after-care within the scope of statutory duties.

In 1962 the Departmental Committee on the Probation Service (known as the Morison Committee) reviewed every aspect of its work, approving the general direction of growth. Since then, however, it has been the reports, committees and legislation focused elsewhere that have had the greatest impact on its development. The work of the service with children, whether offenders, potential offenders or in need of care, has been progressively affected by the Children and Young Persons Act 1963, the White Papers "The Child, the Family and the Young Offender", and "Children in Trouble", and the changes projected in the Children and Young Persons Bill 1969. The Report of the Inter-Departmental Committee on the Business of the Criminal Courts in 1961 led to a great extension in pre-sentence enquiries about offenders by probation officers. The report in 1963 of the Advisory Council on the Treatment of Offenders on the Organization of After-Care has been followed by a great extension of the statutory responsibilities of the service in after-care and also (though this was not then recommended) in prison welfare. The 1967 Criminal Justice Act not only confirmed the transformation of the probation service into the probation and after-care service but resulted in new duties connected with parole.

In Scotland there has been, throughout, a narrower conception of the functions of the service than in England and Wales. Even probation itself has been used less there than elsewhere in Great Britain, and it took longer for it to begin to achieve real recognition as a method of treating adult offenders. This arose partly from differences in traditions, in public opinion and in the sentencing practices of the courts. The Morison Committee attributed it also to the fact that the probation service tended to be regarded in Scotland as a minor local authority service rather than as a service of the courts. They saw scope for its further development and made recommendations to that end.

Again, however, it was the views of another committee that had the greatest effect. The Kilbrandon Report was concerned primarily with children. But once it was accepted that juvenile offenders should come within the scope of the new local authority social work departments, it was argued that what remained of the Scottish probation service would be too small to be viable and that probation officers, and work with adult probationers, should be absorbed into the local authority social work services. There were protests both from the National Association of Probation Officers and from the sheriffs, on the grounds that the change might well result in a setback in the use of probation for adults in the sheriff courts and that it did not take account of the need, in Scotland as in England, to expand the service to provide more social workers for penal institutions and for after-care.[1] The Social Work (Scotland) Bill was, nevertheless, passed in 1968 and the probation service in Scotland will end in November 1969. The remainder of this book concentrates therefore upon the service in England and Wales, though many of the problems it raises and the issues it discusses, will also have to be faced and decided in Scotland.

---

1. See on this Sheriff J. Aikman Smith, *The Social Work (Scotland) Bill and the Treatment of Offenders*, address to the National Association of Probation Officers, Annual Conference, 1968.

2 THE LEGAL BASIS OF PROBATION[1]

From the first, statutory probation in this country was not limited to juveniles, to first offenders, or to a restricted range of offences. Character, antecedents, age, health and mental condition of the offender, the trivial nature of the offence and any extenuating circumstances might all be taken into consideration. But probation could be used by both summary and higher courts for offenders of any age and with no absolute restriction as to criminal record. The only proviso about the offence was that in the higher courts it must be one that carried a sentence of imprisonment. This, in effect, excluded only murder and treason. The provision of the Criminal Justice Act 1948 that the offence must not carry a sentence fixed by law has a similar consequence. This later statute, however, has also expressed in simpler terms the considerations to be taken into account by the court in deciding to use probation: it can be imposed if the court considers it expedient, having regard to the nature of the offence and the character of the defendant. This leaves the maximum discretion to the court.

It was left to a Departmental Committee to spell out the conditions under which an *a priori* case for probation may be held to exist:[2]

"(a) The circumstances of the offence and the offender's record must not be such as to demand, in the interests of society, that some more severe method be adopted in dealing with him.

(b) The risk, if any, to society through setting the offender at liberty must be outweighed by the moral, social and economic arguments for not depriving him of it.

(c) The offender must need continuing attention, since otherwise, if condition (b) is satisfied, a fine or discharge will suffice.

(d) The offender must be capable of responding to this attention while at liberty."

Probation can be used only when an offence has been admitted or proved to the satisfaction of the court. Under the 1907 Act, an attempt was made to help rehabilitation by avoiding the stigma and disabilities attaching to conviction even for minor offences. It was

---

1. Here, and throughout the book, attention is drawn to various salient points relating to the legal and administrative basis of the service. For a more detailed statement of the present position, however, see F. Jarvis, *Probation Officers' Manual*, 1969.

2. *Report of the Departmental Committee on the Probation Service* (Cmnd. 1650), 1962.

provided that a summary court, once satisfied of guilt, could proceed to make a probation order without proceeding to conviction: This provision was dropped in the Criminal Justice Act 1948 since it was argued that it was no more than a legal fiction and contributed to the false idea that probation was equivalent to letting the offender off. Instead it was laid down that if the order was completed successfully the probationer should suffer none of the statutory disqualifications or disabilities normally attaching to conviction. In juvenile courts the expression conviction had in any case been replaced by "finding of guilt".

Though probation, with its sanction of return to court and possible punishment, can be used only for offenders, it should be noted that, since the Children and Young Persons Act 1933, another form of supervision had been at the disposal of the courts in dealing with juveniles up to seventeen found to be "in need of care or protection", or, after the Children's Act of 1963, "in need of care, protection or control". They might be delinquents, truants or in moral danger, they might be neglected by their parents, but if the court considered it for their welfare they could be put under the supervision of a probation officer or a children's officer, and they could be brought back to the court and otherwise dealt with at any time if it appeared to be in their interests.

The Children and Young Persons' Bill 1969 takes the supervision order as the standard method of dealing with those children and young people who still come before the juvenile courts, whether for offences or for other reasons, and who are thought to need treatment but not to need any long-term removal from home. It will thus, in due course, replace the probation order for those under seventeen, even when they have been found guilty of an offence. Even when these new provisions are brought fully into force, however—and it is anticipated that this will take a considerable time—the courts will be entitled to appoint either a probation officer or the children's department as supervisor in the case of young people between fourteen and seventeen. It is interesting, too, to see that the duties of the supervisor are defined in the same terms as those of probation officers in the original Probation of Offenders Act: "to advise, assist and befriend".

This kind of order does not, and will not, need the formal consent of the juvenile. Probation orders, however, have followed the tradition of the recognizance in requiring the offender's consent. There are those who argue that, since the offender will usually agree to probation rather than risk anything worse, consent is another fiction that should be dispensed with. Most, however, would feel that even if given under pressure, it has a real value. It is the fear of something worse that induces people to agree, for example, to a course of medical treatment, but this does not make their consent less valid, or their co-operation less essential. The court has the duty of explaining to the offender what a probation order will involve and the probation officer is required afterwards to make clear to him his rights and obligations. It has been suggested that the element of active participation and responsibility involved in a recognizance (which used to be an actual part of the procedure for making a probation order but was dropped in 1948) could be restored by requiring the offender to sign, perhaps in court, an acknowledgment that he understands and accepts the order.

In the 1907 Act probation was classed in the same section as discharge. In spite of disclaimers, this contributed to the idea that it was equivalent to letting the offender off. In the statute of 1948, the provisions for probation were made quite separate and its distinctness was emphasized by the requirement that, before deciding upon an order of absolute or conditional discharge, the court should satisfy itself not only that punishment was not expedient but also that a probation order was not appropriate. Probation is to be seen, as Dr. Grünhut has put it, as a "third way" of dealing with offenders; distinct alike from discharge and from punishment.[1]

The element of supervision and of treatment distinguishes probation alike from the earlier conditional discharge and from the suspended sentence, first introduced in this country by the Criminal Justice Act 1967. Whereas these both carry, as probation does, the possibility of punishment for the original offence if a further offence is committed, they rely wholly upon deterrence and make no provision for supervision, support or guidance. It has been said that a court should first consider probation: only if it has rejected that as inappropriate in a particular case should the question of a suspended sentence arise.[2]

---

1. *The Selection of Offenders for Probation*, United Nations, 1959.
2. See Lord Stonham, House of Lords *Weekly Hansard*, 4–6 March 1969.

Whilst a court cannot impose a formal punishment and put on probation at the same time for the same offence, it has from the first been able to make a separate order requiring the offender to pay damages for injury or compensation for damage. Since the Criminal Justice Act 1967, it has also been possible for a court to order disqualification from driving and endorsement of the licence in addition to probation. Both these measures may be seen as having a value as a means of restitution and prevention, of encouraging the offender to accept his responsibilities to others. On the other hand they may also be seen as having a punitive element, perhaps as making probation more publicly acceptable in cases where the offender is seen as needing treatment in the open, but at the same time as having inflicted serious harm upon someone else or as being in need of restraint.

To the offender the probation order may appear as a punishment in itself: he is obliged to keep in touch, to receive visits, he has the feeling that the order is hanging over him throughout its duration. Even though such requirements and restrictions are imposed with the intention of helping rather than punishing, they can make probation far more exacting than a fine, which can be paid and forgotten. Far from being let off, the offender is constantly reminded, if only by implication, of his offence and its consequences.

The question is now in the air of whether this should be carried further. Supervision in the community is, in itself, a positive weapon in the hands of the magistracy. Should it be open to the courts, where they see a need both of punishment and of continued supervision and help in the open, to impose, for example, a fine or a short prison sentence in addition to, or as conditions of, probation? Where more than one offence is being dealt with at the same time, it is already possible for a fine (or, where it is applicable, an attendance centre order) to be imposed on one count whilst a probation order is made on another. A fine or attendance centre order can also be used as the penalty for breach of a requirement, without terminating the order. It has been pointed out to courts that they should not impose a probation order and a custodial sentence at the same time, since the two are incompatible. But should they necessarily have to choose, where only one offence is before them, between treatment in the open and some form of punishment? May there not be cases where there is need for both?

To combine either a fine or imprisonment with supervision would seem to take away one of the essentials of probation as it has hitherto been known in this country: the suspension of punishment, even of sentence. Upon this depends the offender's sense of having been given a special chance to make good, and also the possibility of sentence for the original offence if he fails to do so. It may be that the second of these objections could be met, in part, by provision for a fine in case of breach, but it is hard to see how a feeling of grievance about being punished twice could be avoided, a feeling already apparent when statutory after-care follows some form of detention. What seems certain is that if such a measure were introduced it should not be known as probation, and it should not be allowed to take the place of probation. Whilst it may be arguable that it could help the courts in dealing with some offenders, it could do more harm than good if it were allowed to undermine the basis of probation generally.

An essential requirement of a probation order is supervision by a probation officer. The 1907 Act required this officer to be named in the order, thus emphasizing the personal nature of the link between him and the offender. The 1948 Criminal Justice Act substituted, for reasons of administrative convenience, the name of the petty sessional division. At the time there were fears that this would be a first step in undermining the close personal link between probationer and supervising officer to which so much importance was, and still is, attached. Any such intention was denied: since probation officers were by then already organized not merely as individuals attached to particular courts but as members of co-ordinated probation services, the new arrangement seemed simpler and more logical. In that the central importance of the relationship between probationer and supervisor has been stressed more than ever in the development of casework since 1948, fears that the change might weaken it may seem to have proved groundless. In longer perspective, however, there are signs of tendencies to question whether an exclusively one-to-one relationship is the most helpful in all cases, and to think of groups of probation officers as teams, several members of which may be able to contribute to the understanding or rehabilitation of a particular offender, perhaps at different stages. Such an approach may have been encouraged, and would certainly be facilitated, by the removal of the statutory personal link with a named officer.

The maximum period of supervision was set in 1907 at three years. No minimum was then prescribed and in the early days orders sometimes lasted for less than six months, the shortest time then considered desirable.[1] In 1948 the present minimum of one year was added, but the maximum remains at three.

To ensure that the probationer remains in contact with his supervisor, an order also normally includes requirements that he notify the probation officer of any change of address; that he keep in touch with the probation officer in accordance with such instructions as the officer may gave; and that he receive visits from the officer at his home. Various additional requirements as to the offender's way of life (including abstention from alcohol) were explicitly permitted under the 1907 Act. The Criminal Justice (Administration) Act 1914 added to these explicit provision for conditions of residence, which had been used informally, in conjunction with binding over, even before 1907, and which were considered an essential factor in the treatment of some probationers.

Specific restrictions upon a probationer's associations, haunts or habits still occasionally occur in probation orders, especially when the court considers that what is proscribed was closely connected with the offence. Even when such requirements can be justified on these grounds, however, they can be extremely difficult to enforce; it does no good for the probationer to be defying the order without the probation officer's knowledge or without the court being prepared to take action. Very vague and general requirements can also be unhelpful. To be of use a requirement should be both clear and enforceable.

The 1948 Criminal Justice Act replaced the old term "conditions" by "requirements" and made no mention of such provisions as abstention from intoxicating liquor. Its formula was simply that requirements should be such as were thought necessary to secure the good conduct of the offender or to prevent another offence on his part: a criterion more general, and less likely to be interpreted restrictively, than the more detailed examples given in the earlier statute.

At the same time, however, strict conditions were imposed upon

---

1. *Report of the Departmental Committee on the Probation of Offenders Act* 1907 (Cd. 5001), 1909.

the use of two kinds of requirement which might be thought to impinge on important aspects of the probationer's liberty. It was laid down in 1948 that requirements of residence in institutions, whether or not these are probation homes or hostels specially approved by the Home Office, should be made only after consideration of the offender's home surroundings. Further, a requirement of residence in any institution must specify the period, which must not exceed one year. Where the institution is not a probation home or hostel, or a hospital treating the patient for his mental condition, the court must forthwith notify the Secretary of State of the terms of the order. It was also stipulated that a requirement of residence must be reviewed after six months by the court that made it, with a view to its termination if desirable. This last provision, however, was found to be so unsettling for the probationers concerned that it was repealed in 1967, though it is still held that requirements of residence should be kept under review and application made for their early discharge if this seems desirable.

The other extension of probation which could be regarded as a special potential threat to personal liberty was a requirement that the probationer undergo mental treatment, in or out of an institution. This was first fully recognized and carefully restricted in 1948, though it had sometimes been used before that. Though some details of the arrangements laid down then were modified by the Mental Health Act of 1959, the essentials remain. An order can be made only on the evidence of a practitioner with special experience in the diagnosis and treatment of mental disorder that the offender needs, and may respond to, treatment for his mental condition. The doctor or institution to carry out the treatment must be named and the period cannot exceed one year. If at any time during treatment the responsible doctor recommends discharge of the requirement, the probation officer must apply for this and the court must grant it. The offender has, of course, his normal right to refuse consent to the requirement at the time the order is made, and he cannot be dealt with for breach of probation solely on the ground of refusal to undergo surgical, electrical or other treatment if the court thinks his refusal reasonable.

Procedures for dealing in general with breach of probation orders, their discharge or amendment, were made originally in 1907 but considerably clarified in 1948. A probationer may commit a breach either by a further offence or by failing to observe one of the requirements of the order, perhaps failing to keep in touch with the probation officer or to notify change of address. The Criminal Justice Act 1948 distinguished clearly the procedures for bringing the offender back before the court in each of these cases. Where the offender has been dealt with for another offence during his period of probation, the court has to decide whether he should also be dealt with for the original offence, which terminates the order. Where he has broken a requirement of the order, on the other hand, it can either do this or, alternatively, fine him (or make an attendance centre order if a centre is available) and allow the order to continue. The maximum fine in such cases was set at £10 in 1948 but doubled in 1967.

The probationer, as well as the probation officer, has the right to apply to a court for the variation or discharge of an order. Discharge of orders, where desirable, was further facilitated by the Criminal Justice Act of 1967. This provided that the supervising court, instead of the court which originally made the order, should have power to terminate it, unless a superior court had reserved to itself the power to discharge. Thus applications for termination can normally be heard by the court in closest touch with the supervising probation officer and the circumstances of the offender at the time. It was also provided in 1967 that a probation order can be replaced by an order of conditional discharge. This offers an appropriate way of dealing with cases where continuance of supervision is clearly impractical or useless but where the court wishes to retain some hold over the offender.

3 THE LEGAL BASIS OF OTHER DUTIES

Though the supervision of offenders as an alternative to imprisonment was the only activity of the police court missionaries to receive statutory recognition in 1907, it was not the only task they carried over into their work as probation officers. They were already making preliminary enquiries about some of those appearing before the courts to help the magistrates decide how to deal with them. They were trying to assist or reconcile wives and husbands coming to court with matrimonial disputes. They were advising parents who approached them for help with difficult children. And in some areas at least they were involved in the after-care of prisoners. Because they were originally "missionaries" rather than a statutory service, no hard and fast limits had been set to their functions: the range of human need encountered in the courts and at the prison gates was accepted as within their scope. It may be true that, in terms of statutory duties, probation officers started with a single function and accumulated others simply because there was no one else to carry them out. But in terms of the actual development of the service, of the duties accepted by and expected of it, almost all the functions now undertaken were there when it started. The unifying factors were the link with the courts and concern for those in trouble with the law.

The usefulness of enquiries to the courts was acknowledged from the first, though for twenty years they were considered merely a voluntary activity. Even after the Acts of 1925 and 1926 they were included in the rules as a formal duty only in cases where the question of a probation order might arise. Not until 1948 did it become the statutory duty of officers to report, in any case, whether probation was contemplated or not. And this still depends on the directions of the court, which may not ask for a report at all.

The Committee of 1936 pressed very strongly that a report should at least be required before a probation order could be made, pointing out that "In fairness . . . to society, the offender and the probation officer, no person should be placed on probation without full consideration of his previous history and present surroundings . . . without enquiry it is impossible adequately to take into account the conditions which the law prescribes as justifying the use of probation". There was a fear, however, that this might be unduly rigid, perhaps preventing the use of probation in some cases where it was appropriate. In 1968 all courts were urged to make a report a normal prerequisite of probation. Even so, this is still not a statutory requirement.

In some other circumstances, however, courts have been required by statute to consider information about the offender and his background before sentencing. All but the most minor juvenile offenders, and also young adults and first offenders where imprisonment may be contemplated, come within the scope of this legislation. Much expansion has taken place without the need of legislation, encouraged by the availability of probation officers at courts of assize and quarter sessions as well as at the magistrates' courts. The

Streatfeild Report of 1961 confirmed this tendency, and has been followed up by official circulars urging courts to obtain reports on widening categories of adult offenders. The most recent of these makes it clear that a report should normally be obtained before an offender is sent to a penal institution for anything up to two years.

The role of the service in all this has been not only to give fuller information to aid sentencing in individual cases, but to bring into the courts a new way of looking at offenders, a less stereotyped approach to the problem of dealing with them.

Matrimonial work had to wait even longer before it received even partial recognition as one of the statutory duties of the service. By 1922 the services of probation officers in "arranging differences, especially between husbands and wives", were accepted as "essential to the proper administration of justice". But it was not until 1937 that statutory authority was given for the employment of probation officers as conciliators in matrimonial cases. Work with the many wives and husbands who came, and still come, to probation officers for help without being referred by the courts remains outside the range of statutory duties, though accepted as a valuable service.

Perhaps more than any other part of the work of the courts, the handling of domestic cases calls for comprehension not only of the legal position of the parties but of the underlying feelings. Here again the great contribution of the probation service has been to the humanization of justice.

The situation of probation officers as social workers of the courts has also brought them increasing responsibilities for helping magistrates, and more recently judges, to reach decisions relating to the custody and welfare of the children of marriages that are breaking up. Both magistrates' and divorce courts now have power to ask for enquiries in such cases and, exceptionally, to put the children under supervision when making a custody order. The function of carrying out such enquiries or exercising supervision, if required by the courts, is a statutory duty of probation officers, and probation and after-care committees are under an obligation to assign probation officers as welfare officers to every court of summary jurisdiction.

The concern of the service with children in trouble has not been limited, however, to those being dealt with by the courts, whether as offenders or otherwise. Just as in matrimonial cases many have always gone directly to the probation officer, so throughout the history of the service parents have come direct for advice about their children: children who, though they might not yet have committed offences, were truanting, drifting into bad company, or getting beyond control. In this sense the service has long continued to operate as a "family advice service", working with parents on a voluntary basis. Responsibilities both for formal supervision and informal advice in such cases are now being taken over by the children's departments. But both in its continuing matrimonial work and in its long record of availability to parents in trouble, the probation service has played an important part not only in attempts to treat juveniles who have been before the courts but in attempts to forestall trouble at an earlier stage.

The most prolonged controversy about the proper functions of probation officers focused on responsibilities for after-care. Doubts were least strong in relation to approved school and borstal after-care, strongest about accepting responsibility for adult prisoners. During the first forty years of the service, however, many individual probation officers received and accepted requests to supervise and help any of these, without any statutory recognition of after-care amongst their duties.

In the case of children at approved schools, the responsibility for after-care lay with the managers. When, because of distance, they could not have it carried out by their own staff, they frequently requested the probation officer in the child's home area to undertake it. Regularly, outside London, the Borstal Association used probation officers as "associates" to supervise boys during their period of compulsory after-care. The Central Association for Discharged Convicts used them in the after-care of offenders who had undergone penal servitude in the convict prisons. And the Discharged Prisoners' Aid Associations (who were the part-employers of some of the earlier probation officers) often turned to them to help men released from local prisons over whom there was no statutory control.

The question of whether any of these classes of after-care should become a duty of probation officers under statutory rules was debated at length in the early nineteen-thirties. The National Association of Probation Officers was prepared to accept all of them. The Home Office supported this, though lest the service be overwhelmed they would have stipulated that applications for help should not be accepted direct but only through the statutory or voluntary associations.

The 1936 Committee, perhaps because its explicit concern was with the social services directly associated with the courts, took a different view. It feared that such "extraneous" duties might leave insufficient time for the work of the courts, for enquiries, probation, matrimonial conciliation. It had no objection to approved school after-care, which it felt did not involve a great deal of time and effort. It had strong doubts about borstal cases, since they were likely to be more difficult and demanding and might, in addition, involve some risk of contaminating probationers. It condemned outright the employment of probation officers in the after-care of ex-convicts or other prisoners, except in the most scattered rural areas where there was no alternative.

The Criminal Justice Act 1948 nevertheless extended the statutory duties of the service to include the after-care, at the request of the responsible authorities, of those offenders who were required by law to accept supervision on release. They ranged from life prisoners and adults sentenced to corrective training or preventive detention at one extreme to approved school children at the other. This partial rejection of the 1936 recommendations marked official recognition of the role of the service in supervision and social work with offenders released from institutions as well as those adjudged suitable for treatment in the open on probation.

In 1963 the Advisory Council on the Treatment of Offenders recommended that the after-care of that great majority of prisoners who were subject to no statutory requirement of supervision on release should also become the responsibility of the probation service. Looking at the problem in terms of the offender's needs, it could find no justification for providing a skilled, official social work service for those under statutory supervision whilst leaving the rest to voluntary associations which could no longer hope to cope with the burden. Probation officers were still willing to accept it, though it was recognized that it would necessitate a further expansion of the service and a shift in the balance of its duties. So the probation service became the probation and after-care service, and probation officers became responsible for the after-care of any prisoner willing to accept their help.

When this had been discussed in the thirties they had had two doubts about it. One arose from the difficulty of keeping contact with offenders over whom they had no specific authority for long enough to do any constructive work with them. This problem they are still trying to solve. The second arose from the fact that most of these men were released without prior warning or prior information being sent to workers in their home areas. This problem, it is hoped, will be progressively reduced, since the prison welfare service has become part of the probation and after-care service.

Prison welfare is almost the latest, and much the least familiar, of the duties of probation officers. As yet comparatively few have taken part in it. It marks a break in the long tradition whereby the service has concentrated almost wholly upon treatment in the open. It marks the entry of social workers whose concern is primarily with the individual in the community into penal institutions which have traditionally been cut off from the outside world. Ideally it could permit a thread of continuity running through all stages in the treatment of offenders from pre-sentence enquiry to the completion of after-care.

The system of parole, introduced by the Criminal Justice Act 1967, did not begin to operate in this country until 1968. Principal and senior probation officers are involved in the selection of offenders for parole on the Parole Board and local review committees. Any officer may be responsible for supervising a man thus released on licence. This duty has much affinity with other kinds of statutory after-care, but it emphasizes anew the move of the service into closer links with the prisons and responsibility for more serious offenders.

Another link with the penal system must not be forgotten, though it is concerned (like probation) with keeping offenders out of prison rather than facilitating their earlier release. This is the supervision of offenders subject to fines supervision orders. Its history is a chequered one. It was suggested in 1909 that officers could be used to collect instalments of fines as a way of diminishing the very large number of offenders sent to prison for failure to pay. The 1909 Committee dismissed this as foreign to the probation officer's functions. Yet to avoid unnecessary imprisonment had been one of the original purposes of probation, and thousands of very young people, often first offenders, were going to prison in default, even though the court's decision had been merely to fine them. The Criminal Justice Act 1914 therefore gave courts power, where a person was allowed time to pay and was between sixteen and twenty-one, to put him under supervision until the fine was paid, not issuing a committal warrant subsequently without getting a report from his supervisor. Unfortunately these powers were little used, though their value was endorsed by the Young Offenders Committee of 1927 and again by a committee considering imprisonment in default in 1934. Both were strongly of the opinion that probation officers were the proper persons to act as supervisors (as distinct from fine-collectors) and that there was no incompatibility between this duty and the supervision of probationers.[1] The Money Payments (Justices Procedure) Act 1935 (in provisions since replaced by the Magistrates' Courts Act 1952), followed up the views of the committees, requiring courts to consider supervision before resorting to imprisonment of defaulters under twenty-one, and empowering them to use it also for adults. At the same time a Home Office circular confirmed that the probation officer was a suitable person to carry out supervision.

Though probation officers have mixed feelings about this duty, it is still with them. Some think it allows no scope for social work, seeing it merely an enforcement duty, better performed by some other officer of the court. Others think that, in spite of the uncertainty as to how long supervision will last and the limited scope of the help that can be given, it can be of real value in dealing with certain offenders. The Morison Committee emphasized that orders should not be used as substitutes for probation and should not be imposed automatically or indiscriminately: they were most appropriate where the offender was too incompetent or feckless to put aside the necessary savings.

Fines occupy an increasingly important place in the penal system, and efforts are being made from all angles to develop effective means of securing payment without resort to imprisonment. It would be surprising if the service had no part in this. Sometimes a supervision order may be the point at which difficulties and inadequacies that might lead not only to imprisonment in default but further offences, may be identified and dealt with. On the other hand, the whole of this work need not necessarily be carried out by

---

1. *Report of the Departmental Committee on Young Offenders*, 1927; *Report of the Departmental Committee on Imprisonment by Courts of Summary Jurisdiction in Default of Payment of Fines, etc.*, 1934.

probation officers who have also to cover the full range of duties as
social workers of the courts. In a few cases there have been experiments in appointing people, perhaps with more limited qualifications, for this specific task. Much of their work may well be seen as
administrative, but they can look for guidance, where social
problems arise, to probation officers with wider experience. This is,
indeed, one of the areas in which ancillary workers may be recognized as essential if the skilled social worker is to be available to
identify and deal with those in special need over an ever-widening
front.

4 THE SOCIAL-WORK BASIS

That the probation officer was regarded from the first as a social
worker is evidenced not only by the statutory requirement that
he "advise, assist and befriend", but by the account of his duties
included in the report of 1909. The importance of direct personal
influence was stressed first and foremost; so was the importance of
using and improving the social environment. It was assumed that
the solution of various social problems could contribute to helping
the offender out of "the groove that leads to serious crime". Attention was directed to finding work, to encouraging constructive
leisure interests, to the home, to management of financial problems.
Whilst the importance of the court order in maintaining contact and
co-operation was emphasized, it was the relationship between officer
and probationer that was seen as the heart of treatment.

As social conditions and assumptions have changed, and as the
welfare state has grown up on all sides of the probation service, there
have been variations in emphasis and in interpretation. But all
these elements have remained. Some, indeed, which once seemed to
be losing their importance are once more coming to the fore.

The general responsibility for helping people find work has gone
to the employment exchanges. Sometimes the modern probation
officer may approach them direct to discuss work for a probationer,
or accompany him on a visit to the exchange. Much more often he
will encourage the offender to find work for himself, either through
the exchange or directly, perhaps paving the way by discussing with
him the possibilities and difficulties. The full employment of recent
years has in one way made this problem less difficult in most areas
than it was in the days of the first missionaries or in the depression of

the nineteen-thirties. For some delinquents, however, full employment itself had aggravated difficulties: jobs that are too easy to come by are too easily dropped. The new move to automation, the decay of unskilled jobs, as of some of the traditional industries, may well bring the old problems to the fore again. The extended responsibilities of the service for after-care of prisoners, with their special handicaps in finding and settling to work, tends in the same direction. Whatever may be the nature of the link between a bad work record and repeated crime there is no doubt that the two often go together, or that many offenders themselves feel that a steady job is evidence of rehabilitation.

The concern to help probationers find better uses for their leisure is another facet of probation work which has changed almost out of recognition over the course of years, yet keeps recurring in different forms. Youth clubs, in the conventional sense, are unacceptable to many young people now, perhaps most of all to delinquents. Few probation officers attach much importance to their use as a means of treatment. Yet individual officers have experimented directly in providing some kind of substitute—perhaps a discussion or activity group, perhaps weekends or holidays—to widen the interests and leisure resources of probationers, to strengthen their social competence. Now they are being called upon to play a part with the local authorities in the planning and use of a range of "intermediate" treatment measures, designed to permit delinquents to take part with others in stimulating, remedial or educational activities.

The key position of the home in the treatment of child offenders has been emphasized throughout. It has been seen that the earliest experiments in releasing juveniles hinged upon the possibility of sending them home and upon emphasizing their parents' responsibility. One of the purposes of probation was to avoid the removal of child offenders from home where possible. The necessity for co-operation of child and family was still being stressed in the nineteen-thirties:

"It is often better policy to adopt a second best plan with that co-operation than to impose what seems to the worker the better treatment against the wishes of parent and child."

It was stressed, too, that the officer must be in a position to discuss all the needs of the family and act as a link between them and other social agencies.[1]   Since then the influence of psychological and psycho-analytical theories and findings has further emphasized the importance of the family in the development of personality, of family conflicts and failures in relation to delinquency.   The second world war, separating as it did parents from each other and from their children, helped to reveal the conditions under which some of the poorest lived and stressed the need for more personal social services, concerned with emotional as well as material needs.   The children's departments of the local authorities have been pressing further into the field of family care, to the point where they are taking over responsibility for much work formerly done by probation officers.   But the involvement of the service continues in matrimonial work.   And the extension of after-care, the taking over of prison welfare, have brought more concern with the families of adult offenders.

Looking at financial difficulties, even from the first it was stressed that probation was not another relief service.   Though court poor-boxes might be used where there was no other source of help (as they may be today) a probationer in dire financial straits was normally to be directed to other charities, or helped to solve his problems for himself, rather than given doles by the probation officer.   These could merely be a way of dodging or postponing the real difficulties.

Less stress would be laid nowadays upon encouraging the virtues of thrift as such, though that may still be a factor in teaching young people to plan and wait, over comparatively short terms, for things they want.   In modern conditions help in the planning of borrowing, the avoidance of an accumulation of hire purchase and other obligations that cannot be met, is more important to most people than saving, especially since provision for old age, illness and unemployment have become compulsory.   There are always, however, the husbands who fail to give enough housekeeping money, the wives who regularly fail to make it last, and resort to petty offences to stave off trouble.   There are, too, the poorest and most inadequate families who still need continuous guidance and all the help they can get from other services to enable them to keep going at all. Greater affluence has not solved material and financial problems for

---

1. L. Le Mesurier, *A Handbook of Probation*, 1935, pp. 11 and 128.

everyone, and where poverty and bad housing are linked with delinquency some probation officers are feeling they should not stop short at enabling those in their care to use existing social provisions but should join more vigorously in pointing out deficiencies and pressure for improvements.

It is curious that, in this connection too, the new inheritance of the service in prison welfare and after-care has brought second thoughts. What of the homeless boy out of borstal, the man out of prison, who has to start from scratch, with an inadequate or damaged personality, to establish himself in an affluent society? Almost inevitably he will need more than the state allowance. In after-care (just as in the preventive work of children's departments at the other end of the scale) the occasional need of special direct assistance in cash or kind is acknowledged. The concern is no longer to exclude it, as a dangerous alternative to more fundamental and lasting help, but to find means of using it more sensitively, so that it contributes to treatment as a whole.

The sanction of the penal law remains the background of most of the probation officer's work, not only in probation itself but in statutory after-care and parole. But the uses of this tool also have subtly altered, as concepts of treatment have become more sophisticated. It still plays a part in securing the contacts necessary to initiate and maintain treatment at all. For some offenders the limits it lays down are not only seen as controls required for the protection of other people but as helping the probationer himself come to terms with the reality of social demands upon him. A "respectful hearing" and docile acceptance of advice, however, fall short of the active participation the modern officer hopes to secure. Just as it is recognized that, in penal institutions, the "good prisoner" may be a bad risk after he leaves, so in probation or after-care the unduly compliant may slide through supervision with no lasting effect at all. There is, in fact, a deeper understanding both of the dangers and the possibilities of using legal authority in treatment. From this point of view it has gained rather than lost in importance.

Legal authority is not, however, an essential factor in all of the probation officer's work. The police court missionaries welcomed with relief the additional hold over offenders given them by probation orders. But at the same time they continued on a voluntary basis in other areas, notably in dealing with the matrimonial difficulties of those coming to the summary courts. In such cases they and the modern officer alike have to depend upon the personal and social pressures upon husband and wife, and upon their own skill, to provide the continuing motive for contact and co-operation. The direct authority of the court plays little, if any, part, though their link with it may lend weight to what they say. Here they are in the position of many other social workers, whose clients are brought by the compulsion of their own needs and kept, if at all, by their desire to find solutions.

With voluntary prison after-care, however, yet another factor is introduced. Some, though not all, of those who come have little sense of personal need, beyond the need for immediate material help, and little, if any, desire to change. Yet they may have very severe personal needs indeed. At the same time, they cannot be held in contact over a period, as in probation or statutory after-care, to give the probation officer time to stimulate a sense of such needs. This is a problem with which the service, both in prison welfare and in after-care, is only just beginning to try to come to grips.

Whatever the value of the probation order or other legal sanction in itself, it has never been seen as the main instrument in the treatment of offenders by probation officers in this country. The aim, after all, is to secure improvements that will continue after the sanction is removed. From this point of view the legal requirements are important mainly as providing a setting within which the officer can develop and use a relationship with the offender. The nature of this relationship at its best was well described at the start. "Advise, assist and befriend" was not to be interpreted in any superficial sense:

> "What are we to give the tempted and the outcast? Condemnation? . . Mere good advice, often hurled as from a catapult, or dropped at arm's length with an averted face? Such costs little or nothing and is valued at what it costs. Nay, but give love, and that summary of the Gospel which is contained in the word 'Brother'. Grasp the hand of the one you would rescue, and with him ascend the mountain, instead of standing like an inanimate and unsympathetic signpost on the plain which you consider so unsafe for him. Love is the vehicle of all the medicines of Christ."[1]

A modern writer, looking back on them, describes the working of the same spirit in more specific terms.

---

1. Quoted by H. H. Ayscough in "When Mercy Seasons Justice" (C.E.T.S.).

"These founder-fathers were missionaries in the true sense of the word and they used the methods of missionaries—changing behaviour by changing feeling—through 'conversion'. Their methods were persuasion, exhortation and support. They strengthened weak resolution by administering solemn pledges to renounce drink; they gently admonished the sinner while at the same time offering him the helping hand of friendship; they advised him for his own good; they assisted him in many ways to improve his social and economic condition; and finally they prayed for guidance for him and for themselves. These men believed in the supreme importance of the individual to God, and the parables of the lost sheep and the prodigal son were their casework manuals."[1]

Whilst emphasis and methods may have changed the recognition of the importance of feeling, the basis of acceptance, disinterested friendship and support, has remained. It has been reinforced rather than shaken by the powerful influences of psychological and psychoanalytical theory and by the analysis of casework methods. Much of that analysis, indeed, has been devoted to study of its conscious development and its varied uses in treatment. The Morison Committee defined casework as "the creation and utilization, for the benefit of an individual who needs help with personal problems, of a relationship between himself and a trained social worker". The more difficult and demanding the work of probation officers becomes, the more persistently criminal or socially isolated the offenders they try to help, the harder it becomes to establish such relationships, yet the more vital such relationships are if any change is to be achieved.

Concentration upon the relationship between offender and officer as the core of treatment can have, however, the defects of its qualities. It may become unduly exclusive, it may take insufficient account of the natural relationships in the offender's life, which can have a much stronger and longer effect upon him, for good or ill. It may lead to undue dependence upon a particular officer, resulting in breakdown when his support is withdrawn. Some offenders may need, in addition to the single relationship with the officer, the support and stimulation of group treatment. Others need the protection and continuous contacts of a hostel, or perhaps the feeling that some member of the public is specially concerned with them as individuals. All these possibilities have been receiving increasing

---

1. George Newton, "Trends in Probation Training", *British Journal of Delinquency*, October 1956.

attention. They are not seen as denying the value of the direct relationship with the probation officer, but as supplementing it and as still further enlarging the scope of treatment.

5 THE PROBATION OFFICERS

The 1907 Act provided for the appointment of probation officers by the courts and their payment from public funds. Most of the early officers, however, though duly appointed by the courts, were police court missionaries, retaining their allegiance to their voluntary societies and partly paid by them. It was not until after 1936 that they became exclusively public employees.

In so far as they were missionaries, they brought a strong sense of vocation, commitment and certainty. In so far as they tackled at the outset some of the most obdurate social problems, such as chronic drunkenness, they admitted sometimes to being "nearly baffled".

The whole emphasis in the selection of these first missionaries and probation officers was upon "excellence of character and strength of personal influence". Everything hinged upon this. In the words of the Committee of 1909:

> "The value of probation must necessarily depend on the efficiency of the probation officer. It is a system in which rules are comparatively unimportant, and personality is everything. The probation officer must be a picked man or woman, endowed not only with intelligence and zeal, but, in a high degree, with sympathy and tact and firmness. On his or her individuality the success or failure of the system depends. Probation is what the officer makes it."

So great was the emphasis upon the character of the probation officer that no minimum qualifications for appointment were laid down in 1907. Whilst stressing the vital importance of qualities of personality, this had the disadvantage, especially in the earlier days of the service, of allowing many unsuitable appointments. The Committee of 1909 was impressed by the "capacity and discretion" of the large majority of the men and women employed at first. But it soon became apparent that, as the service expanded, less satisfactory appointments were being made.

There was the complaint that "the probation service in England, as well as abroad, is too often recruited from persons too old to work".[1] There was the fact that many officers were paid on a *per*

---

1. Cecil Leeson, *The Probation System*, 1914.

capita system, which meant that they were under a temptation either to tout for custom or (if more scrupulous) to refrain from recommending probation as often as they should for fear of being accused of touting. There was the fact that, even if paid by salary, they were subject to re-appointment annually, and thus kept in constant anxiety as to their future. There was the fact that their pay was almost always niggardly, so that unless they had private means they could not provide for their old age. It was no wonder that many of those appointed had other jobs: apart from the many belonging to religious societies, there were school attendance officers, police, collecting officers, N.S.P.C.C. inspectors and poor law officers.

The Report of 1922 stated categorically that many of these did not appear to be properly qualified to act as probation officers and that their employment was detrimental to the success of the system. It recommended the appointment of full-time officers, adequately paid and with superannuation rights, wherever possible.[1] The recommendation had to be repeated in 1936, however, before a decisive turnover from a largely part-time to an almost entirely full-time service was achieved.

The issue was also raised in 1922 of whether probation officers needed higher educational attainments and more specialized training. It was suggested that the attachment of so many of them to religious societies with strict rules unduly narrowed their outlook. There was general agreement, however, that "a keen missionary spirit, based on religious conviction" was essential, and the Committee were content to hand the problem of education back to the societies, suggesting that they might give their candidates the chance of wider experience and higher education, paying them meanwhile. It was not until 1930 that the Home Office itself started a small experimental training scheme, in conjunction with a few universities and probation officers. It was not until after the war that training became available to the great majority of entrants.

Most of the original officers were men, supervising both men and women probationers. Such women as there were concentrated upon women and children. It was conceded in 1909 that their work, as a

---

1. *Report of the Departmental Committee on the Training, Appointment and Payment of Probation Officers* (Cmd. 1601), 1922.

rule, met with much success, but it was held that men officers were "often as successful, sometimes perhaps more successful" in dealing with cases of adult women. There was statutory provision that, where circumstances permitted, special children's probation officers should be appointed, but this was never generally done except in London. Instead, it became increasingly the practice elsewhere for both women and children to be supervised by women. This was encouraged when, in 1925, the Criminal Justice (Administration) Act stipulated that, wherever possible, women officers should be available to the courts. Subsequently it was provided by statute that girls and women should be supervised by women. It was not until the Criminal Justice Act 1967 that this restriction was withdrawn.

There has never been any corresponding legal requirement that boys and men should be supervised by men, and supervision at least of the younger boys by women has been customary almost everywhere. In London, especially, women have been increasingly involved in the supervision of adult men on probation, and they also deal with men in prison welfare and after-care. Men and women are concerned with both sexes in matrimonial work and in contacts with the families of offenders. The removal of the restriction on the appointment of men to supervise women serves a double purpose. Except in London, men officers are more easily available than women; it can thus ease administrative problems. More important, it restores flexibility in relating the choice of officer to the needs of a particular offender. Obviously there are difficulties, which need to be understood, but these have to be weighed in each case against the possibility of more effective help.

The early feeling that specialized provision should be made for the supervision of children has returned in strength in the White Paper on Children in Trouble and the new statutory provisions for their supervision by the child-care service. Yet the long experience of the probation service, and especially of women probation officers, in dealing with delinquent children and their families in the open cannot be ignored.

Another feature of the probation service in its earliest days also strikes a responsive chord now, after many years out of favour. This was the appointment of part-time and even voluntary probation officers. The Committee of 1909 held that, except in very scattered rural areas, at least one whole-time paid probation officer should be

available to a court. Only so could he regard probation as having
the first claim on his attention and only so could he accumulate the
experience clearly needed to deal adequately with difficult cases.
Whole-time officers should form the basis of the service. On the
other hand the Committee also held that there was a place for the
volunteer and the part-timer. There were, for example, young men
with experience of voluntary work in youth clubs and camps who
would be particularly appropriate as supervisors of the hooligan
type of boy in the big cities. There might be other individuals who
were specially suitable for dealing with a particular case, or class of
cases, whether on a paid or voluntary basis. Such people could
supplement, rather than replace, the work of the full-time officer.

In the process of developing probation into a nation-wide service
the possibilities of using voluntary help were almost inevitably
pushed to one side. The first necessity was seen as securing that all
courts, except those in the most scattered areas, had at least one full
time officer available. The second necessity was seen to be that
probation should become fully a public service, with no danger that
officers would have to devote much of their energy to fund-raising
for the voluntary societies to which so many of them belonged in
earlier days. The third necessity was that probation officers should
be trained as social workers and as officers of the courts.

All these objectives have, in the main, been attained. In the fight
to achieve them, the possible contribution of the part-time probation
officer and the volunteer was inevitably devalued. The use of
volunteers even to assist probation officers dwindled and dis-
appeared in many areas. It was seen as worth while only if it
materially reduced the officer's load, which could seldom, if ever, be
the case. Yet the very fact that the service is now established over
the whole country, and staffed with full-time professional officers,
should make it secure enough in its own position and skills to
welcome the volunteer back. He can appear now not as a threat to
the efficiency of the service but as an addition to it. There is no
longer a danger that he will be used as a cheap substitute for a
probation officer. But he can again bring his individual quality and
experience to the help of particular offenders to whom he has
something special to offer. This renewed interest in the contribution
of volunteers has been associated primarily with the transfer of
responsibility for non-compulsory prison after-care, with all its

existing voluntary links, to the probation and after-care service. But it has been seen as a way of retaining and enlarging community interest and participation in the whole problem of rehabilitating offenders.

From the points of view of lightening the probation officer's load, of the urgent need to expand the service to meet new demands, the revival of the old idea of the part-time officer is likely to prove more important. The modern part-timer may well be neither untrained nor inexperienced. Part-time work can be particularly useful as a method of bringing back to the service the qualifications of women officers who retired when they married or had young families. It may be a valuable way of continuing to use some older officers. It certainly need no longer be feared that part-time officers will enable courts to dispense with full-time ones. And certain specialist duties may be particularly appropriate for part-time workers.

Even the idea that there might be some probation officers who, because of their personalities and experience, should be used to supervise certain classes of offenders has returned. A probation officer is not appointed to specialize in particular kinds of work alone, but two comparatively recent developments have once more encouraged the idea of at least temporary specialization. One is the multiplication of duties: enquiries for courts, matrimonial work, prison welfare, after-care, all have their special demands, to which some officers adapt more satisfactorily than others. It may also be administratively convenient, especially in large urban areas, to have the bulk of these duties carried out by specialists. The second factor is the modern interest in trying to fit types of treatment to types of offender. As yet we have little knowledge about such "matching". But it is recognized that a probation officer's attitudes and way of working are very much influenced by his personality. Again, there are dangers in this approach as well as advantages: both need to be watched as experiments in specialization develop.

There are still traces of the original police court missionary in the modern probation officer. He must still have a genuine concern for other people, and particularly for offenders. His own personality is still a vital factor in his work and he still carries much individual responsibility. His link with the courts remains. But he has added to these not only wider duties and responsibilities but the broadening influences of professional training and of membership of an organized service. He is no longer on his own, or bounded by the outlook of a single court or voluntary society. Leadership in the service has taken several forms and has by no means been the sole preserve of the central department or, for that matter, of the principal probation officer. But it has always tended to broaden horizons and enrich understanding.

6 LEADERSHIP

The first police court missionaries could do their work only with the consent and support of the courts. The first probation officers, though their position was official, were directly dependent upon the courts for their appointment and supervision. The close link between court and officer was seen by the Committee of 1909 as advantageous to both: by following the progress of probationers the magistrates could see the effects of their decisions and gather guidance for the future; by discussing cases with magistrates the officers and probationers could benefit from their wide local knowledge and contacts. The link, in fact, was not only that between employers and employed but between co-workers in the task of dealing with offenders.

The direct employer-employee relationship was modified to some extent by the Criminal Justice (Administration) Act 1925, which authorized the combination of smaller petty sessional divisions into probation areas, which might cover a whole county. Each probation area, whether single or combined, was to have a probation committee made up of magistrates chosen by the courts involved. It was these committees that became the employers of probation officers and responsible for the administration of the service. Moves since then have been towards more combination between areas. The probation committees, moreover, have become, since 1967, probation and after-care committees, required to co-opt a number of non-magistrates with knowledge of prisoners and their after-care. And probation officers seconded to the prison welfare service have responsibilities not only to the principal probation officer, representing the probation and after-care committee, but to the prison governor.

In all these ways the direct link between court and probation officer, as employer and employed, has been reduced. It must be remembered, too, that from the start it has been the local authorities who have been responsible, with grant aid from the exchequer, for the cost of the service. On the other hand, the probation and after-care committees are still predominantly committees of magistrates, themselves deeply concerned with the problems of dealing with offenders and directly interested in the quality of the service in their areas. However necessary it may be to widen administrative areas and expand the range of experience represented in the committees to meet new responsibilities, there would be great reluctance amongst the majority of magistrates and probation officers to see the control of the service pass elsewhere. In the new responsibilities for after-care, indeed, members of the committees have been playing an active part. They, as well as their principal probation officers, are directly represented in regional planning committees, and in some areas at least their members have personally engaged in their old role of arousing local community interest in the needs of offenders. Their concern for the development of the service as a whole has also been expressed in the formation of the Central Council of Probation and After-Care Committees.

The more personal aspect of co-operation between magistrates and probation officers has been perpetuated in case committees. In 1909 it was suggested that one or two magistrates with special interest in probation should informally take on the task of "friendly oversight". In 1925 this was formalized in provision for elected case committees at each court, with the duties of discussing cases, inspecting records, giving any help or advice they could and enquiring into complaints. Since 1948 "inspection" has no longer been specified as a duty. Case committees no longer investigate complaints against individual offenders: this is a matter for the probation and after-care committees. There is more emphasis on general oversight of the work of each officer, including his work in after-care as well as probation. The Morison Committee, like its predecessors, held that this could be of value both in enlarging the experience of the justices and in giving officers the help and stimulus of active, independent laymen. This function can be seen as distinct from the professional case-work supervision now given by a senior probation officer and the administrative responsibilities of the principal probation officer. Its value, to both magistrates and officers, is of a different kind.

Detailed organization of the duties of probation officers and detailed supervision of their casework has passed from the courts to principal and senior probation officers. This would have worried the

Committee of 1909. They rejected the idea of "chief probation officers" because, amongst other things, they thought it would weaken the sense of responsibility of the individual probation officer, who was the person in direct contact with probationers. "His individuality, upon which everything depends, would have less play; he would feel himself merely an agent acting under instructions." It was feared, too, that if the magistrates lost their responsibility for direct supervision of probation officers and had reports on probationers only at second hand, they too would lose their personal interest in the work. Neither of these fears has been justified: a major aim of professional supervision is to enable the officer to use his individuality to the full; and the existence of senior ranks has enabled magistrates to add a wider view of the work of the service in their areas to their direct knowledge of officers encountered in courts and case committees.

The appointment of principal probation officers by probation committees was first authorized in 1926, but very few were appointed until after the Report of 1936. It was probation officers themselves who asked for them then: they complained of a lack of adequate supervision in their work, of a sense of isolation, of having no one to whom they could turn for advice and encouragement, no adequate means of keeping in touch with outside developments. It was to meet such needs as these, as well as to provide probation committees with professional advice on organization, that the Committee recommended the appointment of principal probation officers and, where the number of officers justified it, of senior probation officers as well. Now almost every probation area has a principal officer, sometimes a deputy and assistant principals as well, and supervision and consultation by senior officers is becoming generally accepted as desirable.

For all its fears about chief officers, the 1909 Committee recognized the need for some source of stimulation and information to maintain efficiency and provide the initiative for experiment and growth. They applauded two suggestions: the first that the Home Office should undertake part of this function, the second that probation officers themselves should form an association for the purpose.

One official in the Home Office was, at that time, charged with the duty of keeping in touch with the development of probation work throughout the country and with furnishing any information about it that seemed necessary. In 1922, since development was lagging, it was recommended that the Children's Branch of the Home Office should devote more time and staff to bringing home to magistrates the importance of probation, actively collecting and publishing information. An Advisory Committee was also recommended and established. From this enlarged Home Office responsibility developed informal visits to officers and a series of circulars on various aspects of the work. Following the report of the 1936 Committee, which pointed out that it was misleading for probation to be the responsibility of the Children's Branch, the Probation Division of the Home Office was established; so was a Probation Training Board and an official inspectorate. In 1964 the Probation Division became the Probation and After-Care Department, and there is now an Advisory Council for Probation and After-Care, with an independent chairman and a sub-committee specially concerned with recruitment and training.

The National Association of Probation Officers, formed in 1912, has had a major role in stimulating the service from within. Because the work of probation officers has depended so much upon individual enthusiasm and initiative, opportunities for officers to get together, to exchange views, to support and inspire each other, have been vital to the growth of the service. As senior ranks developed, most principal and senior officers remained members of the association, thus making it a forum within which people with different levels of responsibility could meet on an equal footing, and in which leadership was available from all ranks. Its journal, *Probation*, first appeared within a year of its foundation; through this and through its long series of conferences both at branch and national level, it has contributed to building up the service. It has been concerned both with adequate remuneration and security for all probation officers and with standards of work. It has always been eager to examine new ideas on the service's work or clients. It has formed links with people interested in similar work all over the world.

At this time, when so much affecting the role and position of the service is changing, the association itself has been faced with a decision as to whether to sink its identity in a single unified body of social workers. On one side it has been aware of the pressure of new demands and new relationships needing to be developed by the service, especially with others working in the administration of justice and the penal system. On the other, it has been aware of the pressure to remain within the main stream of social work. It is well aware that its decision is likely to impinge upon those with whom probation officers work as well as upon the service itself. The existing prestige and achievements of the association, and the strong loyalties it has been able to arouse inevitably make the choice a hard one.

7 RESPONSES TO CHANGE

Change in the service over the past ten years has been sweeping, even startling. In England and Wales it has more than doubled in size. It has doubled the number of enquiries it makes for the adult courts, it has doubled the number of offenders under its care. It has embarked upon completely new duties in voluntary after-care, prison welfare and parole. It has found its way into the penal institutions. It has contemplated the prospect of handing over its extensive and traditional responsibilities for delinquent children.

So great have been these changes that to many they seem to constitute a fundamental alteration in the nature and direction of the service. For the future, it is sometimes suggested, there will and should be less concern with juvenile delinquents, more with older adolescents and adults; less concern with first or minor offenders, more with recidivists; less reliance upon individual casework alone, more upon working with groups, enlisting volunteers and involving the community; a less exclusive concentration upon the needs of offenders at home, more upon those in penal institutions or hostels. The increased size of the service and its more onerous responsibilities for the protection of the public, are bringing a more elaborate organization, a greater emphasis upon the role of its senior members. There will be more need for hard decisions where the welfare of offender and community conflict. Comprehensive and realistic assessments will have to be made of what can be hoped for, in the long term as well as the short, with different kinds of offender and of what are the best means of achieving it.

The impact of change can be exaggerated just because it is so new. After-care, though it calls for much fresh thinking and effort at this time, is no novel duty: probation officers have carried responsibilities for it for many years. Probation in England has from the first been concerned with adults as well as children and it has never been restricted to the first offender or the trivial offence. Though it was, and still is, used for a higher proportion of juvenile than of adult offenders, the balance has been changing for many years: less than half of those now on probation are juveniles. Moreover, in spite of all the changes, probation still accounts for over two-thirds of caseloads, after-care for no more than a fifth. Obviously the proportions will change further if few delinquents under seventeen continue to be put under the supervision of probation officers, but even so probation is still likely to constitute the largest part of the supervisory work. Again, though enquiries for the courts may deal with offenders of all kinds and ages, they are concentrated particularly upon first offenders and younger offenders: it is at this enquiry stage that the great majority first come into contact with the service. Nor should it be forgotten that probation officers have many responsibilities arising from wholly non-criminal matters, such as matrimonial disputes coming to magistrates' and divorce courts. Thus to see the future of the service as narrowed down to the treatment of persistent adult criminals alone is to distort the reality.

Above all there is no question of abandoning the basic task of helping offenders to find and keep a place in the community. Rather the service is being called upon to extend to those in greatest need its concern to find alternatives to "offence after offence and sentence after sentence". In addition it is being asked, more fully than ever before, to stimulate members of the community itself to help in rehabilitation. There remains, too, ample scope for initiative amongst all ranks. Senior officers are naturally expected to take a leading part in new developments, but some of the most interesting experiments are being pioneered by individuals. In a service where personalities and personal relationships are the basic working materials, individual decision and individual initiative must always have their scope.

Nevertheless, though the impact of change should not be over-emphasized or distorted, it should certainly not be minimized or ignored. To underestimate the strain imposed upon the service by such radical alterations in its scope and expectations is to invite trouble. If the challenge to its identity and traditions is felt to be too extreme it may lose its cohesion, its self-respect and its impetus at a time when it needs them most. The very fact that it has been one of the pioneers of social work in this country and has built up a tradition of attitudes and duties over many years makes it hard for it to adjust to sudden change. A sense of loss is inevitable when a close-knit service has to face either division or absorption in some larger body.

The course of recent events has hardly been calculated either to allay such fears or to help the service to come to terms with them. In 1960 and 1962, following very thorough surveys, the Ingleby and Morison Committees re-affirmed its existing structure and functions. In the following year came the first indication of a really drastic extension of duties, with the report of the Advisory Council on after-care. On this probation officers were consulted and the proposals made were largely in accord with their recommendations. Though there were fears about whether adequate resources would be forthcoming, there was a general conviction that the service ought to undertake the new duties. In fact not only the functions then foreseen but those of prison welfare and parole were subsequently added to its range. In 1965 appeared the White Paper on The Child, the Family and the Young Offender, which, without any discussion of the work of probation officers in this field, suggested that responsibility for delinquents up to sixteen should be taken over by the local authority children's departments. This and other proposals aroused hot controversy and for well over two years no firm pronouncement of policy was made.

The uncertainties engendered, the difficulty of predicting the future role of the service, the misconception that it would wholly cease to be concerned with young people, were all reflected in the loss of experienced officers and the failure to recruit enough new people for training in the years that immediately followed that White Paper. It is ironical that this should have happened just as the service was being called upon to assume new and exacting responsibilities and whilst it still carries the lion's share of work with young delinquents. It is yet more ironical that this situation should have been produced, at bottom, by the triumph of three approaches to the treatment of offenders of which probation officers were long the major advocates and practitioners. The belief that offenders should be given help in rehabilitating themselves has been, quite logically, extended to cover all who need such help, whether put on probation or sent to institutions. Hence the extension of after-care and prison welfare. The belief that, so far as possible, they should be dealt with in the open has been reflected in the various measures to avoid or reduce imprisonment, including suspended sentences and parole. The belief that children in trouble should, whenever possible, be treated without removal from home and in co-operation with their parents has, equally logically, been developed by children's departments to the point where it is proposed to absorb the care of delinquent children into a comprehensive children's or family service.

Because all these movements are in line with its essential beliefs the service has accepted them, though not unanimously and not without certain doubts and reservations. There have been fears, for example, that if, through excessive caution or shortage of resources, parole is granted too conservatively, the disappointment that results will cause bitterness in the prisons and minimize the chance of helping those most in need when they eventually come out. There have been fears that enough recognition may not be given to children's sense of justice and developing social responsibility. There have been fears that the sharpened distinction between juvenile and adult offenders will heighten the rejection of the latter.

It is not irrelevant to remember, in face of all this change and all these doubts, that the probation and after-care service is not alone in having to face radical new demands. Education, health, welfare and children's services, voluntary societies, approved schools and penal institutions, courts, lawyers and police forces, in fact all the services whose work borders on that of probation officers, have come under scrutiny, have been called upon to re-assess their structures and objectives, sometimes to accept fundamental change or to sacrifice their identities.

Simultaneous attempts are being made to expand their functions in the hope that social breakdown can be prevented or reduced rather than merely treated as it occurs. Such endeavours call both for more material resources and for their more flexible and imaginative deployment by more and better qualified staff. A move away from rigidity and from reliance upon institutional control cannot succeed if it is seen merely as a means of saving money. If the cost of trained educational and social workers, or of necessary hostels, is begrudged, for example, hopes that difficult young people, the mentally ill or the persistently criminal can be treated within the community, must inevitably fail. Alternatives to the heavy expenditure and the waste of life involved in keeping the handicapped or the criminal in institutions for many years are not to be bought cheaply, in terms either of money or of human effort, and they must be accepted as continuing responsibilities.

The widespread upheaval in all these services could affect them in different ways. It could drive each to withdraw defensively into its shell, fighting for its share of scarce resources, anxious to preserve the particular values it upholds, the way of working it has evolved, the special interests of those with whom it is concerned. Alternatively, since all the services are facing similar stress and challenged by new problems, they could respond by drawing together in an exchange of experience. This could be the more fruitful because each, in trying to find fresh approaches, is adopting or adapting the methods of others. Thus schools are beginning to appoint counsellors with functions very like those of social workers, whilst social workers are coming to realize that they may have more to learn from the field of education. Children's departments expect to draw upon the experience of probation officers in dealing with young offenders in the open, whilst probation officers can learn from the child care service about the large-scale use of volunteers, whether as foster parents or as friendly links with the community. Probation is experimenting in work with offenders in groups, an approach hitherto used more in the penal institutions; at the same time these institutions are trying modifications of the casework approach, for long the preserve of the probation officer. It is not likely that the experience or methods of one field can be transferred directly and without modification to another but, in trying to understand each other's ways of working, the various services can both break down walls of prejudice and spark off new ideas for helping their own clients.

Change may be a source of discouragement and confusion, or it may be a source of stimulation. Amongst many probation officers the reaction has been a positive one, a renewed eagerness to experiment and to expand their understanding. This has shown itself in the development of relationships with prisons and penal institutions on one hand and with volunteers in the community on the other. It has shown itself in a range of ventures into groupwork; in cooperation and interest in research; in a willingness to keep on questioning, reviewing and modifying the scope and methods of casework.

Change in the probation and after-care service, as in the social services as a whole, is a product of far broader social change. It reflects the pace of that change, with its accompanying impatience and its conviction that old evils and old failures should not be accepted as irremediable just because no answer has been found in the past. It is part of the attempt to adapt social institutions to meet both old and new needs more effectively and more fully. The possibility of progress depends upon the ability not merely to withstand the strain of change, but to seize and harness its opportunities.

CHAPTER 2

THE SERVICE AND PENAL INSTITUTIONS

1 CONTINUITY

In the eyes of most people there is a great gulf fixed between offenders who are put on probation, fined, discharged, or otherwise left their liberty and those who are "put away", whether they be sent to prison, borstal, or detention centre. To the stigma of the offence is added the stigma of confinement, separation from the rest of society. The very fact that only one indictable offender in five is dealt with in this way emphasizes the conclusion that these are the most dangerous, those most likely to commit further crimes, least likely to respond readily to treatment or to trust. On top of that, in a penal institution they are inevitably in contact with other offenders, they are deprived not only of their liberty but of most of their responsibilities, and even where attempts are made to counteract these evils, they are likely to emerge less rather than more able to stand on their own feet.

The probation service started from a powerful desire to keep people out of prison. Its central concern has always been the treatment of offenders in the open. It has long had some responsibility for a few of those released from penal institutions, particularly the young. Until recently that responsibility has been peripheral. Now it has been brought to the centre.

Statutory after-care has been expanded. Voluntary after-care has been added. And within the penal institutions themselves the probation officer finds himself social worker to a prison, a detention centre, perhaps a girls' borstal or an allocation centre. To understand this it is necessary to look wider than the probation service, even than the probation and after-care service. It is part of a three-fold move to reduce time spent in institutions, to make them more effective and more humane in the treatment of those who must go to them, and to ensure that all who are willing to respond have a chance of help, both before and after they return to the community. In other words, to reduce the traditional gulf and throw some bridges across it.

After-care might have been made the responsibility of a new and separate service. So might prison welfare. In both cases this was carefully considered and in both eventually rejected. The probation service had three things to offer. First it was already a service of considerable size, offering variety of experience and growing opportunities of advancement: its members could thus devote part of their time, perhaps part of their careers, to the care and after-care of prisoners; part, as hitherto, to the service of the courts and the care of probationers and others. A separate service would, in a sense, have perpetuated the gulf between the imprisoned and the rest: a combined service would, by its very existence, form one of the bridges between them. Second, the probation service already had a network of offices, local contacts and local knowledge all over the country: these could be brought into play wherever a prisoner's family might live, wherever he might go on release. Third, the service had a store of knowledge and experience in dealing with offenders generally, as well as a certain amount of specific knowledge of statutory after-care.

That is far from saying that it is already equipped to deal with all the new problems that have suddenly come its way. It is as important to recognize the large areas of ignorance as to remember and try to adapt what has been learned in other fields. Progress depends upon being willing to experiment, and often to fail. Failures, accurately interpreted, can contribute almost as much as successes at this stage, preventing the future misdirection of resources, giving clues as to where effort might better be concentrated.

This may seem a slow and painful process, especially when forces are often spread too thinly upon the ground. It may mean that officers in different parts of the country, connected with different institutions, are adopting quite different roles, following apparently contradictory policies. Given a continued interchange of experience, some principles of general application will no doubt emerge. But the differences between individual institutions, those confined in them, and the communities to which they return, are so considerable that uniformity is never likely either to be attained or perhaps to be desirable. At present those grappling most closely with the new tasks are the readiest to admit their ignorance of what is needed and of how it best can be provided.

It has been suggested that in the long run the probation and after-care service may have an impact upon the penal institutions similar to the impact that it has undoubtedly had upon the courts. There were some in the courts from the outset who were prepared to come half-way to meet the probation officer. Magistrates were amongst those who contributed most to the earlier ventures in the direction of probation. Similarly there are many now within the prison service who are deeply concerned about the humanization of penal institutions and, more specifically, about the needs of individual offenders.

On the other hand, the new direct links between the probation and after-care service and the prisons in after-care have been seen as strengthening direct communication between social workers inside and outside, concerned alike with the welfare of the prisoner and his family. On the level of organization, moves towards regionalization should facilitate this. There are already regionalized prison areas, and probation and after-care areas also have been grouped in regions for the provision of hostel facilities; proposals for a regional-ization of the probation and after-care inspectorate, in areas coinciding with the prison regions, may press the process a step further. The new links have been seen as the means to achieve a continuity of care reaching right through all stages of treatment.

This too is an ideal which has yet to become an actuality. There has been, for example, a very considerable interchange within the probation and after-care service between officers working within the prisons and outside. Yet many probation officers are reluctant to contemplate prison work, even for a short time, and those serving as welfare officers still feel themselves rather isolated from the rest of the service. It is comparatively rarely that the same probation officer can follow an offender and his family right through, say, a pre-sentence enquiry, probation, a failure on probation, visits and contact during imprisonment and eventual after-care. The continu-ity, if it is to come, will usually depend on consistency of aims and standards throughout the service, and a general acceptance of mutual responsibility at all stages.

Whilst the concern for an offender and the endeavour to reduce his criminality may ideally be seen as consistent throughout this continuum, the emphasis on the probation officer's share of responsibility for the protection of the community varies considerably at each stage. In parole it is perhaps at its highest, in voluntary after-care at its lowest. The remainder of this chapter is devoted to a consideration of these variations and of the relation of the probation officer and his work to the various penal institutions. Variations in his casework are dealt with more specifically in a later chapter.[1]

2   STATUTORY AFTER-CARE OF YOUNG OFFENDERS

It is a statutory duty of probation officers to provide after-care for offenders leaving approved schools if they are requested to do so by the managers;[2] for all offenders leaving borstals and detention centres; for all prisoners released on parole; for young prisoners and extended sentence prisoners, even if they are not granted parole, during their period of remission; and for those released from life imprisonment and young persons released from detention during Her Majesty's pleasure. In addition, officers must "advise, assist and befriend" (though not, as in the other cases, "supervise" as well) any other discharged prisoners who come to them voluntarily for help during the first year after release.[3]

This last group have no statutory obligation to contact or remain in touch with the probation officer. All the rest have, and they are therefore frequently referred to as "statutory after-care" cases. Statutory after-care in this sense has been considered necessary for all young offenders, whether they have been to schools, detention centres, borstals or prisons.

Statutory after-care seems to have been instituted with three things in mind. First, an emphasis on training rather than punishment; this predominated in the decision that after-care should be an essential part of borstal treatment. Second, the youth of offenders; this was important in the introduction of after-care for those leaving detention centres: courts were not satisfied to order a short punitive

---

1. See below, pp. 113–131.

2. This duty will presumably disappear if Approved School Orders are abolished under the Children and Young Persons Bill 1969.

3. For a full summary of the classes of offender of all ages subject to statutory after-care, and of the conditions applying to each, see F. Jarvis, *Probation Officers' Manual*, 1969.

sentence alone in such cases. Youth as a justification is also evident in compulsory after-care for young prisoners. Third, the feeling that supervision was needed for certain offenders who might be a particular danger or nuisance to the community, for the protection of others as well as for their own good; this has been an element in parole and to some extent in compulsory after-care for those subjected to the old sentences of preventive detention and corrective training, and to the new extended sentence. Whilst there is an element of control in all kinds of compulsory after-care, and whilst the duty to advise, assist and befriend also runs through all of them, differences in emphasis are discernible.

The stronger emphasis on treatment in dealing with the young is reflected in the fact that, whereas the period of supervision in parole depends on how long the prisoner would otherwise have been held in custody (being shorter the later he is released), in borstal and detention centre after-care it is a fixed period: two years from release for those leaving borstals, one year for those leaving detention centres. In the latter case the period has to be reviewed by the supervising officer with his principal after six months, and discharge recommended to the Secretary of State if thought advisable. In both borstal and detenion centre cases, the Secretary of State can end the supervision at any time, and a recommendation that he should do so can be made by the probation officer. There is no such provision in parole.

The basic requirements of the notice of supervision issued to an offender leaving borstal or a detention centre are broadly similar to those of a probation order, requiring him to keep in touch with the probation officer (who is, incidentally, named in the notice), to be of good behaviour and to lead an industrious life. The borstal licensee, however, is required to inform the officer of a proposed change of address or employment and get his approval, not merely to notify him of a change. And there is no specific mention to home visits by the officer for those licensed from detention centres.

Whereas the sanction behind probation is the possibility that the offender may be brought back to court and sentenced, the sanction in after-care is that he may be recalled to a penal institution. Where a court convicts a person on licence from borstal of a fresh offence punishable by imprisonment, it can order his recall, but the decision to recall for failure to comply with the requirements of the notice of supervision rests with the Home Secretary. A recommendation for recall can be made by the supervising officer through the principal probation officer. In the case of a detention centre, recall cannot be repeated. Thus during the latter part of the period of after-care the sanction may disappear.

The work of probation officers in compulsory after-care of young offenders has to be seen against very depressing failure rates amongst the offenders concerned. Of the youths released from borstal and junior detention centres in 1962, only three out of ten had not been reconvicted within three years. Senior detention centres did little better with four out of ten and approved schools with rather less than that.

If compulsory after-care for young offenders is intended to be, as in borstal training, the second part of a process of treatment begun in the institution, it is particularly important here to think of the process as a whole. For one thing it might be a good idea if courts could formally include the period of after-care in pronouncing sentence: at present, it is too easy for offenders to regard it as a gratuitous addition after they have completed the period in an institution which they regard as their punishment. More fundamentally, the question has been raised of whether after-care can hope to succeed unless the institutional part of training is radically altered. It has been suggested that borstals have been far too much concerned with encouraging conformity within the institution, rather than helping boys in specific ways to adjust to life in the open community. This is, of course, a weakness of all institutions, and lends strength to the proposal that more hostels with skilled staff should be developed, both to follow periods in closed institutions and as alternatives to them.

In so far as that may be seen only as an ideal and long-term solution, there remains the possibility that the direct links now developed between probation officers and penal institutions may lead to a two-way traffic. Not only do probation officers need to know the sort of experience boys undergo in different kinds of borstals and detention centres, but institutional staffs need to know the sort of difficulties the boys come up against after discharge. A beginning has been made in the practice of arranging for probation officers to spend a few days at a borstal and in encouraging visits to individual offenders who will be supervised on release. But there is considerable interest also in experiments like that at Huntercombe Borstal, where some members of the prison staff, co-operating with probation officers, have been able to visit individual inmates for several months after release. As a result, it has been claimed "The many problems experienced by lads after release have also helped to spotlight weaknesses in the training, such as understanding the limitations of the wage packet, the social, personal, financial and domestic aspects of marriage, how to approach official bodies and those in authority."[1]

Though statutory after-care is not a new obligation, the recent expansion of responsibilities to include parole on one hand, voluntary after-care on the other, must lead to fresh thinking and fresh opportunities in the whole field. In particular, it should reduce the old feeling that after-care is peripheral. There are extended possibilities of visiting boys whilst still in the institution. Where this is not possible letters may forge or maintain a link. As after-care hostels and work with volunteers develop, the range of possibilities in helping statutory after-care cases expands. The growing interest in group work may prove particularly relevant here, as many borstal boys will already be accustomed to this kind of approach. In other borstals, where casework methods have been adopted and adapted, there may also be experience to be taken up and carried further. In detention centres, the appointment of social workers from the probation and after-care services, with the express duty of joining with their colleagues outside in preparing for after-care, should give a better basis for continued work in the community.[2]

3 PAROLE

Release on parole under the terms of the 1967 Criminal Justice Act has been described as "discretionary release during the middle third of a fixed sentence of imprisonment, subject to the serving of a minimum of one year". Since most prisoners are automatically released after serving two-thirds of their time, only those sentenced to more than eighteen months can become eligible. It is emphasized that release on parole is not a right and it has been stated that those

1. H. T. Osborne, "Huntercombe Borstal after-care system" (1966), *Prison Officers' Magazine*, Vol. 56, No. 12, p. 319.
2. For a detailed discussion of statutory after-care with young people from the various institutions see M. Monger, *Casework in After-Care*, pp. 151–178.

paroled are continuing their sentences under supervision in the community. If they break any conditions of parole, therefore, or even appear likely to commit further offences, they may be recalled. Though they may make written representations they have no right of hearing.

The probation and after-care service is involved in the processes of parole at several points. At each prison a principal or senior probation officer sits on the review committee. He thus takes part in considering the available information about each man and in deciding whether the recommendation which the committee is required to make to the Home Office shall be in favour of parole or not. He may have the preliminary task of taking a statement from the prisoner of any matters he wants put forward to support his case. When the recommendation for parole is passed on by the Home Office for consideration by the Parole Board, one of the two principal probation officers on that body is likely to be involved in the final decision as to whether release is to be recommended. If the man is paroled, he will come under the supervision of a probation officer, who will be responsible not only for helping him but for reporting any sign of trouble to his principal, who must in turn report it to the Home Office for consideration of recall. Here the Parole Board will have the last word.

Probation officers supported the introduction of a parole system in this country, seeing it as another step forward in penal reform, part of a determined effort to reduce unnecessary imprisonment, a contribution to the rehabilitation of offenders, an acknowledgement that even the public safety might not be best served, in many cases, by unduly prolonged confinement.

Some of the criteria suggested for the selection of men for parole would appear to bear out hopes that there will be an emphasis on rehabilitation. It has been said that it will normally be granted only if the prisoner "demonstrates, by his attitude and response in prison, that he wants to become a law-abiding citizen and if there appears to be a good prospect that, with the help of his supervising probation officer, he will be able to do so by being granted early release".[1] In assessing this, account is to be taken of his past record, the circumstances of his offence, his social background, reports on

---

1. H.O.C. 46/68, 26 February 1968.

him by the prison service and his likely circumstances on release.

There are obvious difficulties however. How does a prisoner demonstrate by his response in prison that there is a good prospect that he is likely to behave well on release? It is only too well known that the "good prisoner", the man who conforms and gives no trouble inside, can be the first to break down as soon as the protective restraint of prison is removed. Yet assessments of response have to be made by members of the prison service, who cannot but be tempted, consciously or unconsciously, to use the possibility of parole as a means of upholding discipline within the institution.

On the other hand, if prisoners can see no direct relation between their efforts to conform to the requirements of the institution, as they see them, and their chances of parole, they may well have a growing sense of injustice. It has been laid down that parole is not a right and that good behaviour in prison alone will not suffice to earn it, but prisoners will still think that if they have kept the rules and taken whatever courses or training are open to them they should be entitled to it. Yet if for any reason it is thought that they would commit further serious crime if released they will not be paroled. Thus a prisoner's past record, the circumstances of his offence, his social background or personal abnormalities may be such that they outweigh any evidence there may be that he has already benefited as much as he is likely to from his time in prison.

There is no doubt that parole in this country has so far been applied in very cautious terms. The primary factor has been the risk to the public thought to be involved in early release. Of nearly four and a half thousand prisoners eligible when parole came into force on 1 April 1968, only a quarter were passed by the Review Committees at the prisons. A half of these were filtered off by the Home Office, leaving only five hundred of those assessed as suitable by local committees. In addition the Home Office referred to the Board over fifty cases which local committees had not assessed as suitable. But of the total put to the Board no more than three hundred and fifty were released, many of them with only very short periods left to serve.

There is justification for great caution in the earliest stages of a new experiment. Failures bring strictures from public and judiciary about the need for stringent selection and for prompt action to recall where necessary. However, those rejected in the first instance are reconsidered regularly, and all cases recommended by review committees are now being referred automatically to the Parole Board. Early in 1969 it was stated that about a fifth of all prisoners eligible for parole were being released, and that only $2\frac{1}{2}$ per cent of those released had failed during the first eleven months of the scheme.

Nevertheless, caution in release will continue and many prisoners will be refused parole. This entails an anomaly that cannot be separated from the conception of parole as part of a fixed term of imprisonment. Precisely those who are most likely to get into further trouble are those who are likeliest to be paroled latest or not at all: those, therefore, who will normally be released without any supervision. It is noteworthy that in America, where over half of all prisoners are already released subject to parole, it has been suggested that a fixed period of parole should follow all sentences of imprisonment, regardless of the proportion served, an arrangement rather similar to the fixed terms of after-care adopted in this country for young offenders who have been to borstals or detention centres.

Another complication arises from consideration of the prisoner's "likely circumstances on release". From the point of view of public safety, and in a prisoner's own interests, there is obviously a much stronger case for releasing him if he has a home to go to and a family, or even a landlady, prepared to stand by him and support him in his efforts to make good. If he is homeless and a place can be found in a good hostel his chances will again be increased. This, however, may again produce a sense of injustice in the case of prisoners with nowhere suitable to go, since they may feel they are denied parole for reasons beyond their own control.

Copies of social enquiry reports made by probation officers before sentence (or, exceptionally, afterwards) are sent to the prison and form part of the parole dossier which is opened when prisoners are admitted. The task of making an up-to-date assessment of home surroundings when parole is being considered, or perhaps of finding hostel or lodgings for a homeless prisoner, again falls upon the probation officer. These enquiries are made only in cases in which, from other points of view, the prisoner seems likely to qualify for parole. This has been justified on the ground that to make visits in all "eligible" cases would raise false hopes. On the other hand, if visits are very selective the hopes raised may be more intense and the bitterness if parole is refused greater. As the parole scheme develops reports may be requested more frequently: if this happens they will become more a matter of routine to the family and the prisoner, and thus less likely to raise false expectations. Quite apart from their usefulness in connection with parole enquiries, they can be seen as an essential part of any efforts to individualize the treatment of prisoners whilst still within the institution and to relate it to their life outside.

The fact must also be faced, however, as in making reports for the courts, that if the probation officer makes this sort of enquiry the offender will recognize his contribution to any decision against releasing him. Similar considerations apply to the contribution of the prison welfare officer to the parole dossier in the prison. These difficulties are all, to some extent, inseparable from the very concept of parole. They have to be recognized clearly because of their effects on the feelings of prisoners and their families, especially in the many cases where parole is refused or long delayed.

The National Association of Probation Officers has advocated from the start that recommendations for parole should not be treated as a separate issue but in the context of the whole of a man's treatment and training in prison. The progress of all long-term prisoners should be made the subject of regular and continuous review, designed to assess progress and adjust treatment. Work, training, hostels, home leave and parole would all come into this, and all kinds of prison staff, including the welfare officer, would contribute. The prisoner would not need to feel, at any one time each year, that parole was the crucial issue or the only important factor in altering his lot. The fact that the new system of documentation introduced for those eligible for parole is being used for allocation purposes, and involves regular reviews, can be seen as a move in this direction.

Where a prisoner is released on parole he is subject to conditions which are again rather similar to the requirements of a probation order: he must be under the supervision of a probation officer, keep in touch with him as instructed, inform him if he changes his address or loses his job, and be of good behaviour and lead an industrious life. He is not specifically required to receive visits at his home but there may be special additional conditions of residence or medical treatment. However, the American habit of imposing all sorts of restrictions upon the parolee's way of life, some of them difficult to enforce, seems unlikely to be adopted here. Requirements to refrain from alcohol or gambling, for instance, are not envisaged.

The principal probation officer is required to inform the chief constable of the licensee's address when he first reports to his supervising officer, and similarly to notify any move to another police area. Probation officers have felt some anxiety about this, though it has been emphasized that the information should not be used by the police in such a way as to handicap the rehabilitation of the offender or impair the relationship between him and his supervising officer. The police, on their side, are required to inform the principal or supervising probation officer at once if the person on parole commits another offence or behaves in a way that suggests he is a risk to the public.[1]

The period of licence usually lasts until the date when the prisoner would, with remission, have been discharged in the ordinary way. Exceptions are prisoners serving extended sentences and young prisoners, who are liable to supervision right up to the expiration of their sentences. In most other cases, however, the actual period is likely to be fairly short, between six and twelve months. It will, nevertheless, cover the critical time immediately after release. And it is clearly envisaged that it will be a period not merely of supervision but of help. To quote the circular issued when the parole scheme was introduced, it should be "possible for support to be given which might not be accepted voluntarily on discharge; and in all cases the relationship established between the probation officer and the licensee and his family, during the pre-release preparations and during the period of compulsory supervision, may encourage the acceptance of voluntary after-care after the licence has expired".[2]

The power to alter the conditions of licence or recall the prisoner on parole rests again with the Secretary of State, but acting on the recommendation of the Parole Board. The probation and after-care service has a duty to notify him not only in any case where contact with a licensee is lost, a condition has been broken, or there has been another charge, but also where there is anything in the offender's response, situation or behaviour that presents an actual or potential risk to the public, that seems likely to bring the parole scheme into disrepute, or that may make it necessary to consider recall. This

1. H.O.C. 66/1968, 19 March 1968.
2. H.O.C. 46/68, 26 February 1968.

may not result in recall but may justify a warning from the Home Office to the licensee.

Although the decision in these matters rests clearly with the Home Office, and although within the probation and after-care service the decision to report them is passed up to the principal probation officer, the wide scope of these requirements for reporting upon the conduct and circumstances of licensees inevitably causes some anxiety to probation officers. They shrink from being instrumental in returning a man to prison where there is no clear breach of conditions. And before the 1967 Act was passed they expressed the opinion that recall should be a matter for the courts, so that the offender could contest the grounds for recall and put his case personally. Though it has been pointed out, against this view, that both the original release and the possible recall are administrative decisions within the framework of a continuing prison sentence, there is little doubt that uneasiness remains within the service on this issue.

4 VOLUNTARY AFTER-CARE

Whilst compulsory after-care for adolescents and young adults has been expanded by the inclusion of those leaving detention centres, there has been a move in the opposite direction as regards adult prisoners. Under the Criminal Justice Act of 1948 all those released following corrective training or preventive detention, as well as the very few persons released from life imprisonment, were subject to compulsory after-care. Under the Criminal Justice Act of 1961 provision was made to add, as soon as the service was able to take this additional burden, all those sentenced to four years' imprisonment or more, those sentenced to six months or more under the age of twenty-six, and those so sentenced who had already been to borstal or been sentenced to at least three months' imprisonment or to corrective training or preventive detention. But the Criminal Justice Act of 1967 saw a change of heart. Preventive detention and corrective training were abolished and the provision for the extension of statutory after-care, which had never been put into force, was repealed.

The decision not to extend compulsory after-care to more classes of adult offenders had as its counterpart and partial justification the decision to make the probation and after-care service responsible for the after-care of all prisoners who desire it. The underlying argument would seem to be that if after-care, in the sense of genuine help rather than mere supervision, is to be of any real use to adults they must accept it voluntarily, and that it is a waste of time in most cases to impose it against their wills.

There is obviously a lot in this, especially as former prisoners feel strongly that they have already paid for their offences and in many cases want to forget about imprisonment and get away from all representatives of authority as quickly as possible. But the same argument could be applied to compulsory after-care following borstal or a detention centre. And the trouble about leaving all but the youngest prisoners to choose whether they will have after-care and how long they will persist in contact is that those most in need of help will often be those least likely to ask for it or to persevere.

Part of the answer may be for prison welfare officers to seek out such men and themselves persevere in trying to show them they have something to offer. This may be very salutary in stimulating new thinking and new methods. But it must be admitted that it is an approach unfamiliar to most probation officers. Much is made of the value, in probation, of the compulsory contact over a set period of officer and probationer. It is pointed out that it gives time for a relationship to be made, plans of treatment to be worked out and worked through. It is pointed out also that the probationer has a sense of being entitled, during the order, to a share of the officer's time and attention. These certainties can exist also in compulsory after-care but are less clear to the prisoner if contact is purely voluntary on his own side and no time limit is set. Time must obviously be allowed to see how far the voluntary system can be developed. There are encouraging signs in some directions. Twenty per cent more prisoners accepted it in 1967 than in 1966, and this momentum was maintained in 1968. But if it becomes clear that the most needy continue to evade it and that some at least of them could be given systematic help if they had to maintain contact, there may be a case for again trying to identify the critical points in the development of recidivism and for requiring after-care for certain classes of offender on the lines laid down in 1961.

Chances to make contact with prisoners, to identify those most in need of or likely to respond to after-care, to begin a relationship that will encourage them to accept after-care, may occur at a succession

of different points. The first may even be before a probation order
breaks down or at the time of a pre-sentence enquiry. Another can
occur when a probation officer sees a prisoner immediately after
sentence to find out whether he or his family are in need of help.
Though there may be much bitterness and even bewilderment at
such times, at least the probation officer can convey that the offender
is not wholly abandoned, can show that his feelings are understood,
and can get pointers to needs which he or the prison welfare officer
can follow up. A third, and vitally important, point of contact lies
with the prison welfare officer when the man enters the institution.
It is here that the heavy pressure of work, especially in overcrowded
local prisons with a high turnover, is a great obstacle to adequate
investigation at a crucial point. Stress has been laid on the need for
an "unhurried initial interview" with each man. This can not only
relieve anxiety and give him an idea of how the welfare officer may
be able to help him, but enable the officer to decide whether he
should take the initiative in seeing more of a particular man and
trying to give him systematic help whilst he is in prison which may
carry on into after-care when he leaves. Meanwhile, it may be
possible for a probation officer in his home area to maintain correspondence and perhaps visit him, thus strengthening the feeling that
he is not forgotten or wholly rejected by those outside and reminding
him that he will have someone to turn to when he gets home. With
such a background the question of whether he wants after-care on
release should gradually cease to be a formality towards the end of
sentence and become instead a question that means something to
the prisoner and holds out hope of a kind of caring he understands
from experience.

In some areas there have been experiments in basing this potential
build-up of concern upon a single continuing relationship, reaching
right through imprisonment into after-care. In connection with at
least one prison serving a largely, though not exclusively, rural area,
probation officers are encouraged to retain casework responsibility
for offenders, visiting them in prison and dealing with their outside
problems as well, carrying on with after-care when they leave. In
another small local prison the continuous relationship may be
provided by a member of the prison staff, as in the borstal already
mentioned. At Grendon the prison psychiatric social worker
specializes in after-care. In yet another prison, taking long-sentence

recidivists, many of whom are without home or friends outside, links are forged by visits from volunteers over a considerable period before release, the same people carrying on as associates after the prisoners leave.

There are many practical difficulties. The pressure of other duties on probation officers may preclude continued contact with prisoners except in a few selected cases. What is possible in rural areas may not prove feasible in the cities where crime and criminals are most concentrated and the problems sharpest. Although the moves towards regionalization in both the prison and the probation and after-care service may reduce barriers of distance and communication, they cannot abolish them. Moreover, however anxious officers may be to promote continuity of care, they cannot ignore the attitudes of the prisoners. To them the relationship with a welfare officer, a voluntary worker, or a probation officer whilst they are inside may be little more than a way of breaking the monotony, valuable at the time but not worth continuing. If, on the other hand, it has developed into more than this, it is likely to be strongly dependent, difficult to transfer to others, or to transform into the kind of relationship needed outside. And militating against the whole idea of continuity is the very natural and indeed healthy feeling of most discharged prisoners that they want to leave prison behind them, to rid themselves of everything connected with it, including after-care. These varying feelings, like the initial hostility of many probationers, have to be recognized and accepted. The special difficulty in voluntary after-care is that they may break off communications at the outset.

Where work has been done with the prisoner's family during his absence it may pave the way to continued contact on release. On the other hand the probation officer or volunteer concerned will often be a different person from the welfare officer who has worked with the prisoner inside. There is some danger, therefore, that he may be viewed with a degree of suspicion on the part of the offender, especially if there is family tension and he is seen as being identified with the rest of the family. If help is to continue to be acceptable it may sometimes be necessary to consider whether a different social worker should take over when the husband returns.[1]

---

1. See Ieuan Miles, *Probation and After-Care*, 1966.

Prisoners who have no home to go back to present other sets of problems.[1] Some, the mentally sick or subnormal, drug addicts and alcoholics, certain of the physically handicapped and elderly, need kinds of specialized provision for after-care that are barely beginning to become available. In a slightly less specialized, but equally demanding way, the totally inadequate, lost and lonely need very long term protective environments in which they can at their own pace be helped to grow into such maturity as they are capable of. Here, too, scarcely a beginning has been made in providing alternatives to a round of repetitive imprisonment.[2]

Almost equally baffling are the needs of those who cannot cope in material terms. Homeless men turn up saying they have nothing but the clothes they stand up in, others have bought clothes and have nothing left for shelter or food. Sometimes they have been on a drinking spree, or eaten too well, or been to the pictures or smoked too much, all natural enough reactions to a period of imprisonment. They may not be telling the truth, they may squander anything that is given them, but what is to happen if they are simply refused? And how are the sheep to be distinguished from the goats? A man whose sentence is three months or less gets no grant on discharge; a man with a longer sentence gets up to four pounds, which will not last him twenty-four hours if he finds a room the day he comes out and has to pay in advance. Certainly the Ministry of Social Security can make a grant. But to go and apply for benefit as the first action on discharge reinforces dependence and frustrates any drive a man may have to get quickly into accommodation and work. It has been suggested that basic needs ought to be met much more comprehensively, without the humiliation of having to beg, demand and manipulate; that prisoners should be restored to society with a change of shirt and underclothes and a razor: a minimum outfit, in fact. A prison governor has already discretion to allow this where it is considered necessary for a man's rehabilitation. It can be argued, further, that the grant of a week's money should be available automatically on release as recognition of a return to independence

---

1. On much of what follows see Georgina Stafford, "After-care in the penal system", *Case Conference*, March 1968.
2. On the use of hostels and volunteers in after-care and on the needs of special classes like alcoholics, see below, pp. 136–160, 168–183.

and normality. This is, of course, a point at which arguments of "less eligibility" are likely to prove powerful. Yet the men must be provided for in some way if they have no private means. The development of prison industries and more realistic prison earnings might enable them to save enough themselves to bridge the gap adequately. Again the interdependence of the prison system and after-care is apparent.

Such measures would certainly not solve all the material problems facing ex-prisoners, but they might leave more time, and provide a better basis, for concentrating on underlying causes and working through problems constructively.

In 1967, out of more than twenty thousand former prisoners seen, a little over half were interviewed more than once.[1] Only about a fifth, however, maintained contact for over three months, only one in ten for over six. There have been very considerable differences between different areas in the average length of contact with voluntary cases. These may be explained partly in terms of the varying conditions to which prisoners return; partly in terms of the kinds of prisoners who choose, respectively, to return home or to lose themselves in large cities; partly in terms of the approach of the probation officers they go to. It has been argued that length of contact should not, in itself, be taken as an index of the effectiveness of after-care. On the contrary, the fact that a man comes only once may mean that he has been adequately dealt with and needs no more help. It is pointed out, too, that the aim should be to encourage independence, and that it is all for the best if a man is able to disappear into society, sever all connection with prison and stand on his own feet. Whilst this may be true of many, especially of those who have been to prison only once and of whom a very high proportion are unlikely to return there, it also remains true that there are a great many men, especially those who return to or drift to the large cities, who do need continuing help if there is to be any hope that they will remain out of trouble for long. The problem for the probation and after-care service is to experiment in getting and holding their confidence, in finding out what can, in fact, be done.

---

1. Total convicted males seen—21,428; one interview only—9,574. See *Probation and After-Care Statistics for 1967, England and Wales.*

5 SOCIAL WORK IN PRISONS

As in voluntary after-care, there is no compulsion upon pr.
accept the help of the prison welfare officer. The practice
prisoners singly or in groups soon after they first come in and .nform
them of the kinds of help the welfare officer may be able to give. It
may be possible also, in individual interviews, to identify some who
are in special need of the assistance of a social worker and call them
up for interviews later, but there is no obligation upon the prisoner to
respond. In most cases the initiative is left to the prisoner, who can
apply at any time to see the welfare officer.

It is nearly a century since the police court missionaries first tried
to break into the round of "offence after offence and sentence after
sentence" by going into the courts to offer treatment in the open as
an alternative to imprisonment. It is twenty years since the role of
probation officers in caring for certain of those who came out of penal
institutions received formal recognition. But it is less than four years
since the probation and after-care service was first called upon to
carry its work into the prisons themselves.

Since the beginning of 1966 the probation and after-care service
has been responsible for prison welfare.[1] More exactly, the probation
and after-care committee in whose area a prison is situated is
required to fill prison welfare posts, normally by the secondment of
probation officers for periods of two to five years. Though some
members of the former welfare service run by the National Association of Discharged Prisoners' Aid Societies and the Central After-
Care Association may remain to work permanently in the prisons,
the great majority of officers will serve there only temporarily, so
that there should, for the future, be a continuous interchange
between social work with offenders in the institutions and in the
community. Most borstals stand outside this arrangement, social
work being carried out by the borstal staff, though still in direct
contact with probation officers. Girls' borstals, however, have social
workers from the probation and after-care service, and since the
beginning of 1969 the same arrangement has been in force for social
workers in borstal allocation centres, detention centres and remand

---

1. H.O.C. 241/65, 5 November 1965.

centres. In these all-male institutions the influence of women is considered a useful adjunct to training, and it has been laid down that the officers appointed should normally be women.[1] A similar argument would seem to justify the employment of more women as welfare officers in prisons, especially, perhaps, married women returning to the service after bringing up their families.

The decision to unite the prison welfare service with the probation and after-care was designed both to improve the quality of the prison welfare service as such, and to promote interchange and collaboration between those concerned with the prisoner's welfare inside and those concerned with his rehabilitation on his return to the community.

As has already been said, the practice still falls far short of the ideal. But much has been accomplished in a short time. When responsibility was first taken over, there were only about a hundred posts for prison welfare officers, ten of them unfilled. This represented one officer to two hundred and sixty prisoners. Within three years the number of posts had been raised to a hundred and eighty-five and the aim is nearly two hundred for 1969/70. Since some posts are still unfilled, the actual ratio is around one officer to a hundred and forty-five prisoners; but average caseloads should be reduced to a hundred and thirty or less when the service is fully staffed. Especially in large local prisons, however, welfare departments still tend to be overwhelmed by the sheer numbers of men coming and going. Appropriate workloads for different types of prisons have still to be worked out. Some have claimed that, to help effectively, prison welfare officers must have caseloads similar to those of probation officers outside, now averaging between forty and fifty. Others argue that the conception should be different: a welfare officer, for example, might be attached to a wing of a hundred and fifty men, "involved with some only in so far as he is helping to create a helping climate in the wing, involved with others in a more personally helpful and well-established relationship".[2] In local prisons, remand centres, allocation and detention centres it is obviously necessary to think in terms not so much of the number of

---

1. H.O.C. 247/68, 1 November 1968.
2. F. E. Edwards, "Prison Welfare—an opportunity", *Prison Service Journal*, October 1968.

inmates at any one time as of the number passing in and out in a day, a week, a year. Account must also be taken of the different types of social work needed and possible in very diverse institutions. Perhaps it is only when their various purposes, and the types of prisoner passing through them, are more clearly defined, that the need for diagnosis, treatment, training or casework can be assessed, the roles of the various staff groups defined, and the number of welfare officers estimated.[1]

Besides the increase in the number of welfare officers, the first three years of their integration with the probation and after-care service have brought, in general, a greatly improved relationship, a new kind of mutual understanding, with the prison service. The welfare officer is responsible, in his capacity as a member of the prison team, to the prison governor; he is responsible, in his capacity as a professional social worker, to his principal probation officer. The possibility of conflicts inherent in thus "serving two masters" has been pointed out.[2] But undoubtedly there have been considerable gains as well. There has been growing co-operation between principal probation officers and prison governors. Some principals have spent up to a month in prisons. In many areas there have been exchanges of staff, prison officers visiting probation officers for several days or spending longer periods attached to prison welfare departments, probation officers from outside spending similar periods in prisons. Welfare officers have been taking a share, formally or informally, in the training of prison staff, and probation officers who have become welfare officers have gone to the Wakefield Staff College to learn about the nature and problems of prison life.

Here again, obviously the picture is not one of unclouded or complete achievement. There are fears on both sides still to be overcome. At the time that the probation and after-care services moved into the prisons, prison officers, or at least an active section of them, had been for some years developing welfare functions of their own and pressing for recognition as social workers rather than mere turnkeys. The reinforcement of the specialist prison welfare departments and their linking with an outside service was inevitably seen by some

---

1. This and many subsequent comments are adapted from *Social Work in Prison*, report of a Working Party on Prison Welfare in London (unpublished).
2. On this see, for example, F. Jarvis, "The Prison Welfare Service", *Probation*, Vol. 13, No. 1, March 1967.

as a check to such aspirations, though it could also prove a key to their fulfilment.

For the probation and after-care service outside, the fear has been in one sense different, in another much the same. Hitherto probation officers had been secure in their status as social workers, concentrated upon their primary task of dealing with offenders in the open, inclined to reject penal institutions as the very symbol of failure. To them the prison appears as a threat, a monolithic and unknown force, opposed in its very nature to the individual treatment and individual responsibility that have been at the heart of probation. Much depends here on how far probation officers are prepared to take their experience as social workers into the penal institutions, adapting it to the kinds of need they find there, carrying on their concern for offenders whatever may have befallen them.

Some are repelled by the fact that to enter prison welfare work means catching up with many failures, the hard core of offenders whose attitudes and problems have proved too much for orthodox forms of casework help, largely derived from experience with clients in quite different kinds of difficulty. Others are attracted by the implied challenge to originality and an extension of their skills. Some are repelled by the setting of authority and control, the ideological conflict. Others find that working in a close-knit environment, where social pressures appear in strong but in some ways simplified forms, contributes to the interest of the work. Some maintain that the concern of the probation and after-care service should continue to be concentrated upon the offender outside prison. Others feel that they can help more effectively on discharge only if they understand more fully what the prison experience means to a man. At least it is encouraging to find that many officers who have so far made the leap in the dark have found, once in, that the experience has been a stimulating and broadening one.

Once in, what is their relationship to the prison regime and the prison staff? Can they "stick to their last", concentrating solely on casework with individual prisoners and preparation for after-care? Or should they be more widely concerned with the work of the institution as a whole, accepting that "It is impossible to divide prisoners up into neat little clusters of therapeutic concern, with the welfare officer confining himself to the prisoner's anxieties about his family, liaising with family agencies and preparation for after-care—

while someone else concentrates on his adjustments to authority, his work habits, his personality difficulties and so on"?[1]

The official view is that the welfare officer should have a four-fold role: as a social caseworker and as planner of after-care, but also as the focal point of social work within the prison and as the normal channel of communication on social problems with the outside world.[2] Most welfare officers accept both sides of this: they see themselves essentially as caseworkers but they also see themselves as part of a "treatment team" within the prison. This has certainly been the ultimate intention.

The Advisory Committee on the Treatment of Offenders held that the social worker "should be in regular and frequent contact with the rest of the institutional staff through whom much of his work may be done". It has been argued that welfare departments should be located near the centre of the prison, so that they should not appear remote and unapproachable. It has been pointed out that it is psychologically bad for the offender to be able to split off "good" and "bad" authority figures; psychologically bad for prison staff to be deprived of helping functions, confined to repressive ones. Not only do attempts by welfare officers to dissociate themselves from the institution as a whole make the prison appear blacker by implication, but it may be asked how is the prison ever to be seen as geared to the task and purpose of rehabilitation if the one person whose activities are most clearly in this direction attempts to dissociate himself from it?[3]

On the other hand some welfare officers reject the notion that they are part of a treatment team: they find it difficult to identify either treatment or team, especially in big local prisons. They see the function of the welfare officer in maintaining contact with the outside world as a complete anomaly in an institution, the main effort of which is directed to cutting off such contact. They have described him as being "in a state of legitimized opposition to the rest of the institution, merely serving to undo some of the harm". Where relationships between staff and inmates are poor, they argue, over-

---

1. R. L. Morrison, *Casework in an Institutional Setting*, Paper read to the Conference of Principal Probation Officers, University of York, September 1966.
2. See. H.O.C. 130/67, July 1967.
3. M. Monger, *Casework in After-Care*.

identification with the institution can endanger any casework relation with the prisoner. Even where relations are better and staff are more concerned with treatment, objectors would still claim that the primary role of the welfare officer lies not in identifying with or influencing the institution but in acting as a link with life outside for both prisoners and staff. They suggest, too, that officers coming in from outside, and for limited periods, know far too little about institutions to hope to influence them effectively, that it is much more likely that any influence will operate in the reverse direction: the caseworker losing just that concern for the individual, just that vivid awareness of the outside world, that should be his greatest contribution.

All these discussions spotlight real difficulties and dangers. To deny differences of tradition and responsibilities, to ignore current conflicts, can only hinder progress. But so can overstatement. The interdependence of all who work in a prison cannot be ignored, least of all in attempts to help individual prisoners. Even in the mechanics of casework welfare officers are highly dependent upon the good will and co-operation of prison staff. And there is much more hope of communicating concern to a prisoner effectively if he sees some sign of it not only in the welfare officer but in the prison officers with whom he spends most of his time and in the handling of decisions about his allocation and training. The point has been made elsewhere that the courts are not treatment teams in the sense usually understood by social workers either: yet officers have succeeded in developing a constructive working relationship with them.

In some prisons the role of assistant governors has been seen as a potential source of confusion. There has been growing emphasis upon social work as an element in their training. In so far as this contributes to understanding of the social and personal needs of the prisoners, and to their consideration in the regime of the prison and the allocation of individuals, it is clearly all to the good. It may also result in a clearer appreciation of the role of the welfare officer. Where, however, assistant governors engage directly in social work with individuals, there may be overlapping. Some clarification of respective roles may well be needed, perhaps on the basis of emphasis rather than hard and fast demarcation. To say that the assistant governor is primarily concerned with the prisoner's adjustment to the institutional regime, the welfare officer primarily with his life before and after as well, may go some way towards clarification; but both are concerned with relating his present to his past and future outside.

The possibilities of working as a member of a genuine "treatment team" are obviously greatest in prisons where other demands on staff allow some part of the emphasis to be upon rehabilitation. This may be the case in a small local prison, where many of the recidivists have become well known to the staff and where prison officers have been encouraged to take a personal interest in groups of offenders. Or the prison, open or closed, may hold a more static community of longer-term prisoners and it may deliberately set out to stimulate inmates and staff to play a part in rehabilitation, to humanize the custodial role and to create and maintain relationships with the outside world. The aims of such a regime are, at least ideally, similar to those of the social workers: to reduce the damage caused by institutionalization; to give prisoners a chance to regain or develop some dignity and separate identity; to build up links with the world outside that will hold after release; in general to increase the prisoner's social ability so that he can return to society a little better able to cope with its demands and less disposed to crime. It is therefore natural enough for the welfare officers to play a part as consultants and trainers, supporting the work of prison staff with individuals as well as undertaking direct casework themselves. It is also natural for them to take part in consultations on many aspects of the running of the institution. In such an institution there is less concern with differentiating the roles of staff members, a sharper focus upon the prisoners and their problems, greater ease of communication and more trust as a result of more confidence and positive relationships.

Few prisons have got as far as this. Even in those that have the achievement is still in some measure precarious, since it inevitably depends a great deal upon personalities. And the great majority of offenders serve their time in the big local prisons where the system seems to militate against concern with individual relationships and individual needs. The sheer pressure of numbers, the short terms being served by many of the prisoners, the constant movement of men, sudden transfers between wings and between institutions, give overwhelming priority to the demands of security, good order and strict timing, with all the depersonalization that they imply.[1] It is in this kind of situation that the welfare department is likely to see itself as an isolated unit, a foreign body working against the grain of the institution, concerned with individuals where everyone else has to be concerned with numbers, concerned with maintaining links with the outside world which the institution must necessarily curtail. It will feel very strongly the pressures and frustrations of a large institution and sense a need to assert its very right to exist within it or to make claims upon the time of the prisoner. The welfare officer has to come to terms with the fact that the legitimate requirements of security and of fairness as between prisoners inevitably limit individualization of treatment in some of its aspects. He may further feel frustrated by lack of understanding amongst some prison staff of the need for an individualized approach in making relationships and in understanding and handling men's problems; by tendencies on one hand to write off social work as sentimental pandering to prisoners, on the other to regard the social worker as a maid-of-all-work who should produce immediate solutions to the prisoners' problems and thus keep down tension in the prison. At the same time there is the difficulty of working at any depth with men who will be in the establishment for only a short time. The welfare officer may feel himself obliged to choose, through sheer lack of time between the vital task of making a thorough assessment of each individual's needs when he first comes in and the urgency of the demands for help that can reach a crescendo just before he is due to go out; between working in greater depth with a few, or doing a little with a great many in the hope that some will profit.

Inevitably welfare officers have been attempting to meet needs at all stages, and inevitably also they have felt that, in attempting too much, they are in danger of doing everything superficially. The ideal is a thorough initial interview when men first come in; speedy attention to all applications for help made by prisoners during sentence; continuous casework with those who seem likely to need and respond to it; an interview with those approaching discharge to identify problems connected with release and, where appropriate,

---

1. See M. Monger, *Casework in After-Care*, pp. 59–60.

set guide-lines for after-care, perhaps jointly with the probation officer who will be responsible outside.

At the stage where an assessment is required for the local review committee on a man eligible for parole, a contribution is specifically required from the welfare officer. But it is to be hoped that his influence will be felt in many other decisions about prisoners. It has been suggested that where a welfare department is fully staffed it should join with other staff in regular comprehensive reviews of prisoners and in decisions about home leave and hostels. It should also take part in staff meetings and staff training.[1]

The extent to which prison officers in the large local prisons can be involved in social work with offenders depends on the adequacy of their own numbers as well as those of the welfare department: many of them simply have not time. It also depends on how much stability of contact is allowed by the prison's organization: if both staff and men are constantly moving around it is impossible to build up any continuity of relationships. Not all prison staff want, or would be qualified to engage in, welfare work. And those who do may have to contend with considerable distrust, as well as the sense of a clash between their custodial duties and their desire to hold the confidence of their charges.

Nevertheless there is much to be gained from taking co-operation as far as possible. The welfare department has at least three things to offer to prison staff who want to move into a more positive role: its experience of social work; its knowledge of the world outside prison and of what becomes of prisoners when they return there; and its immediate links with prisoners' homes and with social agencies outside. The prison staff, on its side, can offer in return greater speed and discrimination in referring men in need of skilled help, and a readiness to share in dealing with many aspects of a prisoner's problems. It has been suggested that in favourable conditions there might be experiments in employing them as ancillary workers similar to those being tried in a few probation areas outside. Another suggestion is that, since much of the routine work connected with prison welfare consists in such tasks as collecting baggage and contacting officials outside the prison, there may be a place for specially appointed ancillary workers in the welfare departments also.

---

1. H.O.C. 130/67, July 1967.

For social enquiries and social work outside the prison, the welfare officer must depend on the co-operation of the rest of the probation and after-care service. And, just as in working with prison staff, the best basis for co-operation is a focus upon the needs of the offender. The quick and efficient exchange of information is of the first importance. When a man is committed to prison the probation officer should send the welfare officer not only copies of reports to the court but information obtained immediately after sentence, including a special note if an early interview is likely to be needed or there are practical matters requiring immediate attention. The prisoner's feelings about the welfare officer, about the probation service and about after-care are all likely to be affected by the way his own requests for help with his outside concerns are handled. The officer outside needs to appreciate something of the intense anxiety that may be felt by a man in prison awaiting an answer to some query affecting his family. The welfare officer needs to remember the difficulties and inevitable delays that may hinder the officer outside. He may have to try to help the prisoner bear the strain of waiting, and often of eventual disappointment; to prevent him jumping to the conclusion that the officer outside has not bothered and that therefore after-care has nothing to offer.

There is always, of course, a danger where two people are dealing with different aspects of a case that one may be played off against the other or that their approaches may conflict. Especially when the officer outside is working with the prisoner's family, he needs to keep in regular touch with the welfare officer. As an increasingly high proportion of welfare officers will be people who have had experience of working in the probation and after-care service outside, and as more and more probation officers will have had at least some experience of work in prisons, misunderstandings and failures of communication should be progressively reduced.

So far the most important result of sending experienced probation officers, women amongst them, into the prisons has not been to increase the number of cases dealt with but to increase awareness of the problems faced by prisoners. There has been a great diversity of experiment and this should obviously continue, making full use of the varying opportunities presented by different institutions and areas. At the same time it would be wasteful if everything remained too long at a local and personal level. Though rigidity is clearly to be avoided, comparisons need to be made, the range of possibilities assessed and principles and standards established.

Research now being carried out at three prisons of different types, Ashwell, Birmingham and Gartree, is designed to determine more clearly the place of social work in prisons. It includes an attempt to assess the number of welfare officers needed and the sort of accommodation and clerical help they require, and also an attempt to discover and define the extent to which prison officers can be involved in social work. Welfare officers have a key role as the bridgehead between the prison service and the probation and after-care service. If they are to develop its possibilities to the full they must have a full complement of staff, the professional and material resources for the job, and support from both sides.

The improvement of prison welfare is inextricably tied to that of the prison service. As long as prisoners in London and the big local prisons continue to be housed in obsolete buildings, with serious overcrowding and equally serious understaffing, these conditions will continue to inhibit attempts to advance towards more treatment orientated regimes. The dilemma with which the probation and after-care service must now wrestle is how to accept its new relationship with the prison service and to be an effective partner, without appearing to give tacit approval to existing conditions and without sacrificing the freedom to advocate change.

One of the encouraging things so far learned is how much there is in common between progressive members of both services. The exchange of ideas and mutual support can enable them to work together toward a coherent and consistent programme of penal treatment. The probation and after-care service can claim some of the credit for the reforms in sentencing practice and the treatment of offenders by the courts which have been effected since the turn of the century. These reforms have resulted from the patient development of diagnostic and treatment skills, and the building up of working relationships with those in allied fields, even when they have not shared the same ideology.

Seen in historical perspective this impetus to reform, currently expressed in after-care, parole and prison welfare, continues to make rapid headway. The gradual growing together of the penal services, far from inhibiting advance, opens up opportunities of moving forward on a broader front, of dealing with offenders less and less in sectional terms, more and more as human beings with a continuing life that needs to be seen as a whole.

6 FAMILIES OF OFFENDERS

When an offender on probation is living at home the probation officer usually sees the family in the course of home visits, though when there is some special difficulty a parent or wife may also see him at the office.

In addition to this, however, officers are required to keep in touch with the families of certain younger offenders whilst they are temporarily away in probation homes or hostels, in approved schools or borstals. In general they act as a link between the home and the institution, keeping the parents in touch with the progress of the offender during training and keeping the hostel or institution informed of any changes in the home circumstances and the attitude of parents towards the boy and his progress. They try also to pave the way for the offender's return by helping to deal with factors at home that may have contributed to his past trouble. They see the youngster with his family again when he is allowed home leave, and they try to help him and his parents to face realistically the difficulties he will have to meet on his return.

The probation officer may become concerned with the families of prisoners in various ways. He may have known them during an earlier period of probation or a wife or child may be under his supervision whilst the husband is in prison. He may have met them during a pre-sentence enquiry. The prisoner may have asked, or agreed, that he should see and try to help them during an interview immediately after sentence or with the welfare officer after arrival in prison. Or the prisoner may have asked for contact to be made later, perhaps owing to anxiety because the wife was not visiting or writing, because of rumours he had heard about her or because of difficulties she was in about finance, housing or the children. Or the initiative may have come from the wife herself as a result of any of these problems or perhaps fears about her husband's return. Or it may have been requested by the prison authorities, to help decisions about home leave, transfer or parole for the prisoner.

Considerable stress has been laid recently upon the extent to which the wives and children of prisoners may suffer, in both material and emotional terms, and their need of much more help than they are at present being given, either by probation officers or by volunteers working with them. It may be that the care of all these families in the widest sense—that of helping them cope with their difficulties as a whole rather than concentrating on problems that seem directly associated with those of the prisoner—is too large a task for the probation service, as at present staffed, to undertake. The Seebohm Committee has suggested that it should be part of the duty of the proposed new social service departments, and even now certain aspects of it may be appropriate to the children's or other departments of local authorities.

On the other hand, in so far as it may be intimately tied up with prison welfare, parole and after-care, probation officers are likely to retain a considerable interest in it, and at present they have a major share of responsibility for making it available, either directly or through volunteers.[1] Moreover, concern with the domestic problems and with the welfare of children is no foreign duty to them. These are important elements not only in their work with offenders but in their extensive duties in civil cases.

---

1. On this whole question see Pauline Morris, *Prisoners and their Families* (1965) and K. Vercoe, *Helping Prisoners' Families*, N.A.C.R.O. (1968).

CHAPTER 3

THE SERVICE AND CIVIL CASES

1 THE BREAKING MARRIAGE

IT is often forgotten that the probation service has for many years been concerned not only with those who break the criminal law but with those whose domestic and other difficulties bring them within the civil jurisdiction of the courts.

Yet the police court missionaries used to try to help those who came to the courts for relief in their domestic troubles and matrimonial conciliation was accepted as one of the primary functions of the service by 1936. Although with the increase of legal aid and the expansion of other duties it has somewhat declined in recent years, it still accounts for a large volume of work. In 1967 well over thirty-three thousand cases were seen; in nearly half of them both husband and wife were interviewed at least once. Many were referred by the courts, before or after the issue of summonses, others came on the advice of clerks, police or other social agencies. Nearly two-thirds, over twenty-one thousand, came to probation officers direct. And in addition there were twenty-six thousand requests for help in other domestic problems. Of late years, too, probation officers have been attached to the divorce courts: their primary functions there are connected with the welfare of children in marriages that are breaking up, but a few cases are referred for conciliation even at this late stage.

It is indeed strange how recently society has begun to concern itself about unhappy marriages and their effects. Outside the magistrates' courts there has been, until recently, little organized help. Yet the consequences arising from the breakdown of marriages have always been far-reaching, although traditionally they were seen only in terms of the personal unhappiness of the individuals immediately involved. Today it is recognized that mental health and social adjustment are directly related to home relationships and upbringing, so that other people's marriages affect us all. It is recognized, too, that mental ill-health and social maladjustment can be self-perpetuating through the children of those affected. Thus the community's concern for satisfactory family life is enormous, and the attempt of the probation officer to bring his trained understanding to the adjustment of such difficulties is potentially one of the foremost contributions of the service to our society. The probation officer has both a statutory obligation to try to help those in matrimonial difficulties referred to him by the courts and an accepted role in assisting those who come to him direct or are referred by other agencies. The Morison Committee held that those referred by courts must be seen by a service "to which the courts have ready and constant access and in which they have proven confidence", and that probation was the only such service. It held also that matrimonial work undertaken at the direct request of husband or wife should continue to be recognized as a desirable and appropriate function of probation officers, and that staffing of the service should take this into account.[1]

Since the link with the magistrates' courts is such an important factor in the matrimonial work of probation officers, it is important that their respective roles should be clear. At some courts people asking in the first instance only for advice on marital problems go direct to the probation officer: if they later decide they want to apply for a summons they are then referred to the court. Those who come initially asking for a summons go direct to the court, though they may be referred from there to the probation officer if they have no *prima facie* case or show signs of willingness to consider reconciliation.

In some other areas, however, it may be laid down that no one shall go to the probation officer for advice without first making application to the court. This appears to be based partly on a feeling that the court should have some control over the work of its officers, and partly on the legalistic views of some clerks that no barrier should be placed in the way of applicants to the courts. They feel, moreover, that legal problems may arise which probation officers are not qualified to solve. There is some truth in this, but the

---

1. *Report of the Departmental Committee on the Probation Service* (Cmnd. 1650), 1962, pp. 51 and 56.

extension of legal aid facilities, together with the improvement of casework method and practice make such objections less relevant. In many other courts there is, on the contrary, a general direction that applicants for matrimonial relief, including those seeking summonses, should first be directed to the probation officer so that the possibilities of reconciliation may be fully explored. This may well be justified, as people often come asking for a summons less because they really want separations than because they feel the need of a pretext to ask for help or draw attention to their plight. Or they may ask for one without having begun to consider the implications for their own future or that of their children. On the other hand, it must never be forgotten that the client has a right of direct access to the court and that nothing should be done to impede this. It seems quite unjustifiable for the court to require, as it does in some busy areas, that the probation officer shall act as a sort of sieve, or at least a brake. If the client desires to go ahead with his application for a summons, it is for the court to decide whether he has a *prima facie* case. Nor is it desirable that the probation officer should be called upon to put the applicant's case to the court for him: it may save the court's time, but it obscures the probation officer's true function as an impartial helper and a caseworker concerned with conciliation between husband and wife.

The probation officer is not, of course, a lawyer and cannot hope to be aware of all the complexities of the law in matrimonial cases. But he needs to have some basic knowledge of the grounds upon which a magistrates' court may make orders for separation, maintenance or custody of children. He needs to be able to identify cases which require qualified legal advice. He needs to be able to give other clients an idea of the possibilities of getting, for instance, a maintenance order on grounds of desertion. Their probable legal position is one of the realities they must face in deciding what they will do: it is thus one of the factors in casework with them.

Some probation officers bring much skill and interest to matrimonial work and have received advanced training for it. Many, however, have mixed feelings about their ability to do it effectively. Doubts may arise from the voluntary and indefinite nature of the relationship, contrasting as it does with the clear-cut framework of probation. There may be a sense of defeat at the outset because so many do not come until it is too late to save the marriage, even though something may still be done to reduce further damage to the couple and their children. There may be a sense of defeat, too, because so many come with the evident hope of using the probation officer or court to punish or coerce their partners. All these factors pose casework problems which will be discussed later.[1]

It needs to be said here, however, that sheer shortage of time militates against the intensive effort needed for their solution. An officer who is hard-pressed already is unlikely to encourage demand for more long-term and exacting casework. There is a feeling that the importance of the work is not fully recognized. Where insufficient staff are available it is often the matrimonial work which is pushed to the wall: the officer has to interview with an eye on the next client. It has been felt that, from the Home Office down through the probation committees, the administration and many seniors, not enough consideration is given to this work and this is reflected at the bottom of the scale by often scrappy and shapeless hand-scribbled records, in contrast to the rather over-long typed recording of statutorily supervised cases.

There is a special need, in dealing with matrimonial disputes, to be constantly alive to the interactions between husband and wife, and indeed within the family as a whole. This is obviously essential to any attempts at lasting conciliation, but it is often essential also as a means of identifying cases, unpromising at first, in which conciliation may prove to be possible. Development of a more "clearly formulated conceptual basis" for social casework in the marital field, involving an analytical approach and an emphasis on dynamic marital interaction, has been pioneered since the early nineteen-forties at the Tavistock Clinic by Dr. H. V. Dicks and by the Family Discussion Bureau. Both have been actively concerned in the training of probation officers, through books and pamphlets, by individual and group methods, by short-term courses for many and long-term courses for a few. The Home Office makes use of this specialized training in marital work by incorporating it into pre-service professional training courses. It is expected, too, that trainees will be given experience in it during their practical placements. Indeed, this approach has now become widespread, since many of those trained have themselves become tutors or teachers to a

---

1. See below, pp. 131–135.

greater or lesser degree, and the example has been followed by other institutions as well as by individual psychiatrists and other professionally skilled people.

Some probation officers, knowing the type of work done by the Family Discussion Bureau, believe that the only useful work with matrimonial difficulties must be by prolonged contact with each party in individual interviews, perhaps by different case workers. At present, time would not allow this in many cases. Probation officers may attempt it occasionally, but usually they have to accept that from one to four interviews are all that they can give, with perhaps a promise of further help if called on, and that limited help at the point of emotional crisis that brings the applicant to the probation officer can be of considerable value.

Even if he can do no more than clarify the situation, both emotionally and intellectually, the probation officer is fulfilling a useful function for those who come to court which no one else at present carries out. Other social workers may be prepared to work with people with marriage problems, though many of them share probation officers' anxieties about them. They are, however, often baffled by the additional legal aspect and the special anxiety engendered by the courts amongst those who are not accustomed to them. On the other hand, solicitors, though at home with the courts and able to give husbands or wives a full explanation of their legal position, will not help them to clarify their own feelings.

In that they are both social caseworkers and linked to the courts, marital casework seems a logical part of the work of probation officers. It is ironical that the new claims of after-care should sometimes be seen as competing with this duty, since much of the success of after-care with adults may hinge on their relationships with their wives and families. Probationers too, whether men or women, can be much influenced by their marital situation.

At the same time it is obvious that probation officers are not the only social workers involved in marital problems. The marriage guidance councils specialize in them. These voluntary councils, however, are available only near the larger centres of population, and their existing counsellors and organization would be unable to cope with a large extension of their work. Moreover their members are likely to be less familiar than probation officers and some other professional social workers with the sort of family in which verbal expression is very limited and a certain amount of violence fairly normal. Certainly there is scope for help from both sources. In many areas there is close co-operation between local probation officers and marriage guidance councils, and consultation may take place on particular cases.

Apart from this, marital and family relationships impinge upon social work in all spheres. All caseworkers need to understand and be prepared to work with them. As departments of local authorities move further into preventive work, they are bound to become increasingly concerned. The logic of any movement towards unified local authority social service departments, and the provision of family advice centres, would seem to be that local authority social workers would gradually take over the responsibilities of the probation and after-care service in helping with marital problems, at least at the stages before they come to court. It is noticeable, however, that this has not so far been discussed very explicitly in official publications. Much will obviously depend on the extent and accessibility of new facilities actually made available. In the meantime, however, matrimonial work is not to be seen as something foreign from the rest of a probation officer's duties but as an essential part of them.

2   THE CHILDREN

The second broad area of civil work in which probation officers are concerned is a series of duties related to the welfare of children and young people where the courts have power to make enquiries or orders affecting them. The children concerned may be those brought to court as in need of care, protection or control, some of them delinquent but others brought because of parental neglect or cruelty. Here the probation officer may report and subsequently supervise in his capacity as social worker for the juvenile court. Or they may be the children of marriages that have broken up, where the court needs to be satisfied as to future arrangements for their care or has to make orders as to access, maintenance, custody or supervision. Here the probation officer may be involved as welfare officer of a divorce court or as social worker of a magistrates' court. Again, the child may be the subject of an application to adopt. Whilst in many cases the duty of making enquiries as guardian *ad litem* would fall upon the children's officer, if the children's department has itself placed the child for adoption the probation officer, as an independent person, is called upon to fulfil this role and report to the court. Sometimes probation officers may also be involved, though to a limited extent, in enquiries for the court in connection with affiliation orders or consent to marriage.

All these may be thought to be matters that could appropriately be dealt with in the future by social service departments, perhaps linked with family courts. For the present they are still the responsibilities of probation officers, again for the reason that they have the necessary familiarity with courts on one hand and with the diagnostic and treatment methods of casework on the other. It is particularly important that they should be well done, not only in the interests of the children immediately involved but because upon their helpfulness may depend how far courts will maintain and develop their general concern for the welfare of children who come within their ambits as a by-product, so to speak, of the troubles and litigation of adults. Whereas the juvenile courts have a long-standing legal duty in this respect, it is something comparatively new in the adult domestic and divorce courts.

The first probation officer to act as a welfare officer in the Divorce Division of the High Court was appointed in 1950. In 1957, on the recommendation of the Royal Commission on Marriage and Divorce, probation committees were invited to make a similar arrangement for every town where matrimonial cases were tried. This was further extended in 1968 by the appointment of officers not only to the divorce courts but to the county courts with jurisdiction to try undefended divorce cases. The primary duty of welfare officers (who remain probation officers, though a few specialize in divorce court welfare work) is to make enquiries, when requested by the courts. The courts have to satisfy themselves as far as possible about arrangements for the care and upbringing of the children of families involved in divorce proceedings. They are, moreoever, empowered to make what orders they think just for the custody, maintenance and education of a child whose parents are being divorced or judicially separated, or even, once a trial has begun, when such proceedings are dismissed. These enquiries may be very extensive, as the officer has to see not only each of the parents and the child or children but any persons of standing who may be able to assist, and much time and travelling may be involved.[1]

The divorce courts' use of their powers to ask for enquiries increased from well under a thousand cases in 1960 to over three thousand in 1967. Practice varies widely between different courts: some call for reports only when custody is contested, some more widely. It seems, however, to many probation officers that the court is frequently satisfied as to arrangements for the future welfare of children on what social workers would consider very flimsy evidence. It is impossible to state accurately the number of children under sixteen involved in divorce proceedings, but a recent estimate gives this as about twenty-nine thousand, of whom considerably fewer than two thousand were the subjects of social welfare enquiries. It has also been felt that there should be more awareness in the divorce courts of the service that could be given, more standardization of practice and uniformity of reports. Perhaps some kind of enquiry, similar to that of the Streatfeild Committee in relation to reports in criminal cases, should attempt to distinguish the kinds of circumstances in which reports should be called for.

The Matrimonial Proceedings (Magistrates' Courts) Act 1960 gave to the domestic courts similar powers to those of the divorce courts, in that magistrates can call for reports by either probation officers or children's officers to help them decide about the custody of children. Once the court has begun to hear a case it has a duty to consider whether it should make any order in respect of the children before either the case is dismissed or a final order made. This means that here too, even if the matrimonial case is not proved, the court can intervene to take action about any children.

Domestic courts may also ask for reports from probation officers when dealing with cases under the Guardianship of Infants Acts. Those concerned may either be illegitimate children whose custody is being claimed by their fathers under the Legitimacy Act 1959, or children one of whose parents wants custody or maintenance for them without seeking a matrimonial order in his or her own right.

---

1. For a full statement of duties of welfare officers see *Memorandum of Guidance for Divorce Court Welfare Officers*, 1968, issued by the Probation and After-Care Department, Home Office. On the whole range of a probation officer's duties in civil cases, see F. Jarvis, *Probation Officers' Manual*, 1969. See also *Report on Divorce Court Welfare*, P.P.O.s Conference, 1968.

As with the divorce courts, however, there is a feeling amongst probation officers that domestic courts do not use enquiries as extensively as they should and that the question of children in matrimonial cases is apt to be dismissed on a superficial discussion between solicitors and parents, or even in circumstances of very dubious benefit to a child on the long-term basis. Much more to prevent human unhappiness could be done by domestic courts if they would really face up to these responsibilities. Once again there should be far more leadership, direction, and instruction in this field of work.

Supervision, either by a probation officer or by a children's officer, of the children of parties to matrimonial proceedings may, in some circumstances, be ordered by the divorce or domestic court when orders are also made about their custody. They cannot, rather illogically, be made in guardianship of infants cases, though it would seem they might be equally necessary as a means of safeguarding the child's future interests. However, their use in other cases has been growing. At the end of 1961 fewer than six hundred children were being supervised by virtue of orders made in connection with matrimonial proceedings in the High Court or the magistrates' courts.[1] By 1967 the number had risen by four thousand and was almost equal to the number being supervised by probation officers as in need of care, protection or control under supervision orders made by the juvenile courts. Orders in matrimonial cases impose no obligations upon the child concerned, except that of being under supervision, which means, in practice, being visited from time to time by the probation or child care officer. There are no sanctions, but the supervising welfare officer may apply at any time for variation or discharge of an order, or (in the case of the divorce courts) for directions as to the exercise of his powers under it. The courts may, at their own instance, vary an order for the custody, maintenance or education of a child who is under supervision. Apart from this, the probation officer may be seen as a source of support and advice to a lone parent of either sex, or to the child itself: for instance a young girl, left as a toddler with her father, will have access to help if problems arise as she grows up.

---

1. For details of these orders and of the procedure for varying or revoking them, see F. Jarvis, *Probation Officers' Manual*, 1969.

There are a few other instances in which the court may ask the probation officer to make enquiries in civil cases. Where a child has been placed for adoption by the local authority, a probation officer is appointed as guardian *ad letem* to report to the court. Applications for consent to marry may also be referred to the probation officer for a report: whilst it is no part of the officer's duty to persuade the parties to change their minds, he may help them to clarify the issues and be of use in the general family situation. Under the Magistrates' Courts Act 1952 officers can still be required to report on the means of parties in domestic and affiliation cases, though now that legal aid is more widely available it should now be less necessary. Nevertheless, there may be times, where, for example, there are difficulties about giving a clear picture of complicated domestic circumstances, when the use of a probation officer is justified.

3 WHO ELSE?

It will be evident that in social work arising from civil litigation, as in so many other things, the probation and after-care service has accumulated an extending range of duties because of its combination of qualifications and because of its availability to the courts. Essentially its contribution has been, as in the criminal court, a humanizing of the law and its administration. On the one hand it has helped to make courts more aware of the social problems and social needs of the men, women and children about whom they have to make decisions; on the other it has helped those coming to the courts for relief to understand better the implications of what they are doing.

Some feel that these functions could well be carried yet further. It is pointed out that a welter of misery and mismanagement, often affecting families with children, comes daily to the notice of the county courts in civil proceedings arising from such matters as failure to pay debts. Some of the worst of these cases are now coming to the notice of probation officers working with civil prisoners in prison welfare or after-care, many of them presenting very complicated social problems. It may be asked whether it would not be better if they could be helped before they reached this stage, and it has been hinted that the presence of probation officers in divorce county courts may open the way to their employment by county courts generally.

On the other hand it may be argued that this, together with the other functions of the probation service in domestic cases of all kinds, would be a proper part of the duties of a social service department. The answer may depend on what is decided about family courts, and what body of social workers they make use of if they are established. It would seem logical that the same body should also serve the county courts.

The important thing is that the growing concern of courts and of society with the social aspects of the law and law enforcement should not be frustrated by lack of resources for adequate enquiry and adequate social help.

CHAPTER 4

CASEWORK: PROBATION

1 THE PROBATION OFFICER AS CASEWORKER

IN 1962 the Morison Report described the probation officer as a professional caseworker employing in a specialized field skill which he holds in common with other social workers. It added that he was also the agent of a system concerned with the protection of society. None of the developments that have since occurred in the role of the probation and after-care service alters either of these propositions, though they have led officers to examine their implications more fully. This chapter is devoted, first, to looking at what many of the offenders on probation are like and what special needs they may have; second to looking at some aspects of casework and seeing how they apply in the context of probation. Their application in parts of the probation officer's work other than probation is dealt with in the next chapter.[1]

The care of probationers was the first duty of probation officers and still constitutes the largest part of their work. It is the sphere in which they are most at home and in which they have had most time to work out and come to terms with difficulties and opportunities. They still tend to assess the demands of other settings, of after-care, prison welfare, matrimonial conciliation or enquiries for courts, in relation to that of probation. It provides, therefore, the best starting point.

---

1. For much fuller studies of certain aspects of casework see, for example, *Relationship in Casework*, published by the Association of Psychiatric Social Workers, 1964; F. Hollis, *Casework, a Psycho-Social Therapy*, 1965; M. Monger, *Casework in Probation*, 1964, and *Casework in After-Care*, 1967; N. Timms, *Social Casework*, 1964; E. Younghusband (ed.), *New Developments in Casework*, 1966, and *Social Work and Social Values*, 1967.
A discussion of the background of social casework was included in earlier editions of this book, see *Probation Service*, 1958 and 1964.

Similarly, though casework is not the only form of social work it is by far the most developed in this country and is central to the social work of probation officers. Many of the principles and attitudes that underlie the use of casework also underlie the approach to groupwork, voluntary help, homes, hostels and other residential resources and attempts to enlist the concern of the community.[1] Each of these is discussed in subsequent chapters. Here it is proposed to concentrate on casework as representing the basic working pattern and set of tools. There are experiments with other tools as well, as the range of work extends and skill and interest develop, but in general these have been used to supplement casework rather than to replace it and they are so far much less developed.

2   THE PROBATIONERS

A person put on probation usually remains within his normal social setting: he lives at home, he carries on with the sort of work to which he is accustomed, he remains in touch with his old associates and interests. In some cases, of course, he may have lost lodgings, a job, perhaps friends, as a result of the offence, and in a few he may be required to go away to live in a hostel for a time. But the general rule is that the probation officer works with him within his accustomed way of life and that the probation order, unlike a penalty involving institutional treatment, makes no necessary break in his social and personal relationships. He thus remains exposed to all the stresses, problems and temptations of the situation in which he committed his offence. This may imply greater risks but it also offers special opportunities. The officer is able to look at his difficulties with him as they arise, to consider their significance and the personal and social resources available to meet them, and to help him cope with them in ways that can continue unbroken after probation ends.

The probation officer has to try to understand the offender's current personal and social situation: his attitudes, the ways he copes with his various social roles, the ways he is helped or hindered by his environment, and particularly the other people in it. In the attempt to understand his present difficulties he and the officer can learn much from his past. The factors in criminality, especially

---

1. See P. Parsloe, *The Work of the Probation and After-Care Officer*, 1967.

persistent criminality, are seldom simple and the constant interplay of the person and his environment produces endless variations.

The probationer's childhood provides clues as to the help he has had to enable him to develop, as to how he felt and feels about his parents, brothers and sisters, as to his attitudes to marriage and family life if he is an adult, as to his attitudes to authority whatever his age. Many of those coming to probation officers have had little chance of helpful relationships with their parents. There may have been a lack of love and so no real basis or security for learning. The probationer himself may have early manifested some personality defect, making him unresponsive and setting up a vicious circle of rejection. There may have been a lack of consistency in discipline or in values on the part of the parents. The probationer may simply have adopted the outlook of a family or neighbourhood in which occasional offences are taken for granted. There may have been poverty and overcrowding, driving him on to the streets. Or there may have been material indulgence combined with emotional deprivation. He may have responded to a sense of being rejected by acting out his hurt and angry feelings and showing early symptoms of defying his parents' control. Or he may have bottled up his feelings for the time, hitting back at parental and general authority only as he grew older. He may even have kept out of trouble with the law for as long as he has had his parents to protect him, appearing for the first time as an adult offender, when home has ceased to act as a refuge and control.

Anything that went wrong at home may have been aggravated or modified by the experience of wider social contacts. These too need to be explored for sources either of disturbance or of help for the future. If it transpires that a probationer who has had difficulties at home has been more successful in relating to some other relative, to people of his own age, to school, work, or married life, he and the caseworker can profitably seek in these areas the clues to his success and try to translate them into his other relationships.

The influence of wider social groups is often important. Sometimes the children and adolescents who do not relate well at home are also excluded from the more acceptable and cohesive groups at school, so that they either remain solitary or drift into more fluid groups of youngsters with various behaviour problems, which may well lead them into further trouble. Sometimes, especially in areas where juvenile offences are commonplace, the insecure form more cohesive delinquent gangs, seeking amongst those of their own kind the excitement, approval and acceptance denied to them elsewhere. There are, indeed, a great variety of groupings, more or less transient in activities, membership and leadership: their members may be closely attached to them or mere hangers-on, they may be drawn to them and remain with them to satisfy different needs. Much older offenders also may feel their only place is amongst others of their kind and may resist any attempts to help them that might cut them off from, for example, other alcoholics or drug addicts.

Many of those on probation lack a satisfactory and regular record of work. Their difficulties are frequently an extension of earlier problems at school, such as poor attendance, inattention, inability to concentrate or to accept reasonable and appropriate authority. They frequently project their inability to manage upon the foreman, the people they work with, the management or anything outside themselves. Their behaviour reflects what they expect of life and unless they can modify such expectations the same kind of thing is likely to happen wherever they work.

The family situation in the present will also be affected by what has been experienced in the past. Apart from the complications already discussed, some will have hardly had any family relationships at all. They may have been brought up in institutions, they may have lost what ties they once had. In either case they may now be isolates, amongst the most difficult to reach, since they have spent much of their lives holding off anyone who may have offered to help them. Some, of course, are still with their parents; others with wives, husbands or children of their own. These close relationships have an important bearing on their behaviour. They can be a source of great support to the offender and if there is promise of this they need to be explored with him and encouraged. If the family situation is not helpful this also needs to be looked at with the offender to see what part he plays in the situation. In either case, and in relation to all aspects of the offender's life, it may be necessary to involve the family as well, both in diagnosis and treatment.

Adolescence is the peak age for delinquency, and there are more probationers between the ages of fourteen and seventeen than in any other age-group.[1] Much has been written about the special problems

---

1. See *Probation and After-Care Statistics for* 1967.

of this phase of life.[1] The Latey Committee firmly rejected "any suggestion that the criminal elements in the age group are in any way typical of the whole", emphasizing that it was "the irresponsible, disturbed and inadequate who become involved in anti-social behaviour, and law-breaking, regardless of age".[2] But a period of life which involves both sharp physical and emotional changes within and strong pressures and frustrations from without is bound to impose special stresses upon the most vulnerable.

Adolescents are striving for independence but at the same time are afraid of its responsibilities; they want to break away from home and yet they want to remain there. This element of desperation, and dissatisfaction with the known means of help available may drive some of them into an indirect search for help through delinquency or uncontrollable behaviour. Because of their insecurity and the fact that society seems to offer them no place, they may make a rigid code, recognized and acceptable to themselves and their fellows but different from that of the grown-up world around them. The gap between the generations has been widened as never before by the speed of scientific and technical progress and of social change. Many adolescents now have high wages and few responsibilities. Many offenders amongst them have aspirations that are not or cannot be realized, and the resulting conflict seems to drive them to delinquent acts. Anxiety and a sense of helplessness in face of world-wide threats like nuclear war produce an underswell of defeatism, a confirmation of the doctrine that as much as possible must be snatched now as there may be no future, and that adults are bankrupt of wisdom and foresight. The idea of a teenage culture, with values exclusive to the young, has been fostered by commercial interests. Drugs have been adopted as a symbol of emancipation as well as a short cut to pleasure and relief from anxiety. All these factors may have to be taken into account as additional elements in the problems of adolescents who fall foul of the law.

Children, too, have their special problems, their different frame of reference, stemming from their stage of mental and emotional development and their dependent situation. Verbal communication

---

1. See, for example, D. Downes, *The Delinquent Solution*, 1966; D. Miller, *Growth to Freedom*, 1964; D. J. West, *The Young Offender*, 1967.
2. *Report of the Committee on the Age of Majority* (Cmnd. 3342), 1967.

and discussion of abstract ideas does not come easily to them, though they expect and accept instruction about their behaviour more easily than adults or adolescents. They can be very much afraid of the strength of their own ambivalent feelings towards those they love, and in need or reassurance that this is normal and understandable. Work with their parents is usually essential. And if they have to face removal from home great care is needed to explain this to them, to prepare them for it and to maintain some reliable link between them and their families whilst they are away. It seems probable that, for the future, probation officers will have far less responsibility for children who commit offences than in the past, though the needs of children will continue to come into other parts of their work, especially in dealing with adult offenders who are parents and with matrimonial difficulties.[1]

The ability of probationers to form relationships, and their willingness to change, are obviously of great significance at any age. There are those whose immaturity, impulsiveness and limited willingness and ability to co-operate make casework a time-consuming and often unrewarding process. There are those whose consciences are undeveloped, who can be deterred only by fear of consequences and who need constant support and reminders of the consequences of failure. There are those who have been so grossly deprived in their early relationships and have so little capacity for entering into a casework relationship because they fear further rejection that it is hard even to begin. There are those who have no desire to change and hold society entirely to blame for the predicament in which they find themselves. There are professional criminals who appear to have consciously chosen a life of crime as profitable, agreeable and adventurous, and who have no intention of abandoning it, in spite of its risks. There are the inadequate psychopaths, some of them homeless, again apparently unable to make relationships or have regard to the effects of their behaviour.

Courts have, in effect, been advised, when deciding whether to use probation, to consider whether the offender needs continuing

---

1. On casework with children, see, for example, J. Rich, *Interviewing Children and Adolescents*, 1968; J. Hotham, in A. H. Denney (ed.), *Children at Risk*, 1968; C. Winnicott, *Child Care and Social Work*, 1964; M. Power, "Casework in the Shoreditch Project", *Journal of the Association of Psychiatric Social Workers*, Vol. 5, 1959.

treatment and whether he is capable of responding to it while at liberty.[1] This seems to imply that offenders selected for probation will have social or psychological difficulties. In deciding this, and the likely response to treatment, the court will normally take into account a probation officer's assessment. Yet it is not always possible at the outset to estimate either need or response. With some offenders these become fully apparent only after a probation order has been in force for some time. This has to be borne in mind in deciding whether probation should be tried and in estimating what can realistically be expected of treatment, and what methods should be employed. Many of those on probation do not, in fact, prove to be facing any serious failure in their social relationships, apart from the fact of their offences, and have no marked psychological abnormalities.

They may have been put on probation less because they needed help in obvious personal problems than because the court regarded their offences as of some gravity and felt they needed a period of discipline and supervision by way of warning. Nevertheless, they share with other offenders, whose social or psychological problems go much deeper, the problem of having experienced a direct clash with society, of having been found guilty of breaking its rules. How much they mind this will depend partly upon the social class and the particular group of family, friends and neighbours from which they come. It is very important, therefore, to discover how far their behaviour is condemned by those amongst whom they live and who are most important to them: how far they are following a common pattern, how far deviating from it. At one extreme the offence may have produced severe shock and rejection amongst associates, perhaps self-rejection and an intense need of punishment within the offender himself. At the other, neither he nor those he cares for will be sorry about anything except the fact that he has been caught. Obviously very different approaches will be needed to help such divergent people to come to terms at once with themselves and with the demands of the law. Yet certain principles underlie the approach of the probation officer, as a caseworker, to all in his care.

---

1. See Home Office, *The Sentence of the Court*, 1964, quoting the Departmental Committee on the Probation Service, 1962.

3 PRINCIPLES OF CASEWORK

The object of all social work may be stated as to help people in personal or social difficulties to find solutions to their problems or come to terms with them, in ways that are acceptable both to themselves and to society. The person in need of help is seen in his social setting and attempts to solve his problems take into account the whole situation. When a probation order is made the need for a solution satisfactory to society as well as to the individual is made explicit. The offender is often explicitly required to meet his several obligations: to "lead an honest and industrious life", to "be of good behaviour". It is the officer's job to stimulate him to want this for himself and find ways of doing it that give him satisfaction without infringing the rights of others. Like other caseworkers, the officer tries wherever possible to plan and act with his client, to enable him to talk about his feelings rather than leave him to work them off in ways that damage others or himself, to encourage him to plan and act for himself rather than to do things for or to him.

Casework can be seen as consisting of interdependent principles, attitudes, processes, and tools, all operating at the same time though at different levels. They are often hard to separate logically. A principle like self-responsibility, for example, can also be seen both as an objective and a means.

The basic principles or assumptions which all caseworkers (and indeed many other people as well) would accept are threefold. First, a belief in the intrinsic worth of each individual human being, quite apart from his talents, virtues or apparent usefulness to the community: respect for him as a person, whatever his conditions; appreciation of his basic human needs and rights. Second, a belief in the possibility of growth and change in people and their situations. Third, an appreciation of the power of feelings, including unconscious feelings often derived from early childhood, to influence attitudes and behaviour, and of the power of new relationships to alter feelings.

From these assumptions stem certain attitudes which include the relationship between the social worker and his clients.

The first is a recognition of uniqueness of each individual, a refusal to look upon him merely as one of a category—a patient, a prisoner, an offender, a child, an old person, a drug addict, a neurotic, a psychopath. This is not to say that certain experiences and tendencies are not common to those in each such class, but to recognize that the combinations and interactions of personality and situation vary endlessly between individuals and change from time to time even within a single individual. Again, whilst it may be possible to identify particular elements to be taken into account in the attempt to understand or treat particular categories, there is also the recognition that, even where people can be assigned with assurance to some definite group, they belong at the same time to others, for whom some other approach seems indicated. This becomes even more difficult when personality differences are taken into account. Being found guilty of an offence and put on probation may mean very different things and arouse very different feelings in different probationers, and the probation officer needs to be constantly on guard against stereotyped interpretations and approaches. His recognition of the whole person, his determination to get beyond the label of thief or pervert to the complexity of the human being and his relationships, is one of his strongest weapons in combating the offender's sense of having been classified and written off by society as nothing but a criminal.

The caseworker's recognition of the individual as a unique person is closely linked with acceptance of him as he is, so far as that can be perceived. This may be very far from approval of his behaviour or attitudes. But if the worker can look at these squarely and with active understanding, and if, aware of what they are like, he can still convey good will and a desire to help, he has crossed his first two hurdles: the relationship will have started on a basis of reality rather than self-deception on either side and there is ground for believing that it will hold whatever may transpire in future. It is acceptance that can ultimately enable the client to use the worker's help. It is acceptance that makes it possible for him to express his feelings, and so begin to come to terms with them or modify them.

Acceptance must be an active going out to a person, not merely passive endurance or intellectual acquiescence. It does not necessarily exclude challenge or the expression of anger at the right time. Indeed, that can itself be an expression of acceptance, a response to the offender as a responsible person. It implies that the caseworker minds how he behaves and it can clear the air and strengthen a relationship. Obviously it should be related to the needs of a

4*

particular client at a particular time, rather than merely a means of relieving the officer's feelings, but even that is preferable to a feigned acceptance, which can convince the offender that the caseworker is not only a fool but a hypocrite.

Genuine acceptance of all offenders is difficult: almost everyone tends to reject certain kinds of people, to feel a special revulsion against certain types of offence. It is necessary for the caseworker to be aware of his own areas of special difficulty, lest he project his own feelings upon these offenders and make it still harder to help them. The ability to accept people of all kinds can be increased to some extent by intellectual learning, by the growing appreciation of the many factors of constitution and environment that can contribute to the development of any human personality, many of them quite beyond the individual's control. But academic knowledge is not enough: like his probationer, the probation officer needs to change and grow at the level of feeling also. This can be partly the product of widening experience in dealing with offenders of many kinds, partly of deeper self-knowledge. It is not an easy process, but it is perhaps the most fundamental part of an officer's whole learning, as a student and as a caseworker, and the most fundamental thing he has to offer in his work with offenders and others in trouble.

There has been a healthy reaction against tendencies to try to impose the conventions and outlook of members of one social class upon those of another. There is more recognition of the wide range of ways of living acceptable in different parts of society, of the fact that no single set of class attitudes or social conventions has the monopoly of good or suits all individuals. All this has made acceptance easier. But it does not mean mere passive "permissiveness". It does not mean that there are no limits and no values. No society can function without some basis of generally accepted morals, if only because there must be some generally fulfilled expectation of how people will behave if anyone is to be able to carry out any purpose effectively. Limits are laid down, especially for probationer and probation officer, by the framework of the criminal law. Values are implied in all that caseworkers try to achieve. The existence of society and the freedom of its members depend upon the acceptance of certain values and limits. There are signs of yet another healthy reaction, in theories of child-rearing and education, against exaggerated permissiveness. There is certainly a place for moral judgments in casework. The point of acceptance is not that these should never be made but that to have any effect they must be worked out within the context of a relationship with which the offender feels free and secure.

The situation in which many social values themselves seem to be changing or dissolving is very challenging to social workers, often very threatening to their clients. The probation officer may sometimes envy the certainties of the old police court missionaries, even whilst he appreciates their dangers. He can feel on a knife-edge between the dangers of too easily assuming he knows what is best and too passively leaving the probationer to make his own decisions. The client may on one hand welcome increasing permissiveness but may on the other feel threatened by the disappearance of landmarks and limits which once offered guidance and protection. Especially in dealing with offenders, it has been increasingly emphasized in recent years that what is required in many cases is not the solution of hidden conflicts but rather basic social education, a reliable relationship that can enable them to mature and to appreciate the demands and rewards of living as responsible members of society. It is not enough to hope that the solution of emotional conflicts will free the individual to behave well according to his lights. He may lack the lights. "Many of those in the compulsory charge of a probation officer", it has been said, "are not clear or stable enough in their own moral values for us to hope that these will 'assert themselves'. Some of them may not have anything coherent enough to be called a 'moral attitude'; others may need help in reshaping their attitude into one more satisfactory to themselves and less of a menace to other people than the attitude they hold now." From this it is argued that the social worker must be prepared to throw his "intellectual moral resources as well as his sympathetic ones into the situation".[1] Both are often necessary. The most powerful influence an officer can have on a probationer's moral values may well stem from the way he himself behaves. The experience of a good relationship can go deeper than arguments and is is a necessary basis if they are to carry conviction.

That comes back again to the fundamental importance of respect

---

1. D. Emmett, "Ethics and the Social Worker", in E. Younghusband (ed.), *Social Work and Social Values*, 1967.

for the individual and his needs. He must be treated as a whole and potentially responsible, human being. And it must be remembered that not only what the social worker says but how he feels and what he does contribute to this. His acceptance of the importance of the offender's own feelings, his rights, his potentialities, can itself demonstrate in action the values in which he believes. Experience of a relationship in which these values are embodied may be the most effective way of conveying them to others, of strengthening morality in a positive way rather than conveying a set of prohibitions.

Rather similar considerations apply to the much discussed case-work principle of respect for the client's right of self-determination. It stems from the belief that the soundest growth comes from within. Florence Hollis puts the case well: such growth demands freedom: "freedom to think, freedom to choose, freedom from condemnation, freedom to make mistakes as well as to act wisely". If the right of choice is to be used wisely there must be opportunities to exercise it. But she has also questioned whether "self-responsibility" would not be a better term than self-determination to describe the individual's primary responsibility for the conduct of his own affairs, since this includes consideration of the rights and needs of others as well as his own.[1]

It is consideration of the rights and needs of others that may oblige the caseworker sometimes to set limits to the client's own rights to decide. How far it is proper for him to do so will depend on the individual's maturity and ability to make responsible choices for himself. Children, the mentally ill and those who are dangerous to others may have to have some choices made for them. It depends also on the legal context in which the social worker is operating. It has obviously an especial application in the work of probation officers with probationers or those subject to statutory after-care or parole. But it should not be forgotten that a children's officer, for example, may also have to take action at times to protect children from each other or even their own parents. Nor should it be assumed that a degree of compulsion or pressure, the setting of limits or the imposition of controls, always militates against the growth of a person towards maturity and self-responsibility. It may

---

1. F. Hollis, "Principles and Assumptions underlying Casework Practice", in E. Younghusband (ed.), *Social Work and Social Values*, 1967.

be a necessary stage and support in such growth, as it so often is in the upbringing of children. The point has repeatedly been made that the failure of control may be interpreted, by delinquents as by children, as a failure to care.[1]

The probation order is both a limitation of the probationer's freedom and an expression of concern for his well-being. He is warned that if he commits another offence or breaks any of the requirements he may be brought back to court and punished for his original offence. He is required to keep in touch with the probation officer and be under his supervision. In this he differs from most, though not all, of the clients of other social workers. In most cases, their clients are assumed to come voluntarily for help, already aware of problems or social pressures for which they need a solution. The probationer, on the contrary, usually comes less because he himself feels the need of help than because others, in particular the court, have decided for him that he needs it. Though the great majority of probationers—all those aged fourteen or over—will have had to consent to being put on probation and to the requirements of their orders, their consent cannot be regarded as wholly free, since they may well have feared some worse alternative and been overawed by the court. The most that can be said is that they have accepted some small measure of responsibility, which the officer can use as a starting point and as a means of ensuring the continuous contact necessary to begin to develop self-responsibility on a much wider basis. In response to the argument sometimes advanced that casework is not possible within a relationship that is compulsorily imposed upon the client, it has been pointed out that some of the most important relationships in life, including that of pupil and teacher at school and that of child and parent, are imposed rather than voluntarily chosen. As with them, however, the probation relationship really succeeds only when it passes beyond compulsion to active mutual acceptance and co-operation.

Experience has shown that the probation officer's use of authority in insisting on regular contacts with his probationer may provide an opportunity for stimulating growth and change. Most people have mixed feelings about authority and probation officers are no

---

1. See, for example, A. Hunt, "Enforcement in Probation Casework", in E. Younghusband (ed.), *New Developments in Casework*, 1964; R. Foren and R. Bailey, *Authority in Social Work*, 1968.

exception, but it is particularly important to them to come to terms
with these feelings and learn to identify themselves with the positive
aspects of authority. The first fact that the probation officer has to
face is that he would never see some of his probationers at all but for
the element of compulsion in the order and so he would have no
chance of establishing any sort of relationship with them. Many
probationers are initially unaware of their need for help, neither
conscious of having problems nor of being problems, and they have
no expectation that people in authority can be helpful or understanding. Secondly, the element of compulsion brings probation
officer and probationer face to face with the whole problem of
authority which may be fundamental to the latter's conflict with
society, so, that, in discussing with him why he has come to the office
or receives visits in his home, the probation officer may get close to
the heart of his problem at an early stage.

Whether or not it proves necessary to set limits to the client's right
to choose for himself, the social worker has an obligation to help him
understand the implications and possible consequences, to himself
and others, of the various choices he might make. He must help him
to face the realities of his situation and must not collude in barren
fantasies or the projection of all blame for what goes wrong upon
other people. These are enemies of genuine self-responsibility. They
are perhaps particularly common amongst offenders.

Another aspect of casework that may give difficulty, especially in
dealing with these same classes of the immature and the irresponsible, is the principle that the client's confidence must be respected,
that what he talks about to the caseworker should not normally be
divulged to anyone else without his consent. This general rule
derives naturally from respect for the individual and his secrets on
one side and from the need to encourage him to express freely his
feelings, his fears, if necessary his sense of guilt, resentment or
hostility. The attitude and skill of the caseworker may encourage the
client to unburden himself of matters which could include infringe-
ments of the law, or indicate a danger to other people. Here the
caseworker sees on one side the need to preserve the general principle
of maintaining the confidential nature of the casework relationship,
upon which much of its value may depend, and the importance of
maintaining a relationship with the client which may have been built
up with much difficulty. Against this he sees his duty as a citizen to

co-operate in the enforcement of the law and the protection of the innocent.

There has been little official guidance about this dilemma. It has been suggested that a probation officer has no duty beyond that of the ordinary citizen to report matters to the police and that, since his function in the community is that of caseworker, it can be argued that, except in cases of very grave crime, the demands of this special role and the interests of the client should have priority. In considering this delicate balance between the welfare of the offender and that of others, it is interesting to see that the new Children and Young Persons Bill provides that, though local authorities have a general duty to treat a child in their care in such manner as to further his best interests and afford him the opportunity of proper development, they may, if it appears necessary for the purpose of protecting members of the public, act in ways inconsistent with that. Moreover, the Secretary of State may direct them to do so in relation to a particular child. In a probation case put to the Advisory Council it was held that where an offender who has committed a sexual offence against children obtains employment which would give him opportunities to repeat his offence his employer must be told, since the need to protect children takes precedence.[1] Obviously the best solution in such a case must be for the offender himself to give up the job, just as when he has committed an offence the social worker's best course is to help him make a clean breast of it to the police himself. But this is not always possible and the case has then to be weighed in the light of all the factors.

In matters short of this degree of gravity, the generally accepted principle in social work is that personal confidences must be respected and passed only with the consent, as well as the knowledge, of the client (except where he is too mentally confused or too young to understand). Even so, it is frequently necessary to make clear to a probationer when the order is served that his confidences will not necessarily be confined to his probation officer, and that other officers, and perhaps magistrates, may need to share them. In particular, a probation officer has a duty to report to a magistrate or the court any breach of the requirements of an order. Though explanation of this at the outset may lead to more reserve on the part

---

1. Home Office *Probation Bulletin*, H.O. 14, 1963 (Item II).

of a client, he is entitled to know where he stands, and it can do far less harm than a feeling that he has been led on and then betrayed.

The duty of the social worker to explain the limits within which he can treat information as confidential can be seen as part of his larger responsibility to tell his client the purposes and the limitations of the agency for which he works. This may be a child guidance clinic, a local authority children's department, a probation and after-care service, a moral welfare organization. Whatever it is, it will have certain objectives, resources, ways of working. These the client needs to know, so that his expectations can be related to reality and so that he may not interpret as indifference any necessary refusal by the social worker to go beyond his own terms of reference, any advice that he should go elsewhere for some particular kind of help.

4   THE CASEWORK RELATIONSHIP

Just as the attitudes of the caseworker stem from his basic principles, his methods of working embody his attitudes. At the heart of them is a professional relationship with those he is trying to help which includes respect for individuality, acceptance, an eagerness to encourage self-direction and responsibility, a concern to maintain confidence. Within this relationship the worker places his knowledge, experience and skill at the service of the client in order to stimulate his capacity for growth and change and to enable him to function more adequately in society.

The relationship is focused upon the client, his needs and his responsibilities. The needs of the caseworker must be kept under control. This is not to say that they should go unrecognized or be denied any outlet. There is a basic satisfaction, deep and enduring, that arises from working with people and serving them in this way. Caseworkers see the heights as well as the depths of human behaviour; they meet people with courage and the capacity for endurance, unselfishness and self-sacrifice far beyond their own. They also encounter, sometimes in the same people, the various weaknesses to which all humanity is prone, and need frequently to remind themselves that they also are heirs to these frailties and that their position *per se* gives them no superiority or immunity. But apart from the general satisfaction derived from the opportunity casework gives for the worker to express love and concern for his fellow men, he should seek no specific emotional gratification in individual relationships with clients. Emotional involvement of this kind may make him want to keep them dependent. It restricts the freedom of both participants by blinding the worker to certain aspects of his role, in particular his need for objectivity, and thus limits the amount of help he can give. He has also to guard against distortion stemming from his own past. For example, his childhood experiences may tempt him to react with hostility to a father who seems overbearing, perhaps to see most fathers as overbearing. If he is aware of such tendencies in himself he will be better able to allow for them. Mere control of feelings by suppression is not what is required. He has to recognize and use his feelings in the client's interest. If he is preoccupied by the need to restrain his anger or appear unshocked or to control his excessive sympathy, his capacity to listen creatively to whatever the client is saying will be impaired. By recognizing for what they are the feelings within himself which the client's behaviour arouses, he is better able to understand the response the client evokes in others and his need to behave as he does.

The client, for his part, whether he seeks help on his own initiative or at the dictates of others, finds himself in a somewhat dependent position. This in itself can make him resentful, even if he conceals such feelings. It also reminds him of childhood experiences, and he therefore tends to cast the caseworker in a role related to the past. The worker may become a father or mother figure, an elder brother or sister, and when this happens the client transfers to him feelings he had in his earlier relationships. Because of this the worker needs to pay particular attention to the attitude the client adopts towards him and its probable significance.

The fact that the caseworker does not retaliate in kind when met with provocative behaviour and can take an objective view, can give the client freedom and security in which to express his attitudes, hopes and fears, the opportunity to change his feelings. On the other hand there are some clients who need to be provoked out of their own apathy, indifference or withdrawal. It may help them more, at such a stage, to feel hostile to their caseworker than to like him. The point is, again, that the relationship with each person must take account of his particular needs at the time, not of the personal inclinations of the officer. Thus seen it provides a medium within which clients can be stimulated to find themselves, particu-

larly that part of themselves which they are uncertain about or afraid
to face alone.[1] And within that framework they can test out both
their hostilities and their ideas and plans for the future.

5   THE PROCESSES OF CASEWORK

In the broadest terms the processes of casework may be seen as
including fact-finding, evaluation and diagnosis; planning; treatment; and preparation for independence. They may be simultaneous as well as consecutive. Caseworkers need to look with each client
at the realities of the situation that has brought him to them
including what it means to him. They need to consider with him his
handicaps and his resources, to seek possible ways of tackling his
difficulties, and plan where to start. They need to engage with him
in active attempts at solutions, whether by modifying his environment or modifying his ways of coping with it, or both. They need to
bear in mind throughout that the eventual aim is to enable the client
to carry on without their assistance. If a period of dependence has
been necessary they have to prepare the way for a return to independence or, if that is not possible, for transition to the care of someone
else.

In probation the process of fact-finding, evaluation and diagnosis
often begins when the probation officer is called upon to prepare a
pre-sentence report for the courts.[2] It will continue, however, as
the relationship with the probationer develops. The attention with
which the officer listens to him in the early stages is an important
element in conveying acceptance. Encouragement and comments
can help him to express and clarify his more painful feelings and to
face the realities of his situation. Thus the process of diagnosis
blends with the process of treatment, reducing hostility, promoting
self-awareness, clarifying what needs to be faced and supporting the
probationer in attempts to understand and take a share of responsibility for his difficulties.

In planning casework treatment it is essential to be realistic about
both facts and feelings. It is no good planning a line of treatment
which is wholly unacceptable to the probationer or his family, or
beyond their resources, physical, mental or emotional. If it is based

---

1. See on this D. W. Winnicott, "The Mentally Ill in your Caseload", in *New
Thinking for Changing Needs*, A.S.W., 1963.
2. On this see below, pp. 110–113.

on an overestimate of what can be achieved and what the probationer can accept, it will lead to disillusionment and discouragement for
both caseworker and client. If it ignores some areas of strength and
potential growth, some new motive for change, it will fall short of
what might have been achieved. The officer has sometimes to guard
against the rationalization of deciding, in a spirit of scientific
assessment, that there is nothing he can usefully do for a particular
individual, having regard to other demands upon him. Even the
professional criminal may reach a turning point in his career where
he is open to change, even the inadequate and dependent may
sometimes be found an environment with which he can cope.

Casework must have some starting point that offers both motive
for effort and the promise of success. And it must be flexible,
responding to changes in the probationer's situation and feelings,
developing at a pace he can stand, but not allowing him to lose
impetus and interest. It is often said that the starting point in
casework should be the problem brought by the client seeking help,
even if the caseworker has reason to believe it is no more than a
pretext, a symptom of the need for aid in deeper but less concrete
worries. Probationers are less likely to be actively seeking help than to
have been sent for help because they are a problem to others. Some
probationers, however, are aware of difficulties, generally in practical
affairs or other people's treatment of them, and they will bring these
forward: perhaps with a genuine desire for help, perhaps to test the
reality of the probation officer's proffered aid, perhaps to hold off
any more searching enquiries into their own feelings and behaviour.
In some cases the offence itself may have been an unconscious plea
for help. On the other hand many probationers have no sense of
having any problems, apart from those arising from the fact that
they have been convicted and subjected to supervision. It will often
be the feelings aroused by this that have to be tackled first, providing
the starting point in casework, and opening up into a more general
consideration of the probationer's attitudes to the demands of
society upon him and his relationships with those with whom he
lives and works.

Casework treatment may be directed to supporting or controlling
the probationer in his developing attitudes, plans, relationships and
behaviour. It may aim at clarifying his situation, so that both he and
the probation officer can see more clearly where he stands and how

he feels and act accordingly. It may aim at increasing his insight into motives of which he is unaware, or only dimly aware, in the hope that this will reduce their power and make it easier for him to control them. It may aim at reducing the stresses in the environments and enhancing its opportunities. The likelihood is that it will at some time include elements of several of these.

Support includes encouragement by word and action whenever the probationer seems to be thinking, feeling or behaving constructively; discouragement if he is drifting the other way. A probation officer may give support by trying to increase self-confidence; by praising efforts to get work or to hold back temper; by admiring a piece of woodwork, a hair-style or a new coat; by going with someone to the Youth Employment Bureau or the Ministry of Social Security; or by just listening sympathetically and trying to understand the probationer so that he is given a sense of his own value.

Control is sometimes seen as the opposite to support but, as has already been indicated, it can often better be seen as another aspect of the same thing. It may include warning a probationer of the probable results of illegal conduct; withholding approval, or showing active disapproval, in ways that strengthen his own powers of self-control; if necessary invoking the law. All these actions, in the appropriate circumstances, demonstrate care and concern, both for the probationer himself and for others whose rights he must learn to consider. All must sometimes be used by a caseworker dealing with delinquents.

Clarification involves helping the probationer to make choices by helping him to understand what is involved in them. It may be a means of stimulating change where the need for it is not felt already. It includes explaining at the outset the effect of the probation order, the obligations and rights of the probationer, the kinds of help the probation officer can offer and his own obligations to the court. It includes helping a person to describe, and so to perceive more clearly, what a situation means to himself and to others in his environment. It may include giving information or embarking upon a measure of social education. Its purpose is to enable the probationer to assess the probable effects upon himself and others of either leaving things as they are or trying to change them.

The development of insight is the most controversial and emotionally loaded of all the techniques of casework. It is the most closely modelled upon the psychotherapeutic and psycho-analytical approach, it presupposes some knowledge and acceptance of theories of personality and the unconscious mind developed by Freud and his followers, and it has gathered to itself a prestige, a somewhat self-conscious mystique, which attracts some people and repels others. In fact many of its basic ideas, if in somewhat distorted form, are now common currency. The task of the caseworker is different from that of the psychotherapist, though there may be some overlap. He needs to be able to recognize the deeper conflicts that may underlie his client's behaviour, but he is not directly concerned with unconscious problems or radical changes in personality. His attention is focused upon feelings much nearer the surface and upon difficulties in relationships with others and in social life.[1] Again, a distinction needs to be made between the caseworker's insight into the unstated emotions in an interview, an attitude, an action or a relationship, and his decision as to whether it will help the client to discuss these with him directly.

The caseworker's own insight should underlie all his relationships with the probationer, including his decision at particular points to use support or control, clarification or environmental modification. It will only be in certain cases, however, that he will discuss these hidden feelings directly with the probationer. Many probationers may lack the will, intelligence or stability to go far in such examination. To some it may do harm. Even when it is advisable it will not necessarily be an elaborate process. It may involve no more, for instance, than bringing into the open a father's unspoken sense that the probation officer is somehow taking away some of his functions by intervening in his family; or speaking with a probationer about the fear or anger he is sensed as feeling, even though he does not voice them, or voices the opposite. It may mean using the caseworker's knowledge of how past relationships and feelings affect present ones. An over-anxious mother, who is unconsciously suggesting to her son or daughter that they are delinquent, may be felt to be reliving in them her own unhappy childhood or adolescence: if she can be given the opportunity simply to talk about her

---

1. See on this an article by A. B. Lloyd Davies, in *The Boundaries of Casework.* Report published by the Association of Psychiatric Social Workers.

own past she may herself link up her youthful days with those of her child, and so find herself freer to react more appropriately to that child's real needs rather than those she has projected upon it. Or a rebellious child may be helped directly if the probation officer can show understanding of his feelings of resentment, caused perhaps by a situation in which the father is dangerously ill, the mother pre-occupied, the family poor and the child himself caught up in fears of death and of the effects of his own naughtiness: for him delinquency may be a sort of defiant distraction from such a painful emotional situation.   More often delinquents respond rather to control and support, a reinforcement of their ability to cope with social demands plus warm encouragement. But an occasional glimpse of the fact that their probation officer also understands some of the pressures within them, and indeed the knowledge that these sometimes frightening and apparently overwhelming forces can be understood, may be very helpful.

Whilst it is generally admitted that modifying the environment, either directly or through the client, is a legitimate part of casework, there has been some tendency to regard it as a very minor part, calling for less skill and somehow less creditable than methods designed directly to strengthen or change the client himself. This is partly a reaction against an older approach, related to much worse material conditions, which tended to plan briskly for the client's good, finding him aid, job or accommodation, and assuming that this, combined with suitable exhortations, would suffice to set him on the right path. Where the lack of these things are indeed the only obstacles that may be so, but it is seldom so straightforward, especially nowadays. It is sometimes argued, therefore, that the probation officer should do as little as possible, since even if he solves current material problems for his clients they will only meet others when probation is over and be no better equipped to meet them than they were to start with. Casework, on this argument, should concentrate upon finding out and dealing with what is wrong within the probationer himself.

There is, of course, a strong element of truth in that, but several qualications need to be borne in mind. One is that many probation-ers can at first appreciate concern only if it is expressed in practical or material terms. Another is that personality and environment are constantly interacting and that a change in some element in the environment may provide the opportunity for changes in attitude: the person has always to be considered in relation to his situation. A third is that some people, even today, are living in conditions, or trying to rear families on incomes, that would tax the powers of the most intelligent and stable. It is because of this that at least some caseworkers are becoming increasingly concerned, through local and national pressure groups and by contributing to research, to call attention to the grosser injustices in society and to get them remedied. Meanwhile, the worst off amongst their clients are often those least able, in terms of intelligence, health and personality, either to cope with difficulties, to find their own way out of them, or to get help from the authorities. Pending social reforms they have to be helped to live in society as it is. And finally, as already seen, changes in the environment need not be, and should not be, imposed: so far as possible they should be brought about by the probationer himself, with the support of the officer; and even where this is not possible they should be fully discussed with and accepted by the probationer and he should play as large a part as he is able in accomplishing them.

Seen in this way, the modification of the environment or the provision of practical help is an important part of casework. Its constructive use calls for as much professional discrimination, skill and insight as any other method. It can convey more meaning to many offenders than any amount of verbal discussion. It must therefore be used sensitively, with awareness of the personality, feelings and situation of the individual concerned. In spite of this, officers sometimes see material and practical help as chores which should not occupy the time of skilled caseworkers, as something quite apart from casework proper. The feeling might be diminished if they could use their clerical staff more flexibly, passing on to them some of the routine but time-consuming tasks of getting in touch with officials or making routine factual enquiries.[1]

Probationers who are very young, or very inadequate, or who are hostile to those in authority and have got on the wrong side of them, may well need intervention by the probation officer, either to put their case or make arrangements for them, or to pave the way for them to do so. The probation officer, albeit with the probationer's

---

1. See on this below, pp. 228–229.

agreement, may himself takes steps to modifiy some aspect of the probationer's life. He may propose to the court a period of residence in a home or hostel; he may arrange a change of school. He may fix up treatment for some physical or mental disability. He may try to help parents, spouse, teachers or employers to understand and help the client better. He may bring some new relationship into his life, like the friendship of a volunteer or membership of a group. He may help him to claim his rights by putting his case or explaining his difficulties to some official or charitable body, or by accompanying him to an appeals tribunal.

The emphasis and choice of method in casework, and indeed the use of other resources such as hostels, groupwork, voluntary help, should depend primarily on the needs of each individual probationer.[1] At the same time it inevitably depends also upon the skill, training and personality of the particular probation officer concerned. This is not wholly a bad thing: we all do best what comes most naturally to us and what we most thoroughly understand. In the probation and after-care service there have, especially of late, been attempts to make use of this fact by allowing certain officers to specialize in work with particular kinds of offender, even experiments in matching individual offenders to the probation officers thought most likely to be able to help them, though as yet we know too little to have got far with this latter move. There are, of course, dangers as well as advantages: if a probation officer concentrates exclusively on the offenders he finds it easiest to accept and the methods he finds most congenial he is likely to confirm his own prejudices, restrict his range of understanding and skills and stultify his own development. He may thus have less ability to adapt to the varying needs even of those probationers he has. And he will be the less qualified, in due course, to take on the responsibilities of seniority and of guiding or training younger workers. This strengthens the case for thorough training of probation officers, both at the outset of their careers and during their service, so as to increase their range and flexibility.

In probation both officer and probationer are aware of when their contact with each other is likely to end. It is within this framework

---

1. On this, see, for example, M. Brown, "A Review of Casework Methods" and E. Irvine, "A New Look at Casework", both in E. Younghusband (ed.), *New Developments in Casework*, 1966.

that they must consider how much they can tackle together and when. It can be a stimulus to get on with things, and at the same time a reassurance to the probationer that he is entitled to help over a certain period. As a rule, the most intensive work, both in diagnosis and treatment, tends to take place during the early part of the order. There are exceptions to this: the probationer may seem to be making little response until some fresh crisis suddenly induces him to seek help. But with the majority contacts become less frequent during the latter part of the order, and the probation officer retires into a more passive role, watching the probationer's progress and giving support where necessary.

This, of course, accords with the aim of encouraging self-responsibility, of reaching a point where the probationer can be relied upon to cope unaided with his difficulties and responsibilities. In some cases the probation officer will be satisfied that this point has been reached before the end of the order. Where that is so he can apply to the court for its early discharge on the ground of the probationer's good behaviour, or it can be replaced by a conditional discharge. This not only releases the officer for other work but can be a great encouragement to the probationer. On the other hand, there are some probationers who are obviously still unable to stand on their own feet as the order draws to its close. They may be inadequate people, isolated or members of problem families, and they are likely to depend upon long-term support. They need linking up in good time with other community services, statutory or voluntary, whenever these are available.

6 THE TOOLS OF CASEWORK

The interview is the major means of developing the relationship with the probationer and, indeed, with those in his immediate environment whose co-operation is needed in treatment. Interviews at the probation office call for some effort on the part of the probationer and underline the activity on his side implicit in the probation order. To fix them at reasonably regular intervals and sometimes to set aside a definite length of time for them underlines the probation officer's side of the obligation and the claim of the probationer upon his attention and help. If the probationer knows what time he can expect he has an incentive to bring up any painful or awkward topic he wants to discuss in good time. If the officer has to cut an inter-

view short, perhaps because of a sudden and unexpected demand for
his attendance at court or action to meet an emergency, he, on his
side, must try to round it off in such a way that his client may feel he
is not being pushed away for something that is more important, but
that this is merely an outward break in his relationship with the
officer, whom he will be seeing again soon. If he can go away in the
knowledge that here is someone who is concerned with him and his
difficulties, he may well be able to go on at the next interview from
where he left off. The purpose is to emphasize continuity so that
there can be real movement in the relationship, in diagnosis and in
treatment. The spacing of interviews, and the way the probation
officer handles unexpected calls at the office by the probationer,
are means of modifying his dependence to correspond with his
changing needs and the stage he has reached in treatment.

Visits to the probationer at his home are also explicitly provided
for in almost all probation orders. Here, too, regularity and concentrated attention can do much to convey continuing concern in
the form of actions as well as words. Visits can allow the officer to
see the probationer better as part of his family. The officer's interest
can help the offender towards a better valuation of other members of
his family and of his own place in it. It can help the family to accept
the probationer and to work in harmony with the probation officer.
This can have a significant place in work not only with children but
with adolescents. Parents need considerable support in tolerating
the moods of a delinquent youngster, and they need also reassurance
that the officer is not usurping their roles. Again the relationship of
an adult offender to wife, husband and children, the way in which
he or she is able to carry the role of spouse or of parent, may be a
vital factor in criminality as well as in social adjustment as a whole.
It is often during home visits that these factors can best be understood and tackled, whether by way of individual interviews or by
entering directly into the interaction of members of the family.[1]

All contacts about the probationer with other people, agencies, all
office interviews and home visits, are entered by probation officers
in their case records. These records are more than a handy source of
reference for themselves and others who may have to deal with the

---

1. On these topics see E. M. Goldberg, "Social Work in the Sixties", *The
Almoner*, Vol. 14, No. 3, 1961.

case later. They are now recognized as an essential casework tool in themselves, helping the officer to plan and disclipine his work. Regular summaries provide the basis for assessments of what has been achieved: of whether progress is discernible; of whether the initial diagnosis and approach to treatment need modifications, and whether there are any factors of personality or situation that have been overlooked and need now to be dealt with or brought into play. They can give the caseworker and his senior insight into the part he himself has played and enable them to consider whether, with advantage, he might have dealt with the situation differently or could plan his part in future interviews more constructively. They can be a useful instrument in teaching casework to students and more advanced workers. If kept in a disciplined way they can have value in research. And as the work of the service extends and the end of probation is no longer regarded as ending such treatment for an offender who is sent to a penal institution, they are likely to provide a vital link in continuity of care.[1]

---

1. See N.A.P.O. Probation Papers No. 5, *Case Recording in Probation and After-Care*, 1968.

CHAPTER 5

CASEWORK: OTHER SETTINGS

1 CASEWORK IN SOCIAL ENQUIRIES[1]

In making a social enquiry, the probation officer is using his diagnostic skill as a caseworker to help the court to decide how to deal with an offender. As a result of his report the court may well order some kind of treatment designed to help the offender. But this will not always be so, since, though the interests of society and of the individual often coincide, they do not always do so. Also, even though a disciplinary or institutional sentence may indeed be the best thing for a particular offender, he and his family may be quite unwilling to accept such a decision. There can be tension, therefore, between the probation officer's desire as a caseworker to do his best for the individual and to carry him with him, and his primary duty in this particular context, which is to report impartially and objectively to the court and, if he is in a position to do so, to indicate what form of treatment he thinks most likely to prevent a further offence. Even if, as may well be the case, he does not feel qualified to suggest imprisonment or borstal training, for example, he may well lead the court to that conclusion merely by giving the opinion that the offender is unlikely to respond to probation.

He also has to recognize that what he considers most likely to advance the welfare of the offender and his family may be unacceptable to the court. Where there appears to be a conflict between the interests of society and the individual, where, for instance, he thinks that a much-institutionalized man might in the long run be rehabilitated on probation but only at the risk of a further offence in the short run, he must put both sides. As a social worker it is his

---

1. On the broader issue of social enquiries in relation to the courts, see below, pp. 185–193.

duty to ensure that the interests of the individual are made clear; as a court officer he must assess, as far as he can, the risk of break-down. The decision rests then with the court.

It has been seen that part of the caseworker's obligation is to help his clients to understand their own situation, to clarify possibilities and get them to face reality. This is the starting point in a social enquiry, when the probation officer explains to the defendant and his family the purpose of the report. They recognize that he has duties to the court as well as to them. They may be hostile as a result. But provided he is frank and does not attempt to deceive either them or himself, they usually accept the position.

Their awareness of it may well lead them to put pressure upon him, consciously or unconsciously, to be on their side, especially to prevent the offender from being "sent away". As a social worker he wants to understand and to help and more often than not clients, even at this stage, sense this attitude and respond. Troubled parents, for instance, may be much relieved to discuss their worries about a difficult child or adolescent. They may equally, however, respond by defending their child, or by covering up a matrimonial difference. Something similar may happen with the spouse of an adult offender. That may in itself sometimes be a sign of health. The probation officer has to show that he has understanding, patience, willingness to accept. He also has to show firmness and his loyalty and respect for the court. He does his best to report fairly. He may check with an employer, a head teacher or another social worker.

From them and from the offender and his family what he wants is information about facts and feelings that will enable him to give a full and fair report about the offender, his history, health, family background and work, about the meaning to him of the offence (if this has already been proved or admitted) and about his prospects for the future.

In so far as this amounts to a tentative social diagnosis he uses his casework skills in arriving at it. In a sense he is also making a tentative prognosis and treatment plan, and laying the basis for whatever treatment the court may order. He will in many cases be trying to assess whether or how the defendant could be helped in a probation relationship; he may be laying the foundation with the family for help and support to be given during a period of possible institutional treatment; he may be seeing a need for medical or psychiatric investigation and action. As a caseworker he will be trying as fully as possible to understand the person and his family and assessing their need for help and capacity to help themselves. He may at the same time, in his interviews, be helping the individual offender or his family to face what he has done, to accept guilt or weakness. He may sometimes, by interpretation and understanding, be deliberately trying to reduce disproportionate feelings of guilt or family disapproval, as for instance in the case of an adolescent exhibitionist or a depressed middle-aged shoplifter.

Most probation officers find that, in spite of the limitations imposed by the context of the court enquiry, it is also often a time of crisis, when feelings are near the surface, when they may be discussed more easily and changes may be effected in them. In the charged atmosphere, a married couple may come to communicate better, a wife to accept her share of blame for a husband's offence, a husband to see his wife's difficulties, parents to face a child's handicap. Sometimes the main work with an offender is done during the enquiry, and subsequent probation may be mainly a period of consolidation.

Whether it is the beginning of a long-term contact or likely to stop at a single interview, this is properly described as casework and is felt to be therapeutic. It is not incompatible with the enquiry for the court and it is expected by the court, which has experience of the sort of relationship and attitude to be expected from a probation officer. Especially if, as is often the case, it is the first contact an offender or his family has had with a probation officer it is also important in paving the way for any future relationship and treatment, whether by the same officer or another, whether on probation, in prison or detention centre, or after leaving a penal institution, and whether focused upon the offender himself or his family. The way he approaches them during an enquiry will give them their first idea of what a probation officer is like and what sort of help he may be able to offer them.

When an offender is being sent away to an institution after, and perhaps partly because of, a probation officer's report, the officer usually tries to see him before he goes to his destination. Reassurances, or assurance of future help or continuing regard, are seldom appreciated at the time, though they should be offered sparingly and may be remembered later. Sometimes the client at this stage may

want to ask for some particular help for a relative. Even mo
he will want to express his anger or despair. If he can do th
probation officer it may save his resentment rankling; it shows him
his officer is not afraid of his anger, and it will help him later to
see him as a real person and so relate to him and to other welfare
officers. This concern for the offender's needs demonstrates again
that the task of reporting to the court, for all its requirements of
objectivity, does not demand a suspension of the probation officer's
attitudes and skills as caseworker, but rather their sensitive application
in a critical situation. Not only as a caseworker but as a significant
link in the processes of criminal justice, the probation officer needs
to treat the defendant with scrupulous fairness and firmness, with
concern for his rights and welfare as an individual and with determination not to write him off.

2   CASEWORK IN PRISONS

Casework in prisons has, in many cases, an emphasis different from
casework in probation. The element of compulsion is lacking:
prisoners are not obliged to see the welfare officer if they do not
want to. There are likely to be more recidivists, more professional
criminals, more inadequate, unresponsive and unpromising people
amongst them. Their situation as prisoners makes them more
resentful and suspicious. The association with other prisoners, from
which they cannot escape and upon which many rely for support,
militates against co-operation with anyone in authority or acceptance of values upheld by authority.

Their problems, too, have a different emphasis. A probationer
can usually carry on in his home and job, or find new ones. The
prisoner, if he had these at all, has suffered a violent break with
them. Both for him and his family material problems usually loom
large. Whatever the underlying emotional problems, the best way
to help in this situation may often be prompt attention to the
material difficulties. To the prisoner in particular, actions speak
louder than words.

The prisoner has two social settings: that of his life outside and
that of the prison. The caseworker in prison may be concerned with
either or both. Obviously the two may interact and the focus shift
from one to another. The emphasis will vary with the length of
sentence and the point reached: the shorter the sentence, the nearer

its beginning or end, the more attention is likely to be concentrated upon dealing with problems outside, maintaining or restoring contacts, paving the way for after-care and rehabilitation in the community. With the longer sentence, with release perhaps far distant, the main concern may be to help the offender cope with the pressures of institutional life.

Whereas in probation the caseworker is usually assured of a continuous period during which he can develop a relationship with the offender and work towards understanding his difficulties and modifying his attitudes, in prison welfare, especially in the big local prisons with their constant comings and goings, he may see a man only once or twice. Moreover, he may be so occupied with the urgent requests for help of men coming in with problems left behind them and men going out with problems awaiting them, that he has little time for continuous casework, the attempt to examine and modify attitudes, with any of them. It has been argued, indeed, that in this kind of setting the welfare officer should "see his own role in providing post-sentence first aid and pre-release preparation for the field worker".[1] Yet despite the pressures, even in the local prisons, attempts are being made to carry out on-going casework with selected men. This can have great value not only in itself but in promoting a deeper understanding of the needs of men in prison and in helping the caseworker, even in his first-aid work, to keep in mind the deeper feelings and longer term considerations that need to be taken into account even in handling sudden requests for practical help which have to be dealt with on a short term emergency basis.

The principles of casework have a special significance in prison. Because prison symbolizes rejection, acceptance, if it can be conveyed, is of particular importance. Because prison robs a man of so much of his individuality and identity, his recognition and treatment as an individual can be of special value. It is not surprising that it is in relation to these two things that the welfare officer often finds himself working against the grain of the institution, that clashes of outlook are most likely with the prison regime and the prison staff.

---

1. A. R. Stanley, "Casework in a local prison", *Probation*, Vol. 12, No. 3, November 1966.

Nor is it surprising that the latter can be so quick to warn the welfare officer of the dangers of being "conned", or feel that the prisoner is getting away with something if he is given special individual attention. Obviously there is substance in the warnings; but the caseworker (in or out of prison) has to cope with the client who tries to manipulate him. This is part of acceptance of the person and the situation as they are. In prison, in particular, the caseworker may need to avoid being monopolized by the demanding and attention seeking, if he is to have any time for the more withdrawn, who may be in much greater need of help. But if he carries the fear of being exploited too far he may lose his chance of helping some whose trivial requests are cover for real needs, who are at least trying to keep some link with the world outside, and who might, if given acceptance and help, move forward in relationship with himself or accept after-care on leaving.

The principle of self-responsibility also cuts across the grain of the regime in most prisons. Even in those most concerned to encourage responsibility, prisoners are necessarily subject to direction in a great part of their lives, and they are largely impotent to influence directly their former environment or their families outside. In many prisons almost all power of decision, and therefore of responsibility, is taken from them. Even the prisoner who is not normally inadequate is forced into a position of dependence. Yet the very fact that there is so little he can do for himself makes it the more important that the caseworker should, wherever possible, help him to write the letter to the housing department or to discuss problems and plans with his family, rather than take these responsibilities off his hands. Again the pressures of time may make this hard for the caseworker: it is usually quicker to do a thing oneself than to help a prisoner to do it. But with so much he cannot do, so much sense of helplessness and defeat, the encouragement and self-respect derived from a small achievement may be out of all proportion to its intrinsic importance.

The diagnostic aspect of casework in prison can be formidable, especially, again, in the big local prisons, where numbers are so large. Ideally, as in pre-sentence enquiries, it should include, first, an assessment of whether each man needs, and is likely to accept and respond to, on-going casework treatment; a decision whether, even if he does not take the initiative in asking for help with specific problems, the caseworker should himself take the lead in offering him regular meetings. Second, there is the need to identify urgent social problems requiring action, either by the welfare officer, by the probation and after-care service or volunteers outside, or by the welfare services in any prison to which the offender may be transferred. Third, the welfare officer may be called upon to give an opinion on a whole range of decisions affecting the prisoners' treatment: in this he will be working as part of a diagnostic team in conjunction with the prison's medical, psychological and educational services. Fourth, if he is to make an accurate assessment under any of these heads he needs to consider not only the problems brought up by the offender but what lies behind him: his home situation, the circumstances that precipitated his crime and imprisonment, and his attitude and probable response to prison itself.

Obviously, attendance at the reception board alone will not suffice to enable him to make this kind of diagnosis. The unhurried initial interview envisaged by the Advisory Council would give more scope if pressure of work allowed for it. Where continuous treatment is possible diagnosis needs to be, as in probation, a continuing process. Prisoners' attitudes change and so do their outside circumstances.

Diagnosis in the case of prisoners cannot be achieved by the individual prison welfare worker alone. In assessing the situation at home, the possibilities of employment, the offender's life outside, he is largely dependent upon the probation service in the open. Hence the importance of a copy of the pre-sentence report, quick notification of anything picked up in a post-sentence interview and the exchange of information between the workers dealing with the prisoner and his family respectively. In assessing the situation in the prison and the prisoner's response to it, the welfare officer is dependent upon the co-operation of the prison staff.

The double social setting is relevant here also. Some attempt has to be made to assess behaviour and attitudes inside the prison in relation to what may be expected outside. This is, of course, likely to be of growing importance as parole develops. How far can apparent responsiveness to treatment be attributed to the "good prisoner" syndrome, perhaps to the hope that it will increase the possibility of early parole? How far is a prisoner using talks with the welfare officer merely to break the monotony and relieve his feelings while in prison? How far, on the other hand, is a more rebellious attitude a healthy symptom? How far are the possibilities of change inhibited by the inmate culture? How far are any apparent gains likely to be carried over on release? As yet the new combination of prison welfare and after-care has not developed far enough, or lasted long enough, for firm guidance on these questions to have emerged. Continuous records of treatment may give the means of assessing the relationship between behaviour and response in the two settings.

The planning of treatment for a prisoner likewise depends upon others besides the caseworker in prison. His family outside may have to be taken into account, the help of the outside service may be needed here also. And inside the prison surgical or medical treatment may be arranged by the medical officer, psychotherapy by a psychiatrist, groupwork perhaps by an assistant governor.

In treatment, as has been seen, the welfare officer is directly responsible for at least three kinds of task: for dealing with immediate problems, for on-going casework in selected cases and for making it possible for others to help the prisoner.

It is easy to dismiss many of the immediate problems put forward by prisoners as trivial and time-wasting, not calling for casework skills or meeting more than material needs. In a large local prison a welfare officer may be besieged by demands for practical help: for property to be retrieved, for families to be contacted, for enquiries to be made of hospitals, housing authorities and all sorts of official agencies. All these things can take a great deal of time. Some kinds of difficulty and enquiry might well be dealt with by other prison staff, if they have time and interest. Others could be carried out by casework aides if these could be made available where welfare departments are hard pressed. But even so there is a very definite place for casework understanding in dealing with this kind of request, in seeing what may lie behind it.

More continuous casework is possible with some prisoners. They have more time on their hands to think about themselves than when they are at large. It may be possible to help them find positive factors and then, when a relationship is well established, to look at some negative aspects also. Or casework may be used simply to minimize the damage of imprisonment. This is not necessarily a purely negative task, since relationships within the prison may be used to improve the prisoner's social adjustment, especially to authority.

The welfare officer may work with people in the prisoner's environment both inside and out. Inside he may draw the attention of a discipline officer, perhaps a chaplain or assistant governor, to the need of a particular prisoner for special interest at a particular time, perhaps suggest a transfer or an educational course. Outside he may involve a probation officer, voluntary associate or voluntary body either in the prisoner's immediate problems or his after-care plans. Directly or indirectly he may involve family or friends in helping the offender or modifying their attitudes towards him, thus acting as a mediator between him and the world outside.

The casework relationship in prison is subject to special difficulties. There has been considerable dispute as to whether it is more helpful for the prisoner to see the welfare officer as part of the prison or as someone belonging to an outside service, but in practice it seems almost inevitable that he will see him as part of the prison, or at least part of the court and penal system that has sent him there. From this point of view the prisoner, even more than the probationer, is likely to view with suspicion offers of help from the authority he knows is punishing him. He knows, moreover, that the bulk of the prisoners are against any collaboration. He may be aggressive in his demands, seeking confirmation of his distrust in any failure to get him what he wants, however unreasonable, evidence of indifference in any delay. If he does form a relationship both his psychological condition and his impotence as a prisoner is likely to make it a very dependent one.

In this kind of situation the importance of clarification in the casework process is evident. One of the objects of the initial interview with an offender coming into prison is to let prisoners know something of the role of the prison welfare department. Since confidentiality must have strict limits in prison this also must be made clear, together with the fact that the welfare officer works within the framework of the prison's rules and security. Likewise, in his hopes and plans for the future the prisoner may need to be steered away from fantasy about his prospects at home or at work and brought towards a more realistic assessment of what he is likely to face and his own ability to cope with it, though often this can be done helpfully and effectively only when the time of release is approaching.

Support, too, can be of great importance in helping a prisoner to regain and keep his sense of identity and self-respect and encouraging him to plan, to decide and to act for himself in so far as it is possible for him to do so. It is also the basis of any attempt at self-examination or greater insight into the causes of his behaviour. It is not only the long-term prisoner who may benefit from these kinds of treatment. Sometimes the sentence may represent an acute crisis for a man serving a short period, and he and his family may be open, as at the time of a pre-sentence enquiry, to new insights and to accepting new attitudes and plans.

3   CASEWORK IN AFTER-CARE

Whatever may be done in an institution to prepare the way for rehabilitation in the community, it is after release that the real crunch comes. Here the probation officer needs a greater sense of urgency than is usual in dealing with probationers. The upheaval will have been more severe, decisions and adjustments have to be made more quickly, the offender is likely to be more anxious. The very fact that he may also be more likely to commit further crime makes it the more necessary for the officer to be quickly available in emergencies and to work with him, not allowing the relationship, though it may be compulsory, to remain or degenerate into one of defensive formality.

Casework with offenders released from penal institutions has to take account of certain common factors, whether they are obliged to accept after-care on a compulsory basis or come for it voluntarily. Other factors apply only to one group or the other.

In most cases there is likely to be more difficulty in accepting an offender in after-care than in probation. The offence or the criminal record is likely to be more serious, the outlook not as hopeful, the personality and circumstances more difficult, the possibilities of growth and change more limited. There are more obstacles in the way of forming a helpful relationship: in many cases the offender may well be more sophisticated not only in terms of crime but in terms of treatment, and his suspicions may be increased if he has previously failed on probation or felt rejected by a probation officer, or let down by a prison welfare officer. Environmental difficulties are likely to be greater than in probation and call for more urgent action: this applies both to the material and to the personal situation.

In some cases the offender may need a place to live and a job to go to, even clothes and money to carry him over until his first earnings come in. In others he needs help in finding his place in a family that has learned to live without him. He is likely to be suspicious of other people's attitude towards him, expecting rejection and sometimes precipitating it by talking about his imprisonment. If he has weaknesses, such as gambling or heavy drinking, he will find himself suddenly exposed to temptation again.

It is particularly important for the caseworker to be aware of the offender's feelings and his own. The attitude of the client in after-care, whether compulsory or voluntary, is likely to include, in addition to more friendly feelings, a certain hostility and resentment, which is unlikely to be lessened, though it may well be concealed, by his sense of dependence and anxiety for the future. These feelings may show themselves in an openly aggressive attitude or, more subtly, in refusal to discuss feelings and problems or in over-dependence. An attempt has to be made to enable the client to face and understand these attitudes in their relevance not only to his relation to his supervisor, but to the demands of society. The recidivist, in particular, knows well how to employ the kind of emotional blackmail implied in the phrases, "Nobody helped me" and "I lost my job when they found out where I came from". Consciously or unconsciously, he will attempt to exploit the law-abiding citizen's confused feelings of guilt, responsibility and compassion, and his demands may be reinforced by his fears and his desire to get even with society. It is thus very necessary for the officer dealing with him to be clear about his own attitudes to authority and to punishment, so that he may be in a position to help without being hampered and confused by, for example, the need to assuage his own sense of guilt.

Environmental treatment is likely to play a bigger part in after-care than in probation, partly because of the break in normal life, partly because many of those concerned are less adequate, less capable of change than most probationers. It is partly because of this that the new interest in hostels and voluntary help is focused largely on after-care. It is partly because of this also that more attention is being given to work with the families of offenders, even whilst they are still in institutions.

The encouragement of self-responsibility will often be both more urgent and more difficult than in probation: more urgent because the offender may need quickly to establish himself in a home and job if he is not to slip back into trouble; more difficult because of the dependence imposed by an institution, which provides at least food, clothes, shelter, occupation and companionship and in most cases almost complete control as well. For those who have been in an institution for a long time there will, in addition, be bewildering changes in economic and social conditions, increasing the sense of helplessness. Yet the fact remains that harm can be done by under-estimating the offender's ability to do things for himself as well as by overestimating it. It has repeatedly been observed, for instance, that jobs and lodgings found for an ex-prisoner or borstal boy are often not taken up, or abandoned after a very short time, whereas he is more likely to stay with those he finds himself.

As social work develops within penal institutions it becomes increasingly likely that much of the planning of after-care, statutory or voluntary, will be started in the detention centre, borstal or prison before the offender comes out, and that his treatment in the institution will be linked to his expected needs on release. Hence it becomes increasingly necessary for the probation officer outside to know what the social worker and others in the institution have been attempting, and also the feelings of the offender about it. Whereas in many instances the officer starts work in probation, or a pre-sentence enquiry, from scratch, in after-care he needs increasingly to take into account what has already been learned about the offender and what response he has shown to treatment.

As has been seen, in compulsory after-care the framework of casework is in some ways similar to that of probation. There is usually a fixed period, the offender is required to maintain contact and keep certain conditions, and during part at least of the period there is the possibility of recall if the conditions are not kept or a further offence is committed. As in probation, too, the probation officer has a measure of responsibility for control, for bringing to the attention of the authorities behaviour that may indicate a further offence or necessitate recall.

In parole the prisoner has to be willing to accept supervision and to agree to its conditions. There is thus, as in probation, a certain voluntary element to build upon. There has also been the fact that, so far at least, parole has been highly selective, so that not only are those freed on this basis the more promising, but they have the special incentive of knowing that they have been singled out from many as trustworthy and likely to make good. At the same time the sanction of direct recall to prison is a powerful one.

In other forms of compulsory after-care there is no element of consent. Supervision may be resented as an additional punishment. Revenge may be taken in open aggression or non-co-operation or in a demanding dependence. Even when the offender reports regularly he can retreat behind a respectful and unreal façade learned in the institution and remain inaccessible to a more genuine relationship. How far he does this may depend partly on how those in the institution have worked with him, partly on how far it has been possible to make or maintain a relationship with him, and perhaps his family whilst he has been there. Even more than in probation, however, it is necessary to try to clarify at the outset the legal framework and the justification and purposes of after-care, and to come to grips with the offender's feelings about it.

The element of compulsion in statutory after-care, as in probation, can work both ways: it can mean different things to different people and often to the same person. It may be felt as interference, restriction, supervision, but also as a measure of security, a claim upon the officer's time and attention, a sense of belonging and a right to long-term concern and support. Even before release the knowledge that a person will become subject to after-care allows for really early contact to be made with him in the institution, either by the probation officer who expects to supervise or by a volunteer or both, so that he can come out to a relationship in which he already has some confidence. In the earliest stages after release, before the offender has had time to adjust to his sudden freedom or to take stock of his environment, an element of direction may be necessary and reassuring, though with all but a few of the most inadequate, this needs to lead on as quickly as possible to support of the offender in making his own decisions and carrying them out.

Probation officers have had experience over many years of case-work in after-care within a compulsory framework. They have had experience over many years of casework in matrimonial and other domestic problems on a voluntary basis. What is comparatively new is casework on a voluntary basis with the whole range of offenders leaving prison. In dealing with many of these, officers are faced with the problem of "selling" casework, perhaps in a single interview, to clients who often do not recognize their need for this kind of help, who lack any strong motive for accepting it and may be deeply suspicious of its sources and motives. Ex-prisoners coming for help to the probation officer often have neither, on the one hand, the strong sense of their own social problems that drives other voluntary clients to seek the help of social workers, nor, on the other, the spur of legal obligation which takes its place, at least at the outset, in launching casework with offenders in probation or compulsory after-care. In voluntary after-care the probation officer has to depend upon his skill as a caseworker alone to establish some sense both of the need and the possibility of personal help in clients who are often deeply inadequate, irresponsible, and suspicious.

Some have homes to return to, though they may need help especially in the early problems of re-establishing themselves in the family and of getting and keeping work. At the other extreme there are some who are so sick, alcoholic, or wholly inadequate and isolated that they need prolonged treatment and accommodation of kinds that are not yet available. Some are the perpetual scroungers, whose sole object is to exploit any source of material aid. Apart from these, there is a wide range of homeless men, especially in the big cities: the sexual deviant; the young, aggressive and demanding; the middle-aged, depressed and demanding; the inadequate, ineffectual and spiritless; the deprived and lonely; those who genuinely want to get on their feet and who decided in prison that they would like after-care in its widest sense; and those others who wanted to make good on their own but are forced to come for specific help.

Unless they have already been contacted by letter or in person before they leave prison, and often even then, they all bring specific problems, almost always the material ones of accommodation, clothes, money, food, work. Whilst these may be genuine and urgent, they may also be seen as justifications for seeking help, like clear-cut symptoms to be taken to a doctor. In some cases to accept the request at its face value may be all that is necessary for the time being: the man may thereby be encouraged to return later and perhaps go further. Or he may see it as an admission that it is all that is needed, feel that he has had his dole and never come back, or come back only for the same. In some cases he may be more likely

5*

to return if his material needs are not immediately met, if some attempt is made at once to look at deeper problems. In others he will shy away and write off after-care as no use to him.

As in other spheres of casework, much depends upon understanding the background and personality of the individual. The use made of material help, immediate or not, has to be related to these. Here again, however, the probation officer is frequently confronted with a comparatively unfamiliar difficulty. In probation and statutory after-care he has normally a report upon the offender to start from. In preparing social reports he has the authority of the court to make enquiries and usually the co-operation of the accused. In marital casework the aggrieved husband or wife can normally see the point of exploring the background and implications of the trouble. But the man coming for help with a job, lodgings, clothes or money on his release may strongly resist any further probing, or any suggestion that he will still be unable to cope unaided even if he gets what he wants. If it was known where he was going the welfare officer will have sent on his record, but he may turn up (especially in London) out of the blue. In that case the probation officer has to feel his way, combining attempts to develop a relationship, to diagnose and to treat from the very beginning.

The principles of really listening to a man and trying to understand the feelings underlying what he says, and of doing things with him rather than for him, may contribute much to all three of these processes. Moreover they can give the maximum value to a single interview, whether or not this is followed up by longer-term casework. Listening with the whole attention carries a tacit recognition that, even if he is cadging, the man matters as an individual. Involving him in the search for work conveys the feeling that he is not helpless and is worth helping. An hour spent in going through papers with him, picking out jobs, discussing their appropriateness, getting the phone numbers and encouraging him to speak to employers himself, even if it is necessary to suggest the right words to him, can have a considerable impact. Even more than most, these men may not really hear what is said to them but may feel what the caseworker does and, even more constructively, what he enables them to do.[1]

---

1. See particularly G. Stafford, "After Care in the Penal System", *Case Conference*, Vol. 14, No. 11, March 1968.

Looking at voluntary after-care from the ex-prisoner's side, it has been remarked that some of the men are well aware that the authorities would like them to seek help and feel that they are entitled to receive it without themselves being under any obligation. They come therefore with the attitude "Here I am, help me in a way that I will determine, and if you fail and I go back to gaol it will be your fault". This aggressive approach may often be associated with embarrassment and anger about having to seek of their own accord the help of the probation officer, with the stigma and admission of dependence that implies. It may also, of course, be part of the familiar process of trying to make others responsible for an intolerable burden of inadequacy and social failure.

Alongside this it is necessary to appreciate how formidable are the practical problems actually facing many prisoners: their jobs, if they had any, filled, their families perhaps broken up, lodgings to be found, savings nil. The ex-prisoner, even if he is not, as so many are, handicapped by personal inadequacy and isolation and a long history of failure, faces severe psychological obstacles in coping with these problems. His anxieties will have mounted as release approached, he may well be convinced that everyone will know he has been in prison, that he is branded with that strongest of all marks of society's disapproval.

Unless he can come to feel rehabilitated he will go on playing the part of the ex-prisoner about to revert to type. And he measures rehabilitation, realistically enough, in terms of a place to live, a job, decent clothes. The way in which his practical problems are handled is thus crucial not only to his material re-establishment but to his self-sespect. Where possible, a generous response to urgent practical needs, such as accommodation, provides tangible evidence of concern and with it the concern of society. Too much caution and hedging in the initial stages is likely to be interpreted by the ex-prisoner as confirmation that he is forever branded as untrustworthy. Of course it is likely in some cases that he will mismanage his life in those early days, not pay the rent, not turn up to the job he had been assisted to obtain, get drunk on his social security money. But it can be argued that if he has not been repelled by an over-cautious approach at the outset, he will be able to return to the probation officer with these problems. It is just those who are like this, lacking in persistence, prone to give in before they have properly started, who most need after-care.

The unreal world of the closed institution, the prisoner's dream of resolving all his problems in the first week after release, has been written about often enough. The shattering disillusionment following release is frequently summed up in the phrase "I didn't think it would be as hard as this". But if the ex-prisoner can say that to his after-care officer it shows that he has come through the illusions to perceive more of the real world, that he has accepted his need of help, perhaps that he will be prepared to go on trying if such help continues.

The extreme importance of environmental resources in all this is evident. It is not possible to respond to urgent practical needs without a firm basis of co-operation within the community and a great deal may be asked of members of the community who accept ex-prisoners as lodgers or employees. The calls upon casework skill in involving and supporting other people in helping the offender are greater in after-care than in any other part of the probation officer's work.

It has been seen that the length of the contact with the probation officer depends mainly upon the ex-prisoner: the caseworker has to adapt to this. Sometimes he may feel that a man who needed further help has not come back for it because he mishandled the initial interview. Sometimes he may feel that a man who keeps on coming with fresh demands is unduly dependent because he has encouraged him to be so. On the other hand, even in probation, wide differences in need are recognized between different clients, and it is accepted that these should be reflected in differences in the frequency of contact, the closeness of support. Similarly in voluntary after-care it is likely that what some men need is a short-term but illuminating relationship, during which certain specific worries or problems can be clarified, perhaps the sort of support already described in finding a job. Others, because they may be so much more inadequate and immature than the usual run of probationers, may need a longer relationship than is normal in probation and to be allowed for a time to be very demanding or dependent.

Here, as elsewhere in voluntary after-care, probation officers are as yet only just beginning to feel their way. As one senior officer of long experience has put it, "I believe that after-care is a challenge, a demand and a gamble. A challenge because we really know so little about it; a demand because we *have* to be willing to learn to experiment, to test out, to discard and try again, going on and on for the third time and the fourth; a gamble because we don't know how much we can achieve, however limitless the time and the skill we spend."[1]

4 CASEWORK WITH PRISONERS' FAMILIES

The focus of casework with prisoners' families varies. It may be primarily upon helping the family for its own sake, trying to reduce the material and emotional difficulties of wife and children arising from the husband's imprisonment. It may be primarily upon relieving the prisoner's anxieties. It may be primarily designed to give those who have to deal with a husband and father in prison and plan his after-care a better understanding of his situation outside. It may be concentrated upon attempts to help the family, and especially the wife, to adjust attitudes and feelings which could have contributed to the prisoner's criminality. It may be intended primarily to prepare the way for co-operation with the family during after-care.

Work with prisoners' families, as with prisoners themselves, is wholly voluntary on the side of the clients. Sometimes a family will want nothing to do with the prisoner any more and refuse even to discuss him or their own difficulties: however hard it may be for the prisoner to accept this, there is nothing the probation officer can do about it. In other cases wives may have taken over from their husbands an attitude of antipathy to authority: sometimes a volunteer may be able to help here better than a probation officer, but sometimes she too will be rejected. Even where the wife asks for help and obviously needs it, her feelings, like those of the prisoner, are likely to be highly ambivalent. There may be relief and gratitude for understanding and help, but also strong elements of humiliation and resentment about the circumstances in which she needs it and perhaps about the source from which it comes.

The recognition of individual differences is as important here as in any other part of casework: the wives will vary from the illiterate to the professional, from the dirty to the obsessionally houseproud,

---

1. G. M. Stafford, paper given at the North-western Region Conference of Senior Probation Officers.

from the helpless, feckless passive inadequate to the efficient, self-sufficient and dominant. Feelings will vary just as widely. To the wife of a recidivist his imprisonment may come as no surprise, to the wife of a first offender, who may not even have told her he was in trouble, it must be a severe shock. Anger may be directed at society, the police, the court, the probation officer, all seen as persecuting her husband. It may be directed at the husband, the offence being seen as a last straw in a catalogue of misdeeds, as letting the family down and leaving them to face the music whilst he himself is out of it all. Occasionally it may be turned inwards upon the wife herself, in a sense of guilt, of having driven the husband to this by nagging or extravagance. Where the full brunt of anger against society is turned upon the person who is trying to help it is not easy to accept and deal with it although, as in working with offenders themselves, such acceptance may be the first step in modifying attitudes to society. Dealing with anger against the husband raises some of the problems discussed later under the heading of casework in matrimonial difficulties. The wife of a prisoner, however, needs especially to have her sense of loss and anger recognized, without it being assumed that anger is the whole of her feeling towards her husband. Anger in the form of self-condemnation calls neither for wholehearted agreement nor whole-hearted denial: the wife needs acceptance of the element of truth in her remorse but at the same time the assurance that in spite of her share in the damage she is still acceptable and can contribute to making good the damage. Whatever the manifestations of shock, anger or mourning, the sense of acceptance is vital in combating a wife's feeling of being outcast. To be with her in an unembarrassed way can often be more helpful than a great deal of bracing advice. This is a sphere in which a volunteer may be able to contribute much.

Alongside feelings about the blame for what has already happened, many prisoners' wives will have a sense of panic about the future, about the responsibility of carrying their husbands' roles as well as their own, especially about managing the household affairs and money. Some women are better at this than their husbands anyway, some wives of recidivists are better off financially when their husbands are in prison and they can rely on regular benefit than they are when they are at large and dole out irregular housekeeping money. But there are many who have to face a great drop in income and often a host of commitments in hire purchase, clothing clubs, rent, insurance, that they cannot hope to meet as they should. The more inadequate may be overtaken by terror and want to run away. They may seem almost paralysed, not doing even what they could to keep things going, allowing debts to snowball, muddles to accumulate, to a point where they seem overwhelming. Exhortation is useless without appreciation of the underlying panic. Attempts at clarification in words alone are often useless at the outset. Support, to enable the wife to discover and use what resources she has, is essential if she is to recover any faith in her ability to cope.

The environmental aspect of casework is clearly important here, in the sense both of modifying and of using the environment. It may well be necessary to explore several statutory and voluntary sources to meet outstanding commitments and bring income and expenditure into balance for the period of the husband's imprisonment. Sometimes the wife can be enabled to earn, or to earn more; sometimes extra help may be obtained; sometimes hire purchase or other instalments may be reduced. Partly this is a matter of clarification. of looking with the wife at the situation, both short-term and long-term, and planning solutions. Here the caseworker's knowledge of the social services and charitable organizations, and the conditions under which they can help, can be of great value. Partly this is a matter of supporting the wife in whatever approaches she can make herself to officials and creditors, or of making such approaches direct where she is unable to do so. The feelings of the wife about her situation may make her particularly awkward and touchy in dealing with officials and unless this is understood she may be regarded as unco-operative and get less help than she might.

Clarification and support are necessary also in another major sphere of anxiety for prisoners' wives, the care of their children. They have to consider what they should tell the children about their father's imprisonment, what they are likely to learn from other sources. They have to consider the possible effects, in various forms of misbehaviour by the children, and the fears and resentment that may underlie them. They have to consider the children's feelings about changes in their own situation due to their father's absence. Wives may also need acceptance and support, perhaps implied rather than fully discussed, in coping with their own feelings of sexual frustration or of relief, perhaps with their guilt about unfaithfulness during the husband's absence and fears about what will happen on his return.

In all these things, as in dealings with the prisoner himself, the caseworker is faced with the complication of two social situations: that of the wife and children as they function in the absence of the husband, and that of the family as it functions when he is there. He has to take into account the way the wife and children adapt on their own, the way the roles change. Perhaps the intervention of the wife's parents or other relatives further complicates the situation. So do the reactions of the prisoner, partly as the probation officer sees or hears about them in the prison, but especially as he perceives them when the family come together during home leave. The officer has to try to recognize, in particular, factors that may help to keep the offender out of further trouble on release or that may make such trouble more likely. They may relate to any of the areas already discussed: the wife's attitude to him, her ability to manage, material difficulties, their sexual relationships, their own roles and those of relatives, the children. Help in coping with difficulties and modifying attitudes, especially if it has kept in step with work with the prisoner himself, may reduce the danger that a man who has responded to treatment in prison will relapse when faced with the old problems outside.

A special problem, affecting only a small group of people but nevertheless presenting serious difficulties, arises where both husband and wife (or an unmarried couple living as such) have been sent to prison. This situation calls for co-operation between those responsible for their care and training in the two institutions, in considering the question of parole and in preparing for after-care.

The point of return, like the point where a man is sent to prison, is a point of crisis. Although there may be excitement and pleasure in the family, there are likely also to be doubts and fears: fears of the wife if she feels the husband will discover that she is in a mess financially or has been unfaithful; fears, especially if she has managed well on her own, about how he will fit in, perhaps whether he will keep out of trouble. If there appear to be no fears at all, the danger is that the family, like many prisoners, has built up a fantasy which will quickly end in disillusionment. Both husband and family need to face the difficulties of readjustment: here too there is a place for clarification and support, perhaps for working towards greater insight. Here the problems of caring for prisoners' families merge into those of after-care.

Whether or not probation officers continue to carry a major responsibility for social work with these families, they will need continuing understanding of their difficulties. Work with offenders, both in institutions and in after-care, must take into account the needs and contribution of those most closely related to them.

5 MATRIMONIAL CASEWORK[1]

In this, even more than in voluntary after-care and prison welfare, it is the client who chooses to come to the probation officer for help, since many come direct without formal referral by anyone in authority. Even those referred by the court are not obliged to co-operate. Again the length of contact is undefined: how far the initial approach is followed up depends much upon the probation officer's efforts to stimulate and sustain the will to face difficulties as well as upon the strength of the fears and hopes the client brings with him.

The likelihood that the problem or request put by the client at the outset does not represent her real need, or at least the whole of her need, is particularly high. Sometimes simple advice on how to get material help for a deserted wife and family, about legal aid or the basic legal grounds for a separation or maintenance order, is all that is needed. Often, there are other complications. It frequently turns out that, given such help, the wife decides not to go on with the case, either because she did not really want to break up her marriage or because, as she has proceeded with her case or discussed it with the officer she has realized more fully the material and social disadvantages to herself and her children. Again, there is the husband or wife who comes belligerently demanding that the spouse be given "a good telling off". It is only after going more deeply into the applicant's own part in the marriage that any direct approach to the other party can hope to be fruitful. In many cases the client needs help with his own doubts and difficulties.

Although it has been emphasized that those who come to the probation officer for help with matrimonial difficulties do so on a

---

1. On matrimonial work in its broader setting, see above, pp. 72–81. See also M. Monger, *Casework in Probation*, Chapter 5.

voluntary basis, it has also to be recognized that they often do so because they hope to make use of his authority as social worker of the court. This applies to many who come direct as well as to those who are referred by the court or other agencies.

They include immigrants who have not yet had time to learn and become accustomed to ways of living in this country, many members of the unskilled working class, and a fair proportion of individuals who tend to express their feelings in actions, such as violence or desertion, rather than in words. Whilst the probation officer needs to establish an atmosphere of understanding with any of these, he must not be unduly influenced by their actions. Sometimes, however, urgent court action is appropriate. On rare occasions the officer may feel that the direct appeal to his authority needs a direct answer. It may occasionally, as in probation, be appropriate to tell somebody "you shall not" or "you must". But it is essential to know what the behaviour means to the people directly involved. It is essential also to know what is culturally acceptable behaviour in the parts of society from which they come and in which they are living now. Without that the officer cannot understand their present attitudes or help them modify them successfully. It is also necessary to talk, in however simple terms, of feelings and expectations. Above all, it is always important to have the married couple as a pair in mind and not take sides. Many people who come for this kind of help can hold only one mood in their minds at a time and do not conceptualize. They cannot remember yesterday's accord in to-day's anger. The officer only colludes with this if he rushes them into immediate action, such as taking out a summons or making an appointment with a lawyer, or writing a letter suggesting the other party cease some bad conduct or come to answer a complaint. The probation officer has to try to help them to look at the whole situation and the whole marriage.

The processes of clarification, legal, factual and emotional, are thus of particular importance. At whatever stage and with whatever expectations the clients come, it is the probation officer's duty to try to help them understand their situation and so reach their own decisions. He has not only to give simple legal information but to help them realize the effects actions will have. The mother of a family has to consider where she will live if she leaves, what will happen to the children. She has to be told the legal position and her rights, but also to be helped to imagine what it will really mean, both now and later, to be separated. Sometimes a husband or wife needs to talk through his or her feelings at length to clarify them before reaching a decision. It may take an hour or more to decide, "He has behaved badly; he may do so again, but we are both getting on in age; I am fond of him and cannot face the loneliness without him"; or "I would rather be with her rowing a little than on my own".

Support can be of many kinds. Sometimes a deserted wife or husband needs to be directed to the Ministry of Social Security or the children's department. Sometimes the need is simply for emotional support to deal with a hurtful situation. It can be of considerable social value to give this when a parent is left with children on whom his or her depression may have ill-effects. There can even be a longer term value in spending time with people whose marriages have broken, since if they do not come to terms with the failed relationship they are likely to plunge into another union and fail again. Again, as we have seen, there may be need in some cases, especially where children are seriously threatened or the client is an immigrant ignorant of basic social and legal standards in this country, of straightforward instruction or warning.

In some though by no means all cases, the probation officer can see a possibility of reconciliation, expressed either in words or behaviour. Here he is faced with the need to look more closely at the relationship between the couple and to talk about it with them. Because this stirs up his own deep feelings about parental and married relationships, he has to overcome a strong natural resistance. Delinquency can be seen with a measure of detachment as a thing apart, but few escape some direct involvement in marital and sexual difficulties. In such relationship problems too, the officer may feel baffled and anxious, unable to wave the magic wand he feels he should possess to make things better. Most casework is about relationship problems of various kinds, but here it is the marriage relationship which is the presenting problem, and others, such as delinquency, housing or illness, are incidental: the issue cannot be avoided. Once the probation officer acknowledges his difficulty and faces his own uncertainty, he can find the courage to look at the troubled people he is to try to help. He can help, however, only with the tools he has. The sophistication of his training and the length of his experience must vary from officer to officer. However, if he offers an un-anxious desire to understand the problem, and a sensitive respect for both husband and wife as people, and for their relationship with each other (however odd this may seem to him), he is making a start and may be able to help each to express his or her feelings and needs. In sensing that they have been understood by the officer, each may perhaps begin to sense the needs of the other party.

Matrimonial reconciliation viewed as peace negotiations—"If he lets you go to your mother's will you let him go drinking on Saturday?"—seldom succeeds. If it does it is probably because of the warmth of feeling created by the officer. Conciliation seen as an attempt to help people communicate with each other may help. The more trained the officer the deeper his insights may be into family interaction. He may be able, with the husband and wife, to explore and help them to see how their treatment of each other reinforces the very behaviour they complain of. He may be able, with them, to recall their experience of their parents' relationships with each other and with them, and see how they are repeating this.

In some cases it may be helpful to the husband and wife to be seen by separate probation officers, or perhaps for one of them to be seen by a child care officer or psychiatric social worker whilst the other continues to be seen by the probation officer. This is the pattern used by the Family Discussion Bureau in their intensive marital casework. It demands a high level of mutual understanding and co-operation between the workers, but it offers a way of sharing the load and of giving clients who have great difficulties in relationships the individual support they may need before they can begin to understand each other's difficulties.

In other cases this is not practicable or necessary and a couple may find it easier to accept, and benefit more from, a single officer seeing both of them. Here the officer has to watch particularly the need to convey acceptance and concern to both, resisting any temptation to become identified with either as against the other.

In yet other cases only one party may be seen, either because the one who first asks for help is unwilling for the other to be contacted, or because the latter is unwilling to come. This does not necessarily mean that nothing can be accomplished. Sometimes it is possible to work successfully with only one partner in the marriage. Sometimes a single interview proves sufficient, at least for the time, to clarify the situation or relieve stress. Perhaps even more than in some other kinds of casework the person in matrimonial difficulties may come back later for further help and be able to build upon what has already been begun.

CHAPTER 6

WIDER INVOLVEMENT

1 VOLUNTARY HELP

THERE has been a marked renewal in recent years of interest in the contribution volunteers can make to the social services, statutory as well as voluntary. The statutory social services can, of course, trace back their ancestry to pioneers who, acting as private individuals, responded to the needs of their fellows. From their example, organized help gradually developed, leading inevitably to the appointment of paid staff and subsequently to the development of professional standards of practice. The struggle to make these services more comprehensive and more dependable often led to the exclusion of the volunteer and an undervaluing of his contribution. It has been seen that this marked a stage in the development of probation from a localized missionary effort to a service available to courts and offenders throughout the country. Even so, in some areas the tradition of voluntary workers alongside the professional service continued, and everywhere the probation officer can function more effectively if he can rely upon or secure the good will and co-operation of members of the public.

Looking at the whole field of social service, most volunteers work within voluntary societies giving practical or personal service to help the aged, or young people or some other dependent group. Recent years have seen the growth of small voluntary societies, like the Samaritans or the Simon Community, dedicated to help particular groups of people alienated from the community at large and in need of intensive personal support.

At the same time, more and more volunteers are being drawn into work in partnership with the statutory social services where there is an increasing awareness of their distinctive co-operation. In the probation and after-care service the revival of interest in the contribution of volunteers was sparked off by the report of the Advisory Council on the Treatment of Offenders on the Organization of After-Care in 1963. In recommending that the service should take over from discharged prisoners' aid societies the responsibility for all ex-prisoners who voluntarily sought after-care, the Council was anxious that the contribution of voluntary helpers should be extended rather than extinguished. In a subsequent circular the Home Office stressed that the volunteer had a vital part to play as a representative of, and a link with, the community to which the prisoner was returning.[1]

The help of volunteers has not, however, been restricted to the ex-prisoners who would formerly have been the clients of the discharged prisoners' aid societies. They have also been brought in to help offenders subject to compulsory after-care, for example on release from borstal or the old sentence of preventive detention. Some of these youths or men may be homeless and friendless and in particular need of support. Volunteers have also taken an active part in helping prisoners' families, both individually and through wives' groups. Some volunteers, again, may more easily start with the less complicated situation and needs of a probationer than plunge straight into the after-care of prisoners.

The idea of using volunteers produced at the outset some qualms amongst probation officers. The Advisory Council saw volunteers as relieving the service of part of the sheer weight of work involved in the care of large numbers of ex-prisoners. It has since been emphasized by the Home Secretary that the use of volunteers cannot and should not be expected to make good any shortage of professional officers.[2] Certainly those who have embarked upon this venture would say that, especially in the early stages, the use of volunteers makes large demands on initiative, time and energy, increasing rather than diminishing the total work required. The justification lies in the possibility of more effective help to the offender rather than in lightening the load of the probation officer.

Another source of some doubts and misgivings was the exact role of the volunteer. Was he to be a new kind of part-time untrained caseworker, brought in again after so many years of efforts to staff

---

1. See Home Office Circular 238/1965, 2 November 1965, para. 2.
2. See Home Office Circular 238/1965, 2 November 1965.

the service with full-time trained officers? Certainly, to be of service, the volunteer must grasp such basic principles of social work as acceptance and respect for confidences. He is not trained, however, in the diagnostic and treatment methods of casework. He is rather an individual with what has been described as a "kind of informed spontaneity", expressing in the ways that come naturally to him a genuine concern for the prisoner, without making demands upon him that he cannot meet. His role has been described as "a representative of normality", attempting to restore the offender's link with the community not by casework or any form of treatment, but simply by offering friendship and practical help without strings.[1]

At the same time it has to be acknowledged that this differs from friendship as normally understood. It is contrived for a particular purpose and is not spontaneous in its early stages. Whilst the volunteer may be a "representative of normality" he is less an ordinary member of the community than an extraordinary one. What he offers is something between a simple act of friendly helpfulness and professional social work.

On this basis volunteers, mostly busy people with full lives of their own, have impressed probation officers by the amount of time they have been prepared to give and the extent to which they have involved themselves. This freedom to concentrate time and interest upon one or two has been seen as a major advantage of the volunteer. It carries, of course, its corresponding danger: the more involved a person becomes with a single client, the more distressed he is likely to be, and the more inclined to blame himself, if the relationship breaks down. This, combined with the volunteer's lack of training in social work, again emphasizes the necessity for him to work in consultation with the probation officer.

A third cause of anxiety has been the official statement that the probation officer "must retain full responsibility" in each case. Attempts have been made to meet the requirements by emphasizing that the volunteer is responsible to the probation officer and that the officer should himself retain contact with the offender; yet at the same time there is great reluctance to tell volunteers just how they should operate, great stress on the value of their natural and spontaneous response. Similarly, though every effort is made to provide

1. *The Place of Voluntary Service in After-Care*, Second Report of the Working Party, H.M.S.O., July 1967.

support, the probation officer cannot be accessible and available to volunteers at all times and places. A comparison with the position regarding direct supervision of probationers may help. There the probation officer has his measure of responsibility to advise, assist and befriend, but the ultimate responsibility for the probationer's behaviour must lie with himself. Similarly, neither probation officer nor volunteer can, in the last resort, be responsible for the behaviour of the client: they can do no more than work together to offer, as acceptably as possible, their different kinds of help.

It was hoped that the transfer of responsibility for voluntary after-care to the probation and after-care service would mark a nation-wide advance in the scale and standards of voluntary help to prisoners on their release. It was decided, nevertheless, that as needs varied so widely between different areas, advertisement or recruit-ment of volunteers on a national scale would be inappropriate. The responsibility for finding and appointing volunteers lies formally with the local probation and after-care committees: they and the local probation services have the task of assessing the requirements of their areas and of keeping the recruitment and preparation of volunteers in step with these. It is evident that the interest of mem-bers of the public should be enlisted as and when it can be directed into active service. Any other course would invite frustration and make it harder than ever to attract volunteers later. For this and other reasons, there has been considerable diversity in methods of recruitment, selection and preparation.

The greatest need for volunteers has obviously arisen in the big cities. London, in particular, has severe problems because of the very large number of clients, especially ex-prisoners, many of them coming from other parts of the country. These problems are aggra-vated by the difficulties of integration in an anonymous city, where accommodation of any sort is hard to come by. In addition, the number of voluntary organizations, though each contributes its distinctive quota of help, creates difficulties of co-ordination. A number of these organizations have been accredited by the Inner London Probation and After-Care service to undertake particular tasks on a "contractual" basis. However, the degree of involvement with the statutory service has varied greatly. One pilot project, Teamwork Associates, now integrated within the National Associa-tion for the Care and Resettlement of Offenders recruits and prepares its own volunteers. They remain members of the voluntary body, though in dealing with the individual offender they work under the supervision of a probation officer. The same body organizes its volunteers into borough teams which meet monthly with one or more probation officers, who act as consultants as well as being available to give advice or reassurance when required.

It has been felt that an arrangement of this sort reconciles the duty of the statutory service to retain general supervision of what is done with the need of voluntary bodies to retain their identities and roots in the voluntary movement and the community.[1] Other bodies, like New Bridge, have remained more independent: their clients come to them direct and do not think of them as being linked with the official after-care system. Others again, like the Simon Community, have no formal links with the probation and after-care service at all. This may make it easier for them to contact people who reject any offers of help from even remotely official sources. Whilst there is obviously a need for a variety of types of help and places to obtain it, steps are currently being taken to effect closer co-ordination. In this also N.A.C.R.O. will be co-operating with the Inner London Probation and After-Care Service.

Looking at the situation on a national scale, the Working Party on Voluntary Service in After-Care emphasized the distinction between long-term help given to a particular offender and "small acts of neighbourliness" to offenders or their families. It suggested that volunteers undertaking the former should be "accredited associates", directly recruited, prepared and organized by or under the delegated authority of the probation and after-care committee. Those undertaking short-term services, on the other hand, might be selected either by the probation service or a voluntary society, which would keep the service informed.[2] This is the general position outside London. If a member of the W.R.V.S., for example, wishes to do long-term work and become an accredited volunteer she does so in her own right. If a probation officer wants some specific help on a particular occasion, however, he may ask the W.R.V.S. to arrange it and the selection and guidance of a volunteer to undertake it falls to them.

1. See Teamwork Associates, *Second Annual Report*, June 1968.
2. *The Place of Voluntary Service in After-Care*, Second Report of the Working Party, H.M.S.O., July 1967.

There is a special value in using people who are members of a voluntary organization. They are involved not merely as individuals but as part of a larger body within the community which is also interested, and influences public opinion. The care of offenders may be the specific object of the society, it may recruit only potential volunteers. Or it may have much wider objectives, only some of its members being concerned with offenders. That is, of course, the case with bodies like the W.R.V.S. It chimes well with a favourite theme of probation officers: that services for offenders should not be wholly cut off from services for other people in need. Thus, whatever difficulties there may be, it is worth putting considerable thought into achieving mutual understanding between the service and the voluntary bodies with which it works. This is not an issue with which the probation and after-care service alone is concerned. All statutory social services now required to work closely with voluntary bodies need to face the issue of allowing those bodies enough room for initiative and decision whilst yet meeting their own legal responsibilities.[1]

Most probation and after-care services have, however, seen advantages in the direct recruitment of volunteers, without any association with an existing organization, although local and informal organizations for the volunteers may subsequently develop. As a means of recruitment probation officers have sometimes approached Rotary Clubs, trade unions, or churches, but often people have been drawn in individually. In some areas a course of lectures or discussions is advertised: this brings in those with an interest in the subject and allows for considerable self-selection as the course proceeds. It is followed up by inviting applications for appointment as volunteers and interview, often by the principal probation officer. Appointments are made for a limited period in the first instance. In other areas reliance is placed mainly upon awakening interest by talks and discussions with various bodies and upon personal contacts made by the service and existing volunteers. In at least one place the expedient has been tried, with apparent success, of getting a prisoner himself to suggest someone he already knows and respects

---

1. On some difficulties see K. Vercoe, *Helping Prisoners' Families*, N.A.C.R.O., Papers and Reprints, No. 3, 1968. On the role of voluntary organizations in the future development of the social services, see *Report of the Committee on Local Authority and Allied Personal Social Services*, (Cmnd. 3703), paras. 495–500.

who might be asked by the probation officer to become his voluntary associate. Where this is possible it has the advantage of providing a natural individual link with the community. It may also give the probation officer a first contact with a volunteer who may subsequently be encouraged to go on to help other offenders.

Whereas the preliminary course has proved a successful device in some cases, in others candidates have found it difficult to learn from this kind of approach and have, as one officer put it, "clamoured to see a prisoner so that they could know what we were talking about". It is perhaps significant that the officer concerned was one of very few who have so far succeeded in one of the objectives stressed by the Advisory Council: that of engaging the sustained interest of lower middle class or working-class volunteers. Most volunteers up to now have been middle class; in this the experience of the service has been the same as that of voluntary organizations trying to help ex-prisoners.

On the whole the probation service seems to be adopting a formal pattern of continued support and education for volunteers. This may be justified partly in the light of the probation officer's statutory responsibilities for after-care. It can also be justified in terms of the needs of volunteers and those they are trying to help. Whatever care is taken in advance to give them an idea of the kind of difficulties and disappointments they will face, the reality of these things appears only in practice. If a volunteer is working in isolation he may easily become discouraged, may lose confidence and blame himself for failures that are inherent in the situation. This will be reflected in his attitude to the offender and result in mutual rejection.

Merely to assure volunteers that advice and consultation is available if they need it is in many cases insufficient. Certainly there are a few whose personality and background enables them to cope very well. Even they, however, can benefit from the probation officer's wider experience in recognizing and dealing with the special problems of ex-prisoners. And it is quite unrealistic, if voluntary help is to be used on any widening scale, to expect that volunteers will prove to be, especially at the outset, fully equipped and adjusted to their task, exactly matched to the needs of the particular offenders they befriend. Those in most need of support and guidance may be unduly diffident about consulting a busy officer unless they have a regular time allocated to them. This is especially likely where the problems appear, as the most important of them well may, vague and subjective rather than specific and definite. Group meetings have proved valuable in providing mutual support, encouraging volunteers to voice their difficulties, and showing them how far these are shared by others. Regular individual discussions with the probation officer give further insight and support in relation to the needs of particular offenders.

The kinds of help that can be given by volunteers are still a matter for experiment. It is undesirable in any case that they should be defined too rigidly or restricted to any one type of approach.

A great deal of interest and effort has been concentrated upon the most demanding and difficult aspect for all, the attempt to give long-term friendship and support to prisoners, usually recidivists, who find themselves homeless and isolated on discharge. Some habitual prisoners have been unwilling even to meet a volunteer. Those who have serious problems of relationships are naturally hardest to help: they tend to reject a friendship which, by the very fact that it is undemanding, is seen as condescending, yet they are too inadequate, too unstable, too preoccupied with their own difficulties, to offer much in return There seems to have been more success with those who are able and willing to communicate and enter into relationships but who, for various reasons including their imprisonment, find themselves without normal social contacts. Some of these, because of their experience, their clashes with the law and the penal system, are unlikely to accept any real relationship with the probation officer but may take to a volunteer.

Some of those who have experimented over a period with the introduction of volunteers to long-term prisoners have emphasized the need for them to meet well before the offender is due for discharge. If they see each other only towards the end of the sentences, when anxieties and fantasies have been building up over years, the prisoner will have unreal expectations of the help that can be given. The result can be that the relationship fails to survive the disillusionment on discharge. A partial answer to this, it is hoped, will be found in the development of the prison welfare service, so that those in need of help and likely to respond can be identified early and their worries and expectations can be kept in better relation to reality. Another part of the answer is to enable volunteers to visit the institution over a prolonged period, so that they make comparatively natural relationships with the prisoners and to a certain extent can pair off on the basis of mutual interest and acceptance. It has been suggested that this would be facilitated if the acceptance of a volunteer by the local probation committee gave him a right to visit prisons similar to that of a prison visitor.

Work concerned with married prisoners seems at least as important as work with those who are socially isolated. In their case success or failure affects not only an individual but a family. It has been estimated that something like half of men in prison are married. Obviously more will be learned about the number of these, and about how many have children, as reports for courts increase, as the practice of post-sentence interviews with those sent to prison grows, and as the prison welfare service develops. The use of volunteers to help families whilst men are in prison differs considerably from one area to another. Some do not use them at all: in rural areas, for instance, it may be thought that local volunteers would cause embarrassment. In so far as work with a prisoner's family is seen mainly in practical and supportive terms it is comparatively easy to see how volunteers can help. The Prisoners' Wives Service in London is an example. In so far as it is seen as a deliberate attempt to identify and modify family attitudes which may be helping to produce crime, it is unlikely that the probation officer will be willing to delegate responsibility.

Yet there is a sense in which the two aspects are inseparable: the practical and emotional support given by a volunteer may themselves modify the attitudes both of prisoner and family. And if the volunteer really has their confidence they may raise with him problems that call for the more skilled attention of the probation officer. Additional complications in work with prisoners' families are the tendency of a volunteer, who knows only the wife and children, to identify and sympathize with them to an extent that may exacerbate the family situation when the husband returns. So once more it comes back to the need for the probation officer to be in close touch with the volunteer, and once more the volunteer must be seen as extending the service to the clients rather than doing the probation officer's job for him.[1]

---

1. On the various points of view of officers see Kate Vercoe, *Helping Prisoners' Families.*

It has been seen that by no means all of the work of volunteers takes the form of long-term relationships either with individual offenders or with their families. There is considerable scope for more limited and specific forms of help, which arouse less initial anxiety on either side and may therefore be easier for volunteers to undertake and prisoners to accept. They may be appropriate for a wider range of offenders. They, too, can demonstrate concern on the part of other people. It is important that they should be given full weight in considering the potential contribution of volunteers. Not only can they be valuable in their own right but it may sometimes prove that they provide the most natural way into more lasting relationships. On the one hand it has been said that some of the best results with homeless and friendless men have been achieved by volunteers who have done nothing in particular but just been around. On the other hand there have been doubts on both sides about "artificial relationships" sponsored by "authority figures". The very word "befriend" has acquired a patronizing ring and those most in need are most likely to be sensitive and suspicious. Approaches with a specific object may be more acceptable.

Thus a volunteer may provide transport to enable a prisoner's wife to visit him, he may look after the children whilst she does so, he may make some urgent enquiry to relieve anxiety about material difficulties, he may help find work or accommodation on release. He may help with practical jobs like decorating, or be able to give advice on some matter like home purchase or income tax. It is obvious that even such services as these cannot be regarded as restricted to material matters or free from emotional complication. The way in which they are carried out, the feelings engendered, can greatly affect the offender's responses, can decide whether he sees them as interference to be avoided in future or support to be sought. The volunteer, on his side, may have to accept that a prisoner is very likely to leave the job or the lodgings found for him with so much difficulty, or become suspicious of any ties that are formed in the attempt to help the rest of his family.

Much stress has been laid upon the careful selection of the volunteer most likely to be able to help a particular offender or least likely to become discouraged in the attempt to do so. In this the special needs and special weaknesses of both have to be considered, as well as any shared interest that may provide a basis for continuing and widening contacts.   Obviously where there are, as at present, comparatively few volunteers in any one locality able to offer this kind of help, and comparatively few offenders willing to accept it, such matching can be very difficult and its failure can result in relationships breaking down at an early stage.   On the whole, however, probation officers have been impressed by the resilience of volunteers in the face of set-backs and their appreciation of the need to persevere.   One has commented that in most cases "fears on both sides have proved unfounded . . . volunteers have been able to like the men they were befriending without blinding themselves to the weaknesses and potential dangers of the relationship".

The special contribution of the volunteer has been held to derive from the fact that he has no axe to grind, no statutory obligation to supervise or to exercise authority.   He can demonstrate that not only the probation officer, whose job it is, but other people as well, want to help the offender back to normal life.   He may be able to make contact with some who reject any approach from an official as a matter of course.   He can help break down barriers within the community which shut the criminal out in so many ways, leaving him isolated or dependent upon others who have also been in trouble.

Whilst many suitable volunteers have come forward and already shown their mettle, it is inviting disillusion to overrate the willingness of the public as a whole to accept and help offenders, especially those who have committed serious or repeated crimes.   It is hard for a volunteer to see himself as a representative of the local community when he is likelier to receive criticism than support from his friends and neighbours.   Far from being prepared to "consume its own smoke" or absorb its own misfits, society will go to great expense to have them kept decently out of its sight, whether they be senile, crippled, mentally deranged, vagrant or criminal.   The probation officer is often exhorted in casework theory to "begin where the client is" and to "go at the client's pace".   This applies as much to the community as to the offender.   No attempt to change attitudes is likely to succeed if it starts from illusion.   So far as offenders are concerned there is much fear, much punitive feeling, and there are many competing, more attractive and more rewarding outlets for individual good will.

It is inviting disillusion also to assume that the bulk of ex-prisoners will welcome and respond to a link with a volunteer. This may be a matter of their personalities, their past experiences, or their circumstances on release. As has been seen, the volunteer seldom comes from the man's own class, from the part of the community in which he is most likely to feel at home, if he feels at home anywhere. This has to be recognized. But to imply that only those of similar social background can help would be an oversimplification unsupported by experience. It may be that some offenders expect the volunteer to come from a different background and find him more acceptable because of it. It may be also that such volunteers bring resources to their work which are a product of their background, education or occupation. Again, the idea that after-care of any sort means no more, or less, than immediate financial help on discharge is likely to die hard if at all. The development of prison welfare services and the chance to get to know volunteers before release may reduce misunderstanding and distrust. But this, too, will take time.

The repercussions of failures or discouragements may well extend beyond the individual offender and the individual volunteer. If a volunteer throws up the sponge he may pass on to others his sense of disillusion, thus confirming rather than combatting the belief that it is a waste of time to try to help a criminal. The systematic effort to help volunteers come to terms, in practice as well as in theory, with the difficulties of their task is an integral part of the responsibility of the probation officer in after-care. For all these reasons it may prove wisest in the long run to go slowly and thoroughly in the development of voluntary help, to compare and evaluate methods of recruitment, preparation and consultation, and the various ways of using it. Here the local nature of developments so far may prove a handicap and there is clear need to establish a means, perhaps through N.A.C.R.O., for pooling information and consultation at a national level.

2 HOSTELS

Hostels for offenders may serve either as an alternative to penal institutions, a means of reinforcing treatment in the open in certain cases, or as a stepping-stone back to more independent life for those who have had to be deprived of their liberty. Approved probation homes and hostels have been recognized as an adjunct of probation orders for young people for forty years. After-care hostels, though voluntary experiments go back for more than a century, have only recently received consistent official support and encouragement. Considerable thought, however, is now being given to their possibilities and functions and this, together with the shift in emphasis in probation towards older offenders, has stimulated fresh thinking also about the role of probation homes and hostels.

Although probation and supervision are basically methods of treatment in the open, the special problems of adjustment, the special dangers and opportunities, which face adolescents and young adults early led to the establishment of hostels and homes for use where a semi-protected environment and intensive social training were considered necessary in the early stages of treatment. It may be thought necessary to remove a probationer temporarily from an intolerable situation at home, or to give him the chance to break off undesirable associations in his neighbourhood. It may be desired to accustom him to regular habits of work or the constructive use of leisure. It may be felt that he needs to learn, by becoming part of a group, how to live acceptably with other people. Hitherto probation hostels and homes have been available for young people between school-leaving age and twenty-one, put on probation or under supervision by the courts. For the future, as a result of the Children and Young Person's Bill, they are likely to be concentrated upon those over seventeen, hostels for younger boys and girls becoming part of the community care provisions. At present only five of the twenty-five hostels for youths are reserved for those between seventeen and twenty-one (though there are thirteen covering the age-range fifteen to eighteen). Only four of the twelve girls' hostels take girls of over seventeen.[1] On the other hand, fresh experiments in probation hostels for adults over twenty-one are probable.

Residence in a probation home or hostel is subject to a requirement of a probation or supervision order. As with other requirements, the consent of the person concerned is necessary, but if he subsequently absconds and refuses to return he may be brought back before the court. To ensure that the implications are fully understood there must be full discussion and agreement between the probation officer, the client and the warden of the hostel or home

---

1. See House of Lords *Weekly Hansard*, No. 719, 25–27 February 1969.

before the court is invited to make a requirement of residence. Apart from explanations of the nature and purpose of the regime, the practice is increasing of taking offenders to see a home or hostel before they make up their minds whether to agree to a requirement. Some offenders do, in fact, refuse to go. The court order is thus not intended to force an unwilling consent but rather, as with requirements of mental treatment, to reinforce the resolution to go through with a course of training once it has been embarked on. Progress is kept under review and application can be made for removal of the requirement if it is no longer considered necessary or desirable. The probationer himself can also, of course, apply for this.

Neither a probation hostel nor a probation home is a "secure" or wholly closed institution. A probation hostel involves less severance from normal life than does a home, as residents go out to work in the ordinary way, pay at least part of their keep and are allowed out during some of their leisure. A home, providing employment on the premises, gives a more enclosed environment for those needing more direct training and for whom greater control is considered necessary. Even so every opportunity is taken to maintain contacts with the outside world, including both the probationers' homes and the local community. In the second part of a period of residence in a home probationers are often allowed to take jobs outside, helping the transition back to full responsibility. Again, the hostel or home is not intended as a permanent alternative to the probationer's own home: requirements of residence are limited to a maximum of twelve months and an important aspect of treatment is the work done by the probation officer for the home area in preparing the probationer's family to accept and help him more adequately on his return. It is most desirable that orders containing a requirement of residence should extend to cover a period of readjustment following home or hostel treatment.

The selection of cases for either of these forms of treatment needs careful consideration, especially in view of the disruptive effect an unsuitable case can have upon the treatment of others who may have begun to make progress. Neither homes nor hostels are suitable for those who are of exceptionally low intelligence or suffering from severe disturbances, nor should they be used as soft option where there is reluctance to commit an offender to borstal. They are inappropriate, too, for those who really need a permanent home and do not specially require training, though they may have a role in preparing a boy from a very bad background for more independent life in lodgings or an ordinary hostel afterwards.

In their different degrees, hostels and homes provide the probationer with some relief from the pressures and strains of his home environment, so leaving him freer to concentrate for a time on the solution of his personal difficulties. In a controlled setting, and in contact with others of his own age and facing similar problems, he can be helped to face the necessity and possibility of a change in his own attitudes. He can come to realize, for example, that adoption, illegitimacy or a broken or affectionless home need not inevitably result in delinquency or immoral behaviour, and should not be used as an excuse for it. He can learn to appreciate his own ability to overcome or withstand his difficulties. Though in the first instance he may accept regular work and a disciplined life merely because he fears being taken back to court, once he realizes his own achievements in these directions he may come to value them for their own sakes and so be on the way to real self-respect and responsibility.

Whilst in residence at a hostel or home the probationer comes under the care both of the warden and of the liaison probation officer, who is responsible to the local court for his supervision. The functions of these two are different but complementary, often overlapping and certainly not independent. The warden is primarily responsible for the community as a whole, its internal organization and discipline: under his care the probationers learn to live as a controlled group. The liaison officer is primarily interested in the probationer as an individual, helping him to understand the difficulties of his individual behaviour within the group and to realize how far these are continued patterns of earlier difficulties in the home setting. This is not intended to imply that the warden is not concerned with individual needs, or that the liaison officer ignores the requirements of the community. The work demands close cooperation, understanding and loyalty between warden and officer. Given this, hostels and homes can potentially provide an excellent setting for intensive group and individual therapy. Over the last five years the practice of regular meetings between the hostel wardens and liaison probation officers in different areas has been developed as a means of improving understanding of roles and responsibilities.

Much of the value of a hostel, as opposed to the closed institution, lies in the maintenance of links with the community, in learning habits of work and leisure amongst non-offenders, in tackling the problems of daily living amidst the realities and demands of ordinary life. Looked at from this point of view, the more closely conditions in a hostel can approximate to normality, the better. It has been suggested that training would be more effective if the sort of freedom normally associated with probation were extended progressively to hostel residents, especially in the handling of their money and in the privacy of their accommodation. Some officers have also thought that the practice of sending probationers to hostels far from their homes, often inevitable in present conditions, can produce some of the bad effects of institutionalization, making it harder rather than easier for them to come to grips with the situation to which they return. This sharp separation between the probationer's home and hostel could be reduced if probation hostels, like those for after-care, were established on a regional basis. There have been limited moves towards meeting some of these points. Home leave at weekends is now generally allowed after the first three months' stay at a hostel. And in a few hostels for senior girls the probationers are allowed, towards the end of their periods of residence, to live in bed-sitting rooms and their keep own wage packets, paying a realistic rent and buying their own food and other incidental requirements. Similar experiments, rather more limited in scope, have begun in several hostels for youths.

As in all institutions, however, there is the danger that the hostel will be used to escape the challenges of everyday life rather than as a means of building up strength and understanding to meet them more adequately and realistically after leaving. When dealing with probationers in these settings, wardens and probation officers need to interpret progress and reactions in the light of their eventual readjustment to independent life. Only thus can what is learned in a protective atmosphere stand the test of life in the open.

In some cases, where the home to which the probationer returns is a fairly good one and the probation officer has been able to work constructively with the parents whilst he has been away, the hostel training may suffice to enable him to settle down satisfactorily.

On the other hand it must be recognized that probationers from more permanently difficult backgrounds, even though they respond well to the regular routine of a probation hostel, may easily slip back if they are obliged to return direct to unhelpful home surroundings. At one time, to avoid this, a girls' probation hostel was linked with an ordinary hostel to which girls could go on, if necessary, when their requirement of residence terminated; thus the return to independence did not have to coincide with a return to a criminogenic neighbourhood or home. This experiment, like some others, terminated largely because of staffing difficulties, but it was an attempt to meet a real need which is as apparent amongst youths as amongst girls. More willingness by existing hostels and organizations like the Y.W.C.A. and the Y.M.C.A. to accept one or two youngsters who have been in trouble in each of their hostels could greatly help. So would more landladies who would accept these youngsters along with others, once they had completed the hostel stage of their training.

All these considerations are likely to apply with still greater force to probation homes than to probation hostels. There have, indeed, long been doubts as to whether homes were an appropriate adjunct to a measure designed to provide for treatment of offenders in the open. There are now only six left. Yet new problems and a new anxiety to explore every gradation of freedom and of treatment short of committal to a penal institution has led to some renewal of interest. There might be a place within the system, for instance, for the kind of home to which people could go for "convalescence" after being weaned from drugs or receiving psychiatric treatment: at a stage where continuous and active medical treatment is no longer required but where they are not yet emotionally ready to face the vicissitudes of work outside. It may be that a new system of community homes may provide this for younger people, but even so the problem of those over seventeen would remain. Meanwhile, to meet the problems of return to the outside world, most probation homes now encourage their residents to go out to work in the last few months of their stay. Some have been linked with hostels, to which residents can be transferred at that stage. Where homes are in areas with suitable work available it may well prove profitable to develop them further in this direction, with the emphasis less upon protection, except in the very earliest stages of settling down, more upon gradually educating offenders in the use of freedom.

A particular difficulty about probation homes and hostels is that their number is so small that specialization in terms of the needs of different kinds of probationers has so far been rejected as impracticable.[1] They have sprung up over many years in different parts of the country where voluntary initiative happens to have been sufficient to establish them, but there has been little systematic consideration of location, and the exact nature of the regime in each is a matter for the local managing committee, and still more the individual warden. This variety has obvious advantages, and gives scope for experiment and flexibility. On the other hand, a more systematic consideration of the kinds of offender for whom probation homes and hostels are used, or could be used, and of the places where they could most usefully be situated, would be a useful parallel exercise to the explorations already undertaken of the need for after-care hostels. It might, for example, be possible to extend the range and value of probation hostels if certain of them had psychiatric support built into their regimes, both to provide direct treatment for residents who needed it and, more generally, to give guidance to staff and supervising probation officers, through individual consultation or regular group meetings or both. This would make it possible for courts to send to such hostels young people who, whilst not disturbed enough to require hospital treatment or confinement, may require regular psychiatric treatment or supervision.

Successive committees have recommended that the number of probation hostels should be increased, even whilst they have recommended also that, where possible, places should be found in ordinary hostels or lodgings for probationers who have to leave home. The Morison Committee faced the essential difficulty about this: that hostels and lodgings willing to take the general run of young wage-earners will not take the kind of young people often sent to probation hostels. In sheer practical terms it seemed to them necessary to retain a series of hostels which could be depended upon by the courts. In addition, the Committee were satisfied that these hostels had, in fact, worked out methods of giving social training to delinquent young people, working in conjunction with probation officers to an extent that could not be expected of ordinary hostels with only one or two probationers amongst their residents.

Whilst it is recognized that the situation is changing, that young

1. See *Second Report of the Departmental Committee on the Probation Service* (Cmnd. 1800), 1962.

offenders may in future benefit from any general extension of hostels for young people and that some after-care hostels will be able to take certain kinds of probationer—there still seems to be a distinct place for probation hostels and homes. They provide support and training, closely linked with probation supervision, for offenders who cannot, for the time being, either be left at home or be found a place in ordinary lodgings or hostels, yet who do not qualify for a penal institution and are not as criminally sophisticated as many of those they would meet in an after-care hostel.

This situation may also sometimes arise in the case of offenders over twenty-one. At present there is no probation hostel catering for them, but probation officers have been urging for some years that such hostels should be established. This case also is strengthened by the new emphasis on after-care hostels. If hostels are necessary for adults discharged from prison it would seem that they could also play a part in dealing with adults as an alternative to imprisonment. Some such probationers may well be placed in after-care hostels catering for their special needs. For example an alcoholic probationer might agree to enter a hostel for alcoholics. But for others, just as for younger probationers, the probation hostel may be more appropriate.

It has been suggested that the regimes of probation hostels for adult offenders should be explicitly designed to meet the needs of particular groups.[1] In particular it has been felt that there should be separate provision for older and younger probationers, since the older would find it very difficult to tolerate the high spirits and aggression of the younger men. Hostels for the older group might meet the needs of inadequate, insecure people, perhaps including women, who might have committed quite a number of offences, none of them very serious, who lacked roots and were known to be frequently drunk though not alcoholics. They would need a homely, supportive atmosphere, combined with a share of personal responsibility in running the hostel. They might initially need to be offered work within the hostel, though the object would be to link them as completely as possible with the life of the local community. For younger adult probationers there might be a number of experimen-

---

1. Letter on Adult Probation Hostels, sent to the Home Office by N.A.P.O. Homes and Hostels Committee, 1967, in *N.A.P.O. on Hostels*, 1960–1968, 1968,

tal regimes in different hostels, geared to what were thought to be the special needs of different types. They might include, variously, provision for group discussion, for psychiatric treatment, for democratic organization, for different degrees of control. All, however, should recognize clearly the adult status of the residents: require them to pay their keep as in any other lodgings; permit them to retain the rest of their earnings for their own use; give them rooms of their own, the right to have visitors and the key to the door. Requirements of residence, if used, might well be for longer than the twelve months allowed for younger offenders but there should always be at least six months' supervision after leaving the hostel before the probation order ends. Hostels for adult probationers, as for younger people, are to be seen not as a solution in themselves, but as a preparation for a better adjustment to normal life.

After-care hostels differ in two important respects from probation hostels. They are designed primarily to provide shelter and support rather than overt training. And their residents enter and remain in them on an entirely voluntary basis, without the sanction of any statutory requirement or court order.

The nearest approach to a compulsory stay in an after-care hostel at present is the prison hostel scheme, whereby selected long-term prisoners are moved into hostels attached to the prisons, from which they go out to work during the last few months before release. It has been suggested that some kind of transitional hostel should also be provided for youngsters, especially the homeless, when they are due to leave borstal, many of them very ill-equipped to face the outside world again. Residence might be made a condition of licence in appropriate cases, but it would probably be better accepted if it occupied the last two months or so of training.

Though much thought and devotion has been invested over the last decades in providing voluntary hostels for inadequate offenders on discharge from penal institutions, only a small part of that problem has yet been touched. In 1966 no more than twenty after-care hostels, providing places for less than two hundred and fifty offenders, qualified for government grants. By 1969 the number had risen to fifty-nine, with places for six hundred and seventy. In addition there are a few hostels for the homeless, or for alcoholics, that may accept discharged offenders. But this whole provision has to be seen against an estimate of something like five thousand home-

6*

less prisoners released every year.[1] Not all homeless ex-prisoners, of course, are inadequate, or would accept hostel accommodation. In some areas most may be quite capable, with support, of finding and sustaining themselves in lodgings or bed-sitting rooms. Certainly many leaving both prisons and borstals are convinced that this is what they want to do. But in the great cities, and especially in London, there are a great many also, particularly the younger ones, who cannot find lodgings or, if they do find them, are desperately lonely and vulnerable to further trouble.

In such areas there are, of course, the very large hostels, such as those run by the Salvation Army and Church Army. These take vast numbers and all kinds of drifters, and they are often housed in old, dirty and depressing buildings. Much smaller hostels are needed, to which men can go for a week or two on release or at times of crisis, where they can be accepted and recognized as individuals and where a probation officer will be responsible for helping them on to the next stage.

The Working Party considering the place of voluntary service in after-care recommended a whole gamut of provisions for homeless discharged offenders.[2] At one extreme they put ex-prisoners capable of looking after themselves, who might do best in lodgings, bedsitters or ordinary hostels; at the other, they put the aged or the severely inadequate, unlikely to change much if at all, needing long-term or even permanent care in hostels, perhaps also sheltered work. For such as these there is as yet hardly any provision at all: they shrink from going to the Reception Centres, which they associate with disgrace and degradation, though they are sometimes agreeably surprised if they do so. In between these extremes the Working Party identified a variety of offenders who for different reasons are unlikely to succeed in the open community without a preliminary period in a protected and tolerant environment, with trained staff to help them work through their difficulties. These groups call for the most specialized hostels and for the greatest skill in treatment. Halfway-houses on the existing pattern may come into that cate-

---

1. House of Lords *Weekly Hansard*, No. 719, 25–27 February, 1969.
2. *Residential Provision for Homeless Discharged Prisoners*, First Report of the Working Party on the Place of Voluntary Service in After-Care, 1966.

gory; so also do the hostels now being developed for homeless young men leaving borstals and detention centres, for very unstable and disturbed adolescents of either sex, for alcoholics needing different gradations of control and treatment, and perhaps for drug addicts.

Perhaps most urgently of all, and underpinning the other kinds of provision, it has been recommended that multi-purpose hostels should be established to provide somewhere for homeless offenders to go when they first leave an institution, or in other emergencies. The availability of such hostels would give probation officers time to assess problems and make arrangements which could not be completed whilst the offender was in prison; to adapt to changes of circumstances and changes of mind; perhaps to smooth the transition from one kind of hostel to another. In particular, wardens of specialized hostels, though they might be uncertain whether a particular man would fit in, might feel freer to experiment if they knew there was somewhere else for him to go in the event of failure.

So severe in the past has been the strain upon the probation service of trying to help homeless offenders to find accommodation in emergencies that in some areas the very attempt has almost had to be abandoned. This has left offenders in a parlous situation which could easily lead to recidivism. Obviously there are dangers in multi-purpose emergency hostels as well, and especially in larger ones where offenders of all kinds are birds of passage. Such hostels should not come to be regarded as an easy way out of difficult family or social situations, or as a substitute for advance planning. Nor should they become a dumping ground for insoluble problems, or take the place of establishments designed to give specialized care or treatment. With these provisos, however, they should prove to be of very great value in allowing both offenders and probation officers a breathing space, time for feelings to cool down and more permanent plans to be made.

The responsibility for establishing and running hostels for offenders still lies with local voluntary associations. It is obviously essential, however, that the nature and distribution of new hostels should be related to national or at least regional needs and resources, and that there should be close links between them and the probation and after-care service. Eight Regional Group Consultative Committees were set up in 1967 to consider and advise upon the need for after-care hostels of various types, to co-ordinate the activities of voluntary societies, and to stimulate the provision of hostels where necessary. They are not themselves executive bodies, but are designed to facilitate communication between the probation and after-care service, local voluntary effort and the local offices of government social services. They include representatives of the prison service, of the National Association for the Care and Resettlement of Offenders (established in 1966 to bring together the voluntary bodies) of the Home Office, and of the probation and after-care service. A principal probation officer is responsible for convening each of the committees and a member of a probation and after-care committee is its chairman.

The decision to survey the need for after-care hostels on a regional basis follows the move to regionalization in the prison service and towards regional discussions amongst principal probation officers. The possibility of extending these arrangements to other aspects of probation and after-care work may be considered in the light of experience.[1]

Local committees keen to establish individual hostels face a number of difficulties, whether the hostel is intended for probationers or offenders leaving institutions or both. First, opposition is very frequently provoked in a neighbourhood by the suggestion that a house be taken over for the purpose. The opposition largely disappears once a hostel has been opened; but before that stage it can stifle or delay the most promising ventures.

Secondly there is the problem of finance. Since the 1925 Criminal Justice Act there has been provision for government contributions towards that part of the cost of maintaining probationers in probation hostels that cannot be met from their own contributions. Since 1948 there has been provision also for contributions towards the cost of establishing, enlarging, improving and carrying on such establishments. Indeed, since then all but about one per cent of the cost of these hostels, after deducting residents' contributions, has been shared between the Exchequer and local rates. The development of after-care hostels, however, may still be hampered by financial stringency and there have been fears that voluntary bodies may have to devote too much of their energies to raising funds.

Thirdly, both probation and after-care hostels are experiencing

---

1. H.O.C. 46/1967, H.2, 20 March 1967.

difficulties in retaining suitable staff, and especially assistant staff, and so in maintaining continuity. Some have even been forced to close, if only temporarily. Undoubtedly this is a crucial problem for every kind of residential institution throughout the social services. Residential staff face the deterrents of low pay, long hours, demanding work, poor prospects and social isolation. They lack any common bond amongst themselves and they often feel cut off from fieldworkers in their own services. Their difficulties are aggravated by the lack, in many cases, of training designed to meet their specific needs or to enable them to understand the approach of the social workers alongside them in the open. With so many alternatives now available to both men and women, it is hardly surprising that the difficulty of attracting and retaining staff is increasing and has begun to be looked at on a wider basis.[1]

If probation hostels are to be regarded primarily as places where offenders can receive treatment and training, rather than as temporary refuges from bad home circumstances, their wardens need skill not only in management and in the difficult task of keeping order amongst a heterogeneous and changing group of adolescents, but in actively working with their probation officers to change their attitudes and habits. They need to be aware not only of what is going on in the hostel but of the sort of surroundings in which the boys will live after they leave. The Morison Committee, commenting on the fact that few of them had had social work training of any kind, observed that this sometimes prevented sufficient understanding by the wardens of the officers' objectives as caseworkers.

At present staffs of probation hostels may attend courses in residential child care. The practice has recently been introduced of seconding newly appointed wardens to the probation and after-care service for a month's observation and practice in social work in the field. Probation officers have suggested that, in addition, they could be kept in touch by participating in group discussions at probation offices. A point should also be made of introducing probation students to the work of the hostels: communication and understanding are two-way processes.

In the field of after-care hostels, where the need for different types

---

1. See on this situation, *Caring for People: Staffing Residential Homes*, Report of a Committee of Enquiry set up by the National Council of Social Service; chairman Professor Lady Williams.

of hostel to meet different varieties of need has been recognized, it has been accepted that higher rates of grant should be allowed to hostels which specialize in the care of very dependent people and incur higher staffing expenses in order to give them adequate support. Financial stringency has limited this concession for the present to hostels specializing in addiction, including alcoholism,[1] but the principle is important. Meanwhile the National Association for the Care and Resettlement of Offenders has recognized the general demand for training, and held its first training conference for the wardens of after-care hostels at the end of 1968.

Training cannot be seen as something apart from salaries. These are especially an obstacle to the retention of good assistant staff in homes and hostels. If training for residential work is to be improved, and especially if it is to include a fair measure of general training in social work, some equivalence in salaries between those who work in institutions and outside will be essential if the residential staffing position is not to become more parlous than ever. Both the National Association of Probation Officers and the National Association for the Care and Resettlement of Offenders hold that any moves to establish professional training and status for residential staffs in the social services as a whole, such as those proposed by the Williams Committee, should also embrace the staffs of hostels for offenders.

The links between all hostels for offenders and the probation and after-care service are of great importance. In probation hostels the main channels of communication are the liaison probation officer or officers who act as links with the court and with the probation officer at home. In the case of after-care hostels, not only has the probation and after-care service an important role on the regional consultative committees, but it is represented on each individual managing committee. At the same time the links between hostels and local community are emphasized by the voluntary nature of the managing committees. In its very nature as an open institution the hostel depends greatly on the support and understanding it gets from outside.

3 GROUP WORK

Discussion about group work has been going on for many years within the probation and after-care service, but interest and experi-

1. H.O.C. 161/1968, July 1968.

ment have intensified since 1960. There have been several reasons for this, including experiments in other fields, but underlying them all has been the feeling that individual casework, even if it includes dealings with an offender's family and others in his environment, is not enough in certain cases and that some people may be more adequately understood or treated as part of a group.

One argument for this approach rests on the common observation that in adolescence the peer group is often the greatest single formative influence, and the deduction that this influence needs to be used in treating young delinquents.[1] The group may be one that already exists, or may be formed of offenders who are naturally gregarious. Or it may be seen as a means of getting through to the more inhibited or withdrawn, perhaps helping them to form relationships more easily. In the case of children, particularly, a group directed to some kind of activity may overcome the difficulties and artificialities of individual interviews.

Although most groups so far run by probation officers have been for adolescents or children, there is evidence from other fields that some kinds of group can be a potent influence at any age: Alcoholics Anonymous is one example. There have been a few interesting experiments in groups for parents of probationers.[2] Recently there have also been experiments with groups of prisoners' wives, run by probation officers or volunteers.[3] All these help people undergoing similar kinds of stress to feel less isolated, perhaps to share their problems, perhaps to give each other mutual support in facing or solving them. In addition it has to be remembered that groups have been used extensively in prisons and borstals in recent years and that this is a kind of approach to which some of those subject to after-care will already be accustomed. Some may reject it for that very reason. Others may prove too sophisticated to benefit. Yet others may miss the support of a group and need some equivalent when they come out.

There is little to support the suggestion that probation officers

---

1. See, for example, H. Jones, "The Group Approach to Treatment", *Howard Journal*, Vol. XI, No. 1, 1962.
2. See articles in *Probation:* by B. Brierley, September 1964; A. R. Stanley and J. McCarthy, November 1965.
3. See, for example, K. Vercoe, *Helping Prisoners' Families*, N.A.C.R.O., Papers and Reprints, No. 3, 1968.

take up group work to save time when they have too many under supervision to see them all separately. It involves considerable effort and preparation, and very few officers see it as an alternative, rather than a supplement, to casework. It might be more to the point to suggest that group work may improve the quality of the care that a probation officer can give to his charges, and increase the amount of time he can devote to each of them: theoretically, at least, he can see five together for an hour when he could have seen each alone only for ten minutes or so. There is evidence that it is in areas where officers have time to think about their work, rather than those with the highest case-loads, that groups have been tried.[1]

Apart from engaging in formal group work, probation officers have in the past used existing community agencies such as clubs, to encourage their probationers to extend their interests or develop their values. It may be partly because these agencies are so often felt nowadays to mean nothing to the majority of young people on probation that groups directly designed to meet their needs are coming more to the fore. From time to time, however, over many years, probation officers have formed the practice in various parts of the country of taking groups of clients on holidays or to camps.[2] This may be seen as a straightforward way of helping them, as a chance of strengthening relationships with them and of understanding them better away from the sometimes formal atmosphere of the individual interview.

What have been called activity groups are in some respects similar, though they are commonly extended over a longer period. In a few cases play groups have been run by women officers for young children under their supervision. Older children and adolescents have been involved in handicraft, educational or recreational groups of many different kinds. Amongst the benefits claimed have been that the young people have been encouraged to express them-

---

1. On this, and many points in this section, see H. Barr, *A Survey of Group Work in the Probation Service*, H.M.S.O., 1966. See also a series of articles in *Probation:* by W. G. Bilston, June 1961; J. A. Waycott, September 1961; P. D. Ashley, March 1962 and November 1965; M. K. McCullough, September 1962; D. Bissell, December 1964; D. A. Jones, July 1967.
2. See, for example, B. W. Steward, "Camping with Probationers", *New Society*, 1964.

selves more freely and form relationships more easily, and that their interests and self-confidence have been enlarged.

This kind of group may be comparatively easy, because it has a clear, ostensible objective apart from its underlying purpose of promoting better understanding and relationships. More diffidence may be felt by many probation officers about the kind of group that requires regular meetings over a period without any such tangible objective or incentive and often with rather undefined aims. There are, in particular, fears about venturing too far into the field of group therapy on the psychiatric model.

Yet much of the present interest in group work in the probation service has been aroused by experiments in the psychiatric field. Of the seventy-five officers who contributed to the survey of group work in probation in 1964,[1] over fifty had already tried what were broadly classed as discussion groups, and the majority of them considered that important aspects of their function in leading such groups were clarification, seeking to give insight and understanding and interpreting behaviour within the group.

Whatever the structure of groups or their overt purpose, however, it has become clearer over the years that all of them have similar dynamic elements, which need to be understood by their leaders. To this end the Howard Centre for Penology has held a two-year training course in group work for probation officers. The first year gives them the opportunity of experiencing and examining group processes at first hand during weekly meetings; during the second the newly trained group conductors have met to examine their experiences of their own groups. In addition, there have been lectures on group dynamics by experienced psychotherapists, who have also played a leading role in the group training. This is a major advance in training and probably foreshadows a further upsurge of interest amongst probation officers in group work methods, with a more extensive use of these methods in the field. A member of the Home Office Probation Training Section is on the steering committee for the Howard Centre course.

In the past much concern has been expressed about the possible dangers of group work in probation and after-care. Most earlier experience of such work had been in institutions, where offenders

1. H. Barr, *A Survey of Group Work in the Probation Service*, 1966.

were living together in any case.[1] Probation officers, on the other hand, must deliberately bring offenders together for the purposes of group work, except in the comparatively rare instances where they are in hostels or hospitals. It is objected that this inevitably raises special problems of contamination, of confidence and of control.

In some cases these arguments can be by-passed by pointing out that those under supervision are likely, in any case, to meet in waiting rooms; or by confining groups to those who already associate with each other naturally. But these are not complete answers and the risks, if such they are, must be faced squarely, for they can cause considerable anxiety to the probation officer.

Although it may seem only too likely that association in a group might be followed by association in crime, and although such an event would attract considerable publicity, there is scarcely any evidence that it occurs in practice. In only one case, out of the seventy-two groups examined in 1964, did it seem possible that meeting in the group had been the sole factor in a subsequent offence. The great majority of the officers concerned saw no reason to be anxious about the formation of associations outside the group.

Fears about confidentiality were more common. But here again, the danger appears more potential than real and group work practitioners do not recall instances in which confidential material, let fall by one member, has been broadcast by others. Despite lack of concrete evidence that confidentiality is in danger, however, it is probably wise to bear in mind the possibility that confidences blurted out as a part of the group process could be spread around, especially if the probationers and their families live near together. Even if this does not happen, the probationer may fear that it will. To explain or discuss the question of confidentiality at the outset may help some groups. Others seem to develop their own code and it has been suggested that members will not, in fact, blurt out personal confidences until this has happened. Also, since most officers see group work as supplementing rather than replacing casework, it is possible to give opportunities for more private matters to be taken up in individual interviews, even though the desire to raise

1. For examples of experiments in group work in institutions, see *Group Work in Prisons and Borstals* 1962–6, Home Office, Prison Department, 1966.

them may have been aroused by general discussion in the group as a whole.

Both in institutions and amongst probation officers there has been a good deal of emphasis on the need to be permissive and non-directive in running a group. This has led to doubts as to whether the role of group leader can satisfactorily be combined with the degree of control and authority required of the officer. Again the problem has proved to be less in substance than in speculation. In any case it is less acute for the probation officer than for the much more directive institutional staff. He is accustomed in casework to combine a measure of authority with an emphasis on encouraging the probationer, as far as possible, to work things out for himself and take his own decisions.

One aspect of control to which he is also accustomed in probation, and to some extent in after-care, however, does not apply to group work. He can insist that those under his supervision shall meet him regularly for individual interviews, but he cannot insist that they meet with each other or that they continue to do so regularly over a fixed period. The normal requirements of a probation order are considered useful in maintaining contact, in giving the opportunity to build up a relationship with a probably reluctant client, and in providing a framework within which casework can be planned. At present group work with probationers is still in an experimental phase: it is not known who may benefit from it and there is much yet to be learned about its nature and use. If it proves helpful, however, there may be a case in the future for making meeting with a group for a stated period a requirement of a probation order for certain offenders, just as a requirement of residence or mental treatment may be now.

Before that would be appropriate, however, much more consideration needs to be given to the sorts of offender whose treatment may benefit from their participation in groups, the sorts of group most appropriate for them, and the objects of group work in relation to the probation officer's other dealings with the offenders.

On the first point, it must be borne in mind that offenders who do not respond readily to individual casework methods will not necessarily respond any better to group work. A study of groups in borstals, for example, has suggested that boys lacking in verbal ability may become worse rather than better after participation in groups.[1] Similarly a very withdrawn or inhibited probationer may become still more anxious if his experience in a group is too threatening or demanding, or if he is picked upon by other members. Group work, like casework, can produce no magic solutions and must be tried with discrimination.

So far there has been much discussion of practical matters amongst probation officers, little attempt to define aims. There may be an implication that these are similar to some of those of casework: to increase independence and self-responsibility, thereby reducing tendencies to impulsive delinquency. It has been becoming obvious that impressions of what happens in groups are not enough and that future accounts of experiments need to include an elucidation of the "imagining" that went into the preparation of the group, a statement of what the leader was aiming at, of how the participants were chosen and of what appeared to be the results.

For purposes of research it would be necessary to define types of group treatment far more accurately, on the basis of analysis of systematic recordings of group discussions and study of counselling techniques. So far we do not know how effective various kinds of group treatment are, any more than we know the results of different kinds of individual treatment. It may well be quite a long time before we do. But research must rest upon continued experiment and increasing accuracy of observation.

Discussions of group work have often ranged round the question of whether methods developed in the psychiatric field can be used by probation officers or are appropriate in the probation setting. Many who have experimented in group work seem to assume that it is only this model that is worth while. A few others, also with considerable experience, argue that this kind of group is far too precious, passive and perilous: what is wanted is a discussion group, which may stimulate and support its members and extend their social awareness but which leaves individual interpretations and direct treatment to be dealt with by casework methods on an individual basis.

In an argument of this sort neither side is likely to be influenced by the other because they do not seem to be talking the same lan-

---

1. P. Shapland, "Groups and the Ability to Communicate", *British Journal of Criminology*, October 1967.

guage: in practice they may come much closer to each other than they would admit. As has been said, an understanding of group processes is needed whatever approach is adopted. And it seems likely, considering the variety in the needs of probationers and the approaches of probation officers, that there are many group models which can be adapted for use in the probation setting. It has been suggested that we might be wise to look towards education for these as much as to psychiatry. And it has been pointed out that, since many officers think groups appropriate for comparatively normal offenders whose problems arise from the influences or stresses of their environments, there should be room for groups that focus upon social education as their primary purpose.

Up to now group work has had a kind of maverick quality: it has seemed faintly unrespectable, innocent and slap happy and it has probably admirably suited the small band of devotees who have practised it in probation. If training becomes more readily available, group work is almost certain to become more respectable, sophisticated and structured. It may be necessary to guard against it becoming as dead and mechanical as casework can become under the same circumstances. There are encouraging signs, however, that practitioners have been, and will continue to be, flexible, imaginative, willing to experiment and willing to have their experiments tested by experience and research.

CHAPTER 7

MEDICAL-SOCIAL PROBLEMS

1 THE MENTALLY ABNORMAL

THE probation officer is involved in the treatment of mentally abnormal offenders at various stages. He will often be the first to notice signs of abnormality and suggest to a court that a psychiatric diagnosis be obtained. He becomes directly linked with psychiatric measures when a requirement of mental treatment is included in a probation order. He has to deal, in the supervision of probationers, with various kinds of maladjustment, various degrees of character disorder. As his work in after-care expands he is likely to encounter such problems in increasing number and intensity. His responses as a social worker and as a representative of authority have been considered in earlier chapters. Here a word must be said about the ways in which his responsibilities in this direction are being affected by wider trends in the penal and the mental health services.

He may become responsible for an offender requiring mental treatment in any of four ways. The offender may be put on probation with a requirement of mental treatment under s. 4 of the Criminal Justice Act 1948. Or he may be subject to supervision following conditional discharge from Broadmoor, Moss Side or Rampton, or from another mental hospital to which he has been sent by a court under s. 65 of the Mental Health Act 1959. Or after-care, voluntary or compulsory, may follow a sentence of imprisonment during which he has received mental treatment through the prison medical service. Or mental treatment may be a condition of licence on parole.[1]

A number of safeguards for the offender are attached to a require-

---

1. For details of the requirements governing each of these kinds of supervision, see F. Jarvis, *Probation Officers' Manual*, 1969.

ment of mental treatment under a probation order. As with other requirements, it cannot be made without the offender's consent. It can be made only on the basis of a medical report. It cannot extend beyond twelve months. It must specify the hospital, clinic or doctor the patient is to attend. Reasonable refusal by the patient of surgical, electrical or other treatment is not to be regarded as breach of the requirement. The responsible medical practitioner can, with the consent of the patient, vary the place of treatment, and if he considers the patient no longer needs or is susceptible to treatment he may discharge him. It is thus clear that a requirement of mental treatment, even in a hospital, cannot be regarded as a substitute for imprisonment. The probationer is unlikely to be held in secure conditions and he may be discharged at any time, though this would not normally be done without consultation with the probation officer. It has, indeed, been suggested that the requirement of treatment should include a stipulation that the probationer abide by the rules of the hospital, since there have been instances where offenders have brought pressure on doctors to discharge them by deliberately disruptive behaviour.

Mental treatment can be linked with probation only in cases where the offender's condition is not serious enough to justify compulsory detention in a mental hospital. The Criminal Justice Act 1948 limited the responsibility of the probation officer whilst the offender was under hospital treatment to the formal supervision necessary for discharge or amendment of the order. The intention was to avoid any interference with the psychiatrist's control of the case as a medical problem. In practice, however, so rigid a distinction has proved unhelpful. The Morison Committee agreed with the opinion of medical witnesses that the part to be played by the probation officer should be much more flexible. He could often do much to befriend the probationer, keep in touch with his family and prepare for the time when he returned home and came under normal probation supervision.

The value of this co-operation between psychiatrist and probation officer, reflecting the interaction of psychiatric and social factors, was further emphasized by the observation that a social enquiry report, in addition to the mandatory psychiatric report, was likely to be specially valuable in cases where a requirement of mental treatment was being contemplated. It must also be remembered that the probationer required to receive treatment for his mental condition may not be in hospital at all: he may be carrying on his normal life whilst attending a specified clinic or doctor. In this case again the probation officer must work throughout in close co-operation with the psychiatrist.

As the result of a study of probationers subject to requirements of mental treatment in 1953, on whom full medical information was available, Dr. Grünhut found that seventy per cent were discharged with a favourable medical prognosis and almost as many (including some whose prognosis was not so favourable) had not been reconvicted within a year after the end of their probation. In other words they had done as well as the normal run of probationers.[1] The Morison Committee concluded that "mental treatment requirements are a valuable part of the probation system and should be retained. . . . The provisions meet the needs of offenders whose mental condition is susceptible to comparatively short-term treatment but who appear to need non-medical supervision thereafter". The continuity of social care is certainly an important advantage of this kind of order.

The question of responsibility for the offender subject to mental disorder was tackled in another way by the Mental Health Act of 1959. This empowers courts to make orders of hospital treatment or guardianship in any case where the offence is punishable by imprisonment and the offender is suffering from mental illness, mental subnormality or psychopathic disorder of such nature or degree as to warrant such an order. In these cases the consent of the offender is not required. It is necessary, however, that two doctors agree on the diagnosis and that admission to a hospital can be arranged. It is also necessary that the court decide to use such an order in preference to some form of treatment within the penal system, such as imprisonment or probation. Whereas any court can make a hospital order, only quarter sessions or assizes can add a restriction order, limiting the right of the hospital authorities to discharge the offender as soon as they think fit by requiring them to obtain the prior consent of the Home Office. Even in these cases the patient may have considerable liberty within the hospital. And

---

1. See M. Grünhut, *Probation and Mental Treatment*, 1963; *Report of the Departmental Committee on the Probation Service* (Cmnd. 1650), 1962, p. 36.

it is only in these graver cases, where a restriction order was imposed, that he can be subjected to conditions, including a condition of supervision, on his discharge (though hospitals sometimes resort to the stratagem of allowing "home leave" without discharge of the order). In restriction order cases there may be a requirement that the offender attend a psychiatric out-patient clinic and he may be put under the supervision either of the probation officer or of a local authority mental welfare officer. He can be recalled at any time whilst the restriction order lasts if there are signs of further mental disturbance, a fresh offence, or any other reason to take him back into hospital in his own interests or those of public safety. The probation officer is required to report any deterioration to the hospital or the Home Office and to send regular reports to the Home Office where the offender has been discharged from Broadmoor, Moss Side or Rampton. In such cases, therefore, he has a heavy responsibility, but he has also the assurance that the offender can, if necessary, be recalled to hospital quickly.

This is not the case with the third category of mentally abnormal offenders he may have to deal with; those discharged from prisons. Although mental hospitals have frequently been exhorted to provide secure units for offender patients, and especially psychopaths, they show little inclination to do so. Modern hospitals (apart from hospitals for the sub-normal) are in general unable to cope with patients who require control other than control by drugs. The idea runs contrary to their present policy of open wards and quick discharge wherever possible. Prisons can offer a degree of security and control which hospitals seldom do. Accordingly courts often decide that prison must be the choice. They may hope, and even say, that an offender will be given treatment for his mental condition whilst he is there. Whether this happens depends on whether he is identified as needing such treatment, whether he will co-operate, and whether psychiatric facilities are available to give it. Since the Report on the Organization of the Prison Medical Service in 1964 considerable efforts have been made to make psychiatric treatment in prison a reality. Consultant forensic psychiatrists have been appointed to work part-time in the prisons, part-time in teaching hospitals. The Grendon prison hospital, with a medical superintendent as governor, has provided within the penal system specialized psychiatric facilities combined with security. There is now, it has been claimed, "a logical and promising recognition that, since the habitual offender and the psychiatric patient overlap, it is quite inevitable that any services which are effectively to deal with them must also overlap".

Unfortunately the recognition tends to be less marked where these offenders are no longer in prison. There is no provision for continuity of care even at the crucial point when they leave prison. There is no formal provision for their after-care unless they happen to be amongst the few now qualifying for compulsory supervision by probation officers. Few of them are likely to ask for after-care voluntarily or to maintain contact long if they do. Rather optimistically the Working Party on Voluntary Service in After-Care observed that, if the established trend towards psychiatric treatment in prison continues, "the after-care service is likely to be called upon to accept a higher proportion of, we hope, recovered or adjusted psychiatric offender-patients."[1] The process of recovery and adjustment is hardly likely to have been completed in prison. It has been said that "the probation officer is found to be more appropriate than the mental welfare officer for dealing with some types of offender-patients". Certainly he, more than many other social and medical workers, has had to come to grips with the problem of the unwilling client. But this is a matter of degree: if he is to go further, he himself will need more co-operation.

The probation and after-care service has derived much benefit from consultation and group discussions with individual psychiatrists. In London particularly there are clinics specializing in forensic psychiatry to which officers can turn for help with individual patients. In other parts of the country, however, they are often handicapped by the need to refer an offender to a psychiatrist through his own doctor, who may be unsympathetic. Similarly, whereas a patient who has been treated in a mental hospital can return there if necessary with a minimum of difficulty, there is no equivalent provision for an offender who has been treated in prison. He cannot go back to the environment and doctor he knows and it may be hard to secure his admission to a mental hospital if he comes within the category of "psychopathic disorder" rather than mental illness.

---

1. Second Report of the Working Party on the Place of Voluntary Service in After-Care, 1967.

In attempting to help the persistent and apparently incorrigible offender, whether on probation or subject to any kind of after-care, the probation officer looking for guidance to a psychiatrist is likely to be met with something like this: "The man's a psychopath. He's not a medical problem but a social one. It's a matter for you. You should deal with him as you would with a child." But in open society, where he is expected to fulfil the responsibilities of a man and is a potential danger to others, such an offender cannot be dealt with like a small child, unless he is very fortunate indeed in his family, employer or landlady. The reaction of the probation officer to so unpromising a situation may well be to turn his main attention to cases in which his time and energy are likely to be employed more rewardingly. As things stand this is eminently reasonable. But it leaves the problem of some of the most difficult offenders to rankle unsolved.

Certainly no solution is likely unless it is acknowledged that these problems are neither exclusively medical nor exclusively social, but an inextricable mixture of both. It is on such lines that attempts are being made to tackle them elsewhere, notably at the Hersted-vester prison near Copenhagen and at the Van der Hoeven Clinic in Utrecht. Though the two institutions differ in many respects, certain basic principles emerge.

First, in the earlier stages of treatment these offenders need an environment specially adapted to their capacities and needs. Second, both psychiatric and social treatment is required and the two must go hand in hand. Thus at the Van der Hoeven Clinic individual and group psychotherapy are carried on in the setting of social therapy within the institutional community. Whilst the former proceed on a personal basis and at quite a deep level, the latter includes learning to earn a living and pay one's way, taking part in managing the affairs of the clinic, living together in small units with the staff, fostering ties with families or substitute families outside. Third, restoration to the open community must be gradual: the way must be prepared by the patients going out to work, to develop new contacts, to visit families who befriend them and to make acquaintance with the problems of normal life. Fourth, intensive care in the open, either directly by the staff of the institution or by others with supervision and guidance from them, is as important as the institutional treatment itself. Fifth, there must be provision for temporary return to the institution where social breakdown occurs or threatens. Sixth, at all stages there must be close co-operation between different kinds of staff responsible for treatment: doctors, psychologists, social therapists and workshop instructors.[1]

Such continuity and flexibility, such close links between psychiatric and social workers concerned with the treatment of these offenders inside and outside institutions, are so far almost entirely lacking in this country. Yet there are a few straws in the wind. Steps are being taken to improve the mental health services of local authorities and it has been suggested that they and the probation and after-care services should co-operate more. It is hoped that the development of better psychiatric services in the prisons, linked with hospitals outside, will increase the number of psychiatrists and clinics with an interest in the special problems of offenders. This could be of help both to courts and probation service in diagnosis, in consultation, and in direct treatment of offenders subject to probation or after-care. It has been proposed that special diagnostic, treatment and research centres might be established; these could perform similar functions as well as carrying forward the exploration of the kinds of medical and social therapy most appropriate for the variety of persistent offenders. It may well be that such clinics or centres should be formally linked with the probation and after-care service as well as with prisons. Certainly the service has equal need of their advice and support.

It has been suggested, moreover, that they might serve as recall centres to which patients could return if there were signs of further breakdown. Similarly there have been proposals that certain prisons specializing in treatment should have hostels not merely as a bridge to the outside world when offenders are leaving but as a refuge to which they could voluntarily return for a time if they got into too much difficulty. Whether or not such proposals offer the best solution, they show an appreciation of the fact that some such safety valve is needed if serious attempts are to be made to find a place in society for these offenders. It will not be done easily or without relapses; it may threaten at times the harmony of a hostel and the treatment of others. It calls for concentrated effort from medical

---

1. See A. M. Roosenburg, *The Unwilling Patient*, First Denis Carroll Memorial Lecture, 1966; A. K. Stürup, *Treating the "Untreatable": Chronic Criminals at Herstedvester* (Isaac Ray Award Lectures), Baltimore, 1968.

and social workers alike. The most promising approach may be through the hybrid prison-hospital or hostel-clinic, but neither is likely to succeed unless linked with continuing care and adequate resources in the community.

2 ALCOHOLICS

Alcoholics and drug addicts are groups that overlap with the mentally abnormal. Like them, they present both medical and social problems. Many, though not all, are much more of a danger to themselves than to other people. And there is still a great lack of knowledge about their varying needs and a great lack of provision for their treatment.

There were between four and five thousand offenders in prison in 1967 for drunken offences. Many more, of course, appeared before the courts for various offences connected with drunkenness. Not all these, of course, are alcoholics, but repeated convictions for offences of this kind have, in themselves, been held to indicate alcoholism. Social enquiries are rarely asked for in such cases, though if there seems any ground for hope of a change in the offender, or he is obviously not of the regular mould, the magistrate may ask for one. That this happens seldom is not because of any lack of feeling on the part of the court but because there seems so little hope, with existing facilities, of providing sustained help or treatment for most of the people concerned. Very few alcoholics are young: their average age could be set at about forty. The majority are isolated: they live alone or have no homes at all; they have either never married at all or left their wives. Most are below average in intelligence, illiterate, often given to lying. Some have psychiatric difficulties, some personality disorders.

Different devices have been tried in various parts of the country to avoid bringing them to court. In one city they may be taken by officers of the Ministry of Health and Social Security to a reception centre. In another police may take them to a voluntary hostel. Few are put on probation by the courts for offences of drunkenness, but probation officers may find themselves supervising alcoholics as a result of other offences, and they may, of course, come under the head of voluntary after-care, having served prison sentences, short or long. Attempts to help them have to be on a day-to-day basis, with frequent lapses to be expected, and with increasing difficulty in securing their entry to hostels or any other accommodation following such failures.

Apart from this, the great difficulty about using a probation order to deal with an alcoholic, especially if he is homeless, is that he is most unlikely to keep the terms. If he fails to do so the officer cannot allow the order of the court to be flouted, but there is little to be gained by bringing him back to court as no constructive alternative can be offered and he is probably impervious to imprisonment. The addition of a requirement of treatment at a hospital or hostel for alcoholics seldom succeeds either. A very few hospitals have small units for alcoholics or will accept them for treatment, but none claim much success. In any case the offender is likely to need the shelter of a hostel for a time after he leaves if he is not to relapse almost at once.

The prison system is equally unable to solve the problem. It has no means of either assessing or treating the many alcoholics who pass in and out. Alcoholics Anonymous, prison staff and prison welfare officers have tried to help groups of alcoholics in prison. but it is difficult to inject much reality into this whilst they are completely cut off from the pressures they will have to meet when they leave. The meths drinker, in particular, is unlikely to persevere once outside. Even if the hope is that offenders will eventually cease to be sent to prison for such offences as being drunk and disorderly, alcoholics are still likely to go there for other offences. It is felt, therefore, that there should be one or two specialist alcoholic units in the prison system, staffed to enable proper rehabilitation to be attempted, and working in close liaison with the probation and after-care service and with hostels capable of providing support after discharge.

Section 91 of the Criminal Justice Act 1967 stipulates that the Home Secretary shall not bring into force the provisions abolishing short-term imprisonment for offences of drunkenness unless he is satisfied that sufficient suitable accommodation is available for the care and treatment of the offenders concerned. There are still very few hostels to which the alcoholic can go for treatment, either direct, from the court, or from hospital, or from prison. There are not much more than a dozen in the south of England, providing something like a hundred places, and some big northern and midland cities have none. Alcoholics, even when offered the chance, are often reluctant to go to special hostels and they seldom stay in them for any length of time. If they relapse, the hostel is usually unable to accept them back. It may be necessary to accept that the majority of alcoholics will drift in and out of hostels if they use them at all.

The tendency has been for hostels specializing in their care to start by admitting the less promising, the vagrants and confirmed alcoholics, but gradually to restrict admittance to those more able to respond. Rathcoole, the experimental hostel established for vagrant alcoholics in London, began on the basis of re-admitting men in spite of repeated lapses, in the hope of building up long-term relationships with them. Obliged to concentrate to start with on simple supportive measures, it found that at least some of the men could maintain sobriety and keep in employment for several months, though very few stayed as long as a year. Even these could not be regarded as cured. Almost all resisted attempts at more active therapeutic measures, such as group discussion and were very unwilling to be involved in decisions on hostel policy. It was decided, therefore, that a vigorous directive approach was needed, designed to foster self-help rather than passive dependency and to involve all residents in such awkward decisions as whether a man should be re-admitted after a lapse.[1] Group therapy is now used and higher demands are made on the residents. But this means that the person entering the hostel must have a strong desire to succeed and be considered likely to benefit, and he must understand that a relapse will result in rejection.

It has been estimated that only about one alcoholic in five is willing to accept treatment. The Simon Community is prepared to try to help them without requiring them to give up alcohol, and Simon Houses, apart from their humanitarian objects, serve to take the men off the street and reduce the nuisance to others. It may have to be accepted that this is the most that can be achieved with many.

Small hostels may prove to be suitable only for the more hopeful, those who already have some will and ability to change. Many others, who lack either will or ability, seem likely to continue to reject the idea of hostels and to resist attempts to involve them in treatment. A few may go to hostels willingly; a few may be reinforced in their intention to stay and to co-operate by probation

1. See T. Cook, H. G. Morgan, B. Pollak, "The Rathcoole Experiment", *Probation*, Vol. 4, No. 2, July 1968.

orders; but for many some less demanding atmosphere than that of the small hostel may be required. During the period, a year or two ago, when the majority of alcoholics from the London courts were being sent to Spring Hill Prison, many of them seemed well content in the open community there, hardly missing their drink. It may be that such as these need a new form of care, perhaps a similar community outside the prison system but reinforced by a new kind of court order, perhaps on the lines of a hospital order. It may prove rewarding to look at overseas experience with various kinds of working colony, farm or other community in which alcoholics can live either voluntarily or on the order of a court as an alternative to imprisonment.

3   DRUG ADDICTS

Among the new challenges recognized by the probation service during the 1960s has been the rapid rise in the incidence of drug abuse and dependency in this country.[1]

It is well known that, when the first Brain Committee reported in 1961, drug addiction was still considered to be a very small problem on this side of the Atlantic. Even though numbers of registered heroin addicts showed a sharp rise in 1960 there were still less than a hundred of them in that year, most of them over fifty and none under twenty. The number for 1968 was two thousand two hundred and forty: about a third of them in their teens. Many, though by no means all, come from good social backgrounds.[2]

The older drugs like heroin, cocaine, cannabis, have not been by any means the whole of the problem. The second Brain Committee also drew attention in 1965 to the widespread abuse of new drugs, increasingly marketed and prescribed since the war. Amphetamines and similar stimulants affecting the central nervous system were mentioned in particular.[2] In 1966 it was estimated that a hundred and sixty thousand people were misusing amphetamines in this

---

1. For a clear, brief survey of the whole problem, see W. D. M. Paton, "Drug Dependence—a Socio-Pharmacological Assessment" (Public Lecture delivered on 26 August 1968 at the Dundee Meeting of the British Association), in *The Advancement of Science*, Vol. 25, No. 124, December 1968.

2. For stages in this progression see: *Report of the Inter-Departmental Committee on Drug Addiction*, H.M.S.O., 1961; *Second Report of the Inter-Departmental Committee on Drug Addiction*, H.M.S.O., 1965; Home Office figures for 1967, reported in *New Society*, 13 and 22 August 1968; P. D. Scott and D. R. Willcox, "Delinquency and the Amphetamines", *British Journal of Addiction*, No. 61, November 1965.

country, and the habit has become widespread amongst adolescent delinquents.[1]

Under the Dangerous Drugs Act 1965, unauthorized possession of heroin, cocaine and cannabis and certain other drugs is punishable by up to twelve months' imprisonment on summary conviction, ten years on indictment. Under the Drugs (Prevention of Misuse) Act 1964, unauthorized possession of amphetamines, L.S.D., and other similar substances is punishable by imprisonment up to six months on summary conviction, two years on indictment. New legislation and stricter enforcement, designed to combat the continuing rise may well have brought more drugtakers to light. Charges of illegal possession of drugs and forgery of prescriptions, as well as the theft and sale of prescriptions and drugs, have appeared regularly on court lists, not only in London but in other urban areas. Probation officers in the big cities have been well aware of what has been going on and have been in the vanguard of pressure for adequate treatment provision and for precautions during drug manufacture and distribution. They began their own research and study, seeking ways of recognizing and helping those in their care.[2]

Though closely related to the numerically much greater problem of alcoholism, drug dependence has aspects which arouse even more anxiety in the social worker. These include the youth of most of those now affected, the rapidity of deterioration in appearance, health and behaviour, and the real risk of early death—if not from overdose, at least from secondary causes.[3] Because so many drug abusers are adolescents, parental involvement and family interaction is still very much part of the problem, even where they are estranged.[4] Acutely anxious parents often need as much help as the addicts themselves. What is more, the really dependent young person is usually unable to work, penniless and often homeless. Any money

---

1. Bewley, *Bulletin of Narcotics*, Vol. 18, No. 4, 1966.
2. PE/EM. "Beyond Brain", *Probation*, July 1966; F. Dawtry (ed.), *Social Problems of Drug Abuse*, 1968, N.A.P.O.
3. See Glatt, Pittman, Gillespie, Hills, *The Drug Scene in Great Britain*, 1967; Wilson (ed.), *Adolescent Drug Dependence*, ref. Helpern, Camps and Louria, 1968; I. P. James, "Suicide and Mortality amongst Heroin Addicts in Britain", *British Journal of Addiction*, No. 62, 1967: Fish, "Barbiturate Addiction", *Proceedings of Teach-in on Drug Taking*, Merseyside Council on Drug Taking, 11 May 1968; C.I.B.A. *A Symposium on Hashish*, Churchill, 1965.
4. H. Ganger and G. Shugart, "The Heroin Addict's Pseudoassertive Behaviour and Family Dynamics", *Social Casework*, December 1966; Sandler, *Psychopathology of Addiction*, Paper to Society for the Study of Addiction, 5 July 1966.

he is given goes on drugs. He is unkempt and unacceptable in lodgings. He relies for support and understanding on a group of others like himself, and fears to break away from them. There is an urgency and intensity in such situations that require the devotion of a great deal of a probation officer's time and can sometimes engender an understandable ambivalence about accepting responsibility for the case.

It could therefore be asked whether the problems of drug addiction, any more than those of alcoholism, are a proper preoccupation for a hard-pressed delinquency service. If addicts are primarily sick people, and if special treatment facilities have been provided for them, is the law-breaking not purely incidental, and are the staff of the official clinics not the right people to take them on? Undoubtedly this is very often so.[1] The fact remains, however, that many drugtakers appear in court, where the bench will frequently wish to have a probation officer's report. Moreover, some drug takers are there on charges not recognizably associated with drugs until enquiries are made; some refuse treatment; and others are already on probation before the drug taking is observed.[2] It has sometimes been suggested that drug taking in this country is the prerogative of young middle class intellectuals, but there is evidence that it affects all classes, including the alienated and criminal amongst the working classes as well.

The courts are valuable for the discovery of addicts, and from them those able to make use of treatment can be directed towards it, either freely or as a requirement of a probation order, or under the Mental Health Act if the offender's mental condition justifies this and if facilities are available. The probation officer has an important diagnostic task which goes beyond recognition of addiction. The addict's sickness is a symptom, not the only characteristic of the person.[3] In considering whether prison, borstal, approved

---

1. A. Kaldegg, "Heroin Addiction", *New Society*, 2 February 1967; M. Nyman, "Hazards in Relation to the Treatment of Drug Addiction", *Case Conference*, October 1967; Wilbur and Connor, "Intensive Casework with the Drug Addict", *Case Conference*, April 1966; Dale Beckett, *The Salter Unit*, Paper to Society for the Study of Addiction, 31 March 1967.

2. James, 50 *Male Heroin Addicts Seen in Prison*, Paper to British Society of Criminology, 12 December 1967; *Report on Drug Survey*, 1967, Middlesex Area Probation and After-Care Service.

3. M. Silberman, *Aspects of Drug Addiction*, Royal London Prisoners' Aid Society, 1967; F. Dawtry (ed.), *Social Problems of Drug Abuse*, 1968.

school, probation or straight referral to medical care is the most appropriate disposal, there are other factors to consider. Is the offender a "pusher"; was he already delinquent before he took drugs; is he just an adolescent lost in the search for definitions and controls; what are the social pressures, what the boredom to be faced if he should allow himself to return to the reality from which he has escaped? Many drug takers seem to be covering up a depression that can be better unmasked and treated in its own right in hospital. Others have such fears or psychopathic tendencies that they could not meet the obligations of a requirement of mental treatment on probation for very long, and to recommend such a condition is to invite breach of the probation. Some hospitals prefer their patients not to be tied to treatment in this way. Others feel that such a requirement strengthens the motive to stay, if the probationer knows that to leave without permission, or to provoke discharge, will definitely mean reappearance in court.

Addicts sent to penal institutions are kept off drugs during their stay but need in addition active treatment directed to the cause of their drug-dependence and to showing them the positive gains of a cure. Whether an addict has been in a penal institution or a hospital, his first few days, even his first few hours, at liberty are crucial. He can easily slip straight back into the social setting in which his addition is taken for granted and so back to drug-dependence. To avoid this he needs both an initial motivation to make the break and intensive after-care.

Sometimes the probation officer may find the underlying problems are more familiar to him than to medical people. On the preventive side, some drug takers, using small quantities of "soft" drugs, may be recognized and helped by probation before medical intervention is required. In any case, the out-patient centres established at teaching hospitals for the treatment of addiction and the supply of drugs have been created to deal mainly with heroin and cocaine users and have not so far been given either the space or the staff to take on the much larger number of people misusing other types of drugs.

Thus it seems certain that probation officers will continue to be involved, both inside institutions and out. This has been officially recognized by inclusion of a probation officer on the Standing Advisory Committee on Drug Dependence, which was set up at the suggestion of the Brain Committee. It has also to be recognized in training. Probation officers now need to know the principal drugs of abuse and their effects. Drug addicts remain people: ordinary casework skills apply to their treatment, with due allowance for the inevitable lies, the relapses, the irrational and infantile responses of the really dependent person, who needs to transfer his dependency and hostility to the worker while relinquishing the drug. Because of the importance of a continuing relationship in the early phases of weaning from the drug, it has been found necessary very often to try to retain the same supervising officer, even if it means travelling over divisional boundaries, and courts have recognized this. Addicts on probation may be able also to use the growing experience and training of the service in group work, as they move from total isolation and dependence towards the next phase of mutual commitments in normal social relationships.[1]   It seems likely that half-way houses and even self-help groups such as exist in the United States will become necessary, and they may well call on the probation service for liaison and other co-operation.[2] Daytop Lodge, one of the self-help communities for addicts in America, began as Drug Addicts Treated On Probation.[3]   Working with addicts also involves co-operating closely with hospitals, and it has extended the scope of liaison work with specialized in-patient units and out-patient clinics.

There have been peaks in drug abuse patterns before in England and on a large scale in the United States, Sweden and Japan.[4] Epidemiological factors make it possible that certain forms of drug dependence will become prevalent from time to time, while others are forgotten.   Methods of prediction and prevention may be developed when causation is better understood, and probation files will continue to provide material for research into these problems, as well as into the actual effects of certain drugs and the crimino-

---

1. See M. M. Glatt, "Group Therapy with Young Drug Addicts", *Nursing Times*, 21 April 1967.
2. Geis, G., "Halfway House for Narcotic Addicts", *British Journal of Addiction*, No. 61, November 1965.
3. B. Sugarman, "Daytop Village, a Drug Care Co-operative", *New Society*, 13 April 1967.
4. *Drug Addiction*, Office of Health Economics, October 1967.

genic quality of drug abuse.[1] It seems unlikely, however, that addiction will die away completely as have more ephemeral manifestations of youthful unrest. The probation service is therefore facing another long term need, making big demands on its strength, training and time.

All this has again highlighted the general need in the service for adequate diagnostic facilities, readily available consultation and psychiatric support for officers in their work. Treating addiction has demonstrated the need to ensure that the various symptoms of people in contact with several agencies should not be treated in isolation. A closely communicating team can show concern for the person as a whole and arrive at a more reliable prognosis.[2] Work on these lines has led to the spontaneous development of one or two centres where reporting to the probation officer and seeing the medical team can be combined. This saves weakly motivated probationers the discouragement of extra travel. The geographical rapprochement allows for regular case discussion between those involved, and it promotes a common approach to local problems. Inter-disciplinary barriers have come down and communication has been established through the participation of probation officers with other social workers, teachers and doctors in numerous associations, working parties and research projects devoted to the prevention of addiction, its incidence, treatment and after-care.[3] While this better co-ordination and appreciation of common aims is a by-product of the community concern that has arisen around one form of dangerous and deviant behaviour, it is a dimension that has often been sought after less successfully in other areas of the probation officer's work, and can profitably be carried over into the general field. What has not yet developed in this country is any scheme to enlist the help of ex-addicts themselves in the team.

---

1. A. T. Wood, *Drug Dependence*, Bristol Council of Social Service, 1967; Eddy, Halbach, Isbell, Seevers: "Drug Dependence: Its Significance and Characteristics", *W.H.O. Bulletin*, Vol. 32.

2. *Services for the Prevention and Treatment of Dependence on Alcohol and other Drugs*, W.H.O. Expert Committee on Mental Health, 14th Report (1967); M. Nyman, "Birmingham Tackles Addiction", *New Society*, 9 February 1967; J. Owens, "Integrated Approach", *British Medical Journal*, 20 May 1967.

3. *Proceedings of Teach-in on Drugtaking*, Merseyside Council on Drugtaking, 11 May 1968.

CHAPTER 8

THE SERVICE AND THE COURTS

1 A CONTINUING RELATIONSHIP

EARLIER chapters have given a picture of the probation officer as a social worker, but a social worker who is employed by a committee consisting largely of magistrates and whose relations with his clients are coloured by their varying legal positions. In this chapter attention is focused particularly upon his role as social worker of the courts and the special duties and loyalties which this carries with it.

It is sometimes suggested that probation officers are moving away from their role as social workers of the courts into that of social workers of the penal system. It might be more accurate to say that they are moving further into both these roles. Probationers still make up a good two-thirds of the probation officer's caseload. It is true that he has become involved in fresh responsibilities in penal institutions and after-care, dealing with offenders who have not been directly placed under his supervision by the courts. But all these offenders have been sentenced by the courts in the first instance. Moreover, the employing committees and the case committees attached to the courts are now concerned with the oversight of probation officers' work in after-care as well as in probation. Above all, there has been a great extension in recent years in the number and scope of reports prepared by probation officers to help courts decide upon sentence in the first instance. In the decade 1955 to 1966 the annual number of pre-sentence enquiries more than doubled, from 75,000 to 165,000. In 1967 there were well over 181,000.[1] And this was before the recent advice that courts

---

1. See *Probation and After-Care Statistics for 1967, England and Wales.*

should consider reports in still more cases before using probation or sentencing offenders to penal institutions.

It may, perhaps, be suggested that all this is becoming less relevant because the powers of courts to decide sentence are being gradually eroded, because the decision as to the institution in which a sentence shall be served and the exact length of time an offender shall spend there is being increasingly prescribed by law or handed over to the executive. For example, successive statutory restrictions have been placed on the powers of magistrates' courts to imprison. And it rests with the executive to decide when a boy shall be licensed from borstal or a prisoner released on parole. Against this tendency, however, must be set the fact that the courts retain the most fundamental decision of all: whether or not the offender must be deprived of his liberty, either in the first instance or following failure on probation, conditional discharge or suspended sentence. Moreover they are showing great concern to improve their sentencing, through such means as sentencing conferences. The reports of probation officers are seen as a vital contribution to such improvement. The probation and after-care service may in future play an important role in subsequent decisions about the treatment of offenders in institutions, in parole or other forms of licence. But his primary contribution to decisions is still made in the courts and in his supervision of probationers under their direct authority. These two major fields of co-operation will be considered in turn.

2 SOCIAL ENQUIRY REPORTS

The authority for the preparation of home surroundings reports for the courts in the case of children and young persons charged with offences or alleged to be in need of care or protection was contained in the Children and Young Persons Act 1933, s. 35(2). In most areas up to the present these reports have been prepared by probation officers. So far as adults are concerned, the probation officer has a duty, prescribed in the Fifth Schedule to the Criminal Justice Act 1948, to make investigations, in accordance with any direction of the courts, with a view to assisting their decision as to treatment.

The Report of the Departmental Committee on the Business of the Criminal Courts dealt comprehensively with the question of what information the courts now require to enable them to select the most appropriate treatment for offenders, and with arrangements for providing them with this information. It emphasized that modern courts were concerned not merely to punish the offender for his past crime, but to influence him and others in such a way as to prevent further offences in the future. To do this they needed information not only about the offence but about the offender and his social background. This principle obviously applies to the decisions of magistrates' courts as well as to those of quarter sessions and assizes (with which the Streatfeild Committee was primarily concerned) and the report has in fact influenced the attitude of courts at all levels.

It raises a series of practical issues. At what stage should enquiries be made: before trial or between conviction and sentence? Is it necessary or practicable to have them in all cases and if not how should priorities be decided? What should be included in reports? Who, besides the court, should be entitled to know their contents? There has been controversy on all these points.

As to timing, the Streatfeild Committee favoured pre-trial enquiries, at least for certain classes of case coming before the higher courts. Its main argument was that they avoided the delay in sentencing which must result from a remand enquiry. It saw no objection to them in principle, provided the defendant (through his solicitor if he had one) was first told what was involved in the enquiry and given the chance to object. If he did object, the enquiry should not be made at that stage, though the court could ask for one later if there was a conviction. The committee held that, given such safeguards, an enquiry could properly be made even in cases where the defendant intended to plead not guilty, a point on which many officers would still have considerable doubts. But apart from that the practice of pre-trial enquiries is now well established in connection with cases coming before the higher courts, except in Inner London, which has special arrangements for dealing speedily with requests for enquiries after conviction.

In some magistrates' courts, also, it has long been the practice for pre-trial enquiries to be made before cases are heard. Particularly in country areas, where courts sit infrequently, there is usually time for this to be done between notification by the police that a case is coming to court and the day of the hearing. By the same token, the delay saved by a pre-trial enquiry may be considerable. Some town and city courts also have reports prepared before the case is heard. Others rely on adjournments. Where this is done it is important that sufficient time should be allowed for a full social enquiry, including visits to the offender's home and, if relevant, interviews with his family as well as himself. The practice of putting back a case for an hour or two only, allowing the officer barely time to interview the offender, can seldom be justified.

In making an enquiry at any stage, especially in preparing a written report for the higher courts, the probation officer needs to take account of others who will also be reporting to the court. He needs to know, but not recapitulate, what is included in the police statement of antecedents. Where the defendant has already been in custody he needs to know what is being said about him by the prison authorities. These authorities, on their side, need to be aware of the defendant's social background. Arrangements have accordingly been made for co-operation between police, prison and probation at this stage, though each service still prepares and presents its separate report.

It has been seen that there is no general requirement that courts shall consider reports on all adult offenders, though they are required to have background information on all but the most trivial juvenile cases. It may well be that it is unnecessary as well as impracticable to have reports in dealing with the majority of the offenders, at present fined or discharged by the magistrates' courts.

Short of attempting to make enquiries on all of them, selection may be at the discretion of the court and probation officer, taking into account any special features in individual cases. This is possible and desirable in addition to any attempt to lay down categories on whom enquiries should be made as normal practice. Such categories may be based on factors relating to the offender (like age or sex), on factors relating to the offence or record (like the trivial or serious nature of the offence, whether it is the first time or not), on factors relating to the kind of sentence the court may be contemplating (such as whether probation or some period of detention is likely to be considered). In fact, and probably rightly, the categories laid down so far in legislation or suggested to the courts have related, variously, to all these considerations. And they have never been exclusive.

The classes of case defined in the Streatfeild Report as calling for pre-trial social enquiries in the higher courts were:

(1) persons aged under 31 at the date of committal for trial;
(2) persons aged 31 or over at the date of committal who have not previously been convicted since reaching the age of 17, of an offence punishable by imprisonment;
(3) persons who have recently been in touch with the probation service (e.g. on probation or for after-care).

These recommendations have, in general, been accepted by the courts.

Section 57 of the Criminal Justice Act 1967 empowered the Secretary of State to make rules requiring a court to consider a social enquiry report before passing a particular kind of sentence, such as imprisonment or some other form of detention. This power has not yet been used.

However in 1968 the Home Secretary addressed a circular to all courts, magistrates' included, recommending that they should, as a normal practice, consider a social enquiry report on any offender aged 17 and over before imposing sentences of:

(1) detention in a detention centre;
(2) borstal training;
(3) imprisonment (including a suspended sentence) for two years or less, where the offender had not received a previous sentence of imprisonment (including a suspended sentence) or borstal training.

They should also normally have reports before:

(4) any sentence of imprisonment on a woman;
(5) committing an offender to quarter sessions for sentence;
(6) making a probation order.

The Streatfeild Committee held that the probation officer's report might be relevant to all the objectives of sentencing: it might have a bearing on the view taken of the defendant's culpability, or even upon the probable effect of a sentence on others in the area. But the main stress was laid upon its relevance to the possibility of preventing the offender himself from continuing in crime.

The officer must keep in the forefront of his mind his primary duty of providing, as accurately as possible, the information relevant to this required by the court. Accuracy and objectivity do not demand that he shall include in his report to the court all the facts he may have collected in the course of his interviews with the defendant, his family or others, though these, together with his impressions and the sequence of the interviews, may well form a useful part of his records if social work with the offender or his family continues. Apart from any local considerations about the form of report which a particular court finds helpful, the basic fact has to be borne in mind that the report is written for the use of lay magistrates or of those whose specialist training has been in the field of law rather than psychology or casework. Moreover, it must be remembered that, whilst modern courts may use welfare agencies to achieve their objectives, they are not themselves such agencies, at least in the narrow sense. Their fundamental duty is to protect the public and to watch over the interests of all concerned, administering the law as it exists. The part of the probation officer in this process is to produce a report which will help the court decide upon sentence or treatment.

In considering sentence a court takes account, deliberately or otherwise, of three things. First, the crime, its gravity and the circumstances under which it was committed; second, the needs of the public for whose protection the court exists; and third, the offender who is part of the public and will continue to be a member of society, for good or ill, whatever the sentence. The court's problem is to balance the needs of society, which has been injured and stands in need of protection, against the needs of the offender who yet remains part of society. The material considered by the court in deciding this problem in each case is provided by the prosecution in presenting details of the nature and gravity of the crime; perhaps by the defence in putting forward mitigating features; by the court itself with its knowledge of society's needs and of the provisions of the law; and by the probation officer's report, which shows the offender as a person in his social setting.

Thus the probation officer's report should give to the court a picture of the offender as seen against his history and background, revealing aspects of his personality and attitudes which may not be evident during the earlier hearing of the case.

In interviewing the defendant or his family the probation officer takes a background history in as full detail as possible. He prepares notes of the offender's childhood, adolescence and maturity; the quality of his relations with his family and associates at these stages; how he has reacted to misfortune and stress; his intelligence and educational attainment; how he has coped with employment problems; his medical history and present health; his apparent response to any previous measures of treatment or punishment. Valuable as these details are to the caseworker, to be of help to the court they must be assessed in relation to the offender's present position as a delinquent or criminal. Those aspects of his background which appear to explain or have a bearing (positive or negative) on his present position are therefore mentioned briefly in the report.

From the offender's history, the way he has dealt with situations in life and the quality of his relationships, the probation officer is able to make a tentative assessment of his personality: whether, for example, he is reasonably mature and able to face reality or is emotionally immature and still exhibiting much childish conduct; whether he is over-anxious, aggressive, inhibited or otherwise handicapped. In conveying this to the court it is out of place to use any kind of technical language, nor is it necessary to go into great detail about the relevant symptoms. What the court requires is a word picture in ordinary language of the strengths and weaknesses in the offender's make-up, and the relevance of these to his offence. Here the probation officer may try to assess the quality of the offender's attitudes to society, the values by which he steers his conduct, and the possibility of modifying them. It is perhaps on this part of the report more than any other that the court relies to help it reach its decision regarding sentence, the decision as to whether, amongst other things, the offender requires treatment in the open or training entailing deprivation of liberty, or indeed whether he is so fixed in his attitudes that he appears unlikely to reform at all in view of the present limits in our knowledge and methods of treatment.

The responsibility implied by this fact may well tempt an officer to step occasionally into the role of defending counsel, confining himself to pleading mitigation. This may sometimes be acceptable to the court which is thereby given the opportunity to be magnanimous, but such departures from impartiality are unlikely to lead to the form of treatment most helpful to the offender in the long run, and tend to undermine the reliance which can be placed on probation reports generally. The report is made for the court and not for the defence. In this connection it is worth bearing in mind that s. 43 of the Criminal Justice Act 1948 places on the court, not the probation officer, the responsibility of giving a copy of the officer's report to the defendant or his legal representative, thus emphasizing that the report is prepared for, and belongs to, the court itself.

The Streatfeild Committee held not only that the officer should select the information contained in his report on the basis of its relevance to sentencing—itself no easy task—but that he should, where in a position to do so, give an opinion as to the offender's likely response to probation or some other form of treatment. The Morison Committee agreed that he was qualified to express opinions about the likely response to probation but held that it would be a long time before he would be equipped, either by the experience of the service or by the results of research, to comment upon other measures. Since then the position has somewhat changed. Through extended responsibilities for after-care, prison welfare and parole, the service is learning more about penal institutions, their effects and after-effects.

Another difficulty about giving opinions has been the idea, held by some courts and some probation officers, that this amounts to telling the court what it ought to do, to usurping its function in sentencing. A tendency to refer to opinions as "recommendations" strengthens the impression. It needs to be stressed that the opinion relates only to the expected response of a particular offender to a particular form of treatment. The court has also to consider other aspects of sentencing, such as the gravity of the crime and general deterrence. These may sometimes take priority. If, in such a case, the court and the officer have seen his opinion as a recommendation, he will feel his advice has been rejected. If they have seen it as only one factor in the decision, even though an important one, there need be no sense of this on either side.

The feelings of the defendant and his family about all this have also to be considered. The situation during enquiries is discussed elsewhere from the casework point of view.[1] The defendant must understand that the officer's first duty is to the court; that the report

---

1. See above, pp. 110–113.

resulting from the enquiry will not be confidential—in some cases may even have to be read aloud, though this is very undesirable; and that it will not necessarily be favourable to him. Some officers would maintain that the detachment and objectivity needed for a court enquiry precludes the possibility of any casework relationship at all with the defendant and his family at this stage, and that any desire to help them, even in facing their immediate problems, must be firmly resisted; they would argue that it is wrong to become involved in casework of any kind until the decision of the court is known. Others, whilst agreeing that they are not justified in anticipating the decision of the court, feel that in certain cases the decision to make a probation order is so likely that they are justified in preparing the way for this and treating the enquiry as the first stage in casework diagnosis. The newer responsibilities of the service in prison welfare, in work with prisoners' families and in voluntary after-care extend the scope and relevance of this argument.

In general, adult offenders are entitled to know the full contents of the probation officer's report. If it is given orally they will hear it, if it is a written report (as is usually the case at least in the higher courts) the defendant or his counsel is entitled to see a copy. In a juvenile court the child and parents respectively must be told of the substance of anything in the report relating to their character or conduct that has a bearing on the magistrates' decision. Obviously there is a risk that any adverse comment will inhibit a helpful relationship between officer and offender subsequently. But such a relationship must be based, in the long run, on an attempt to face honestly the behaviour and needs of the offender. And many officers find it helpful to discuss such comments with the offender in advance. In any case, the interests of justice have to be considered. The greater the influence of probation officers' reports upon the decisions of the courts, the more important it is that defendants should have the opportunity to challenge facts and opinions contained in them. Where the defendant is represented this can be done by questioning the probation officer, where he is not, and does not know how to proceed, the clerk of the court may, for example, ask the offender whether or not he agrees with what the officer says.

It is sometimes argued that not merely the defendant but the general public should know what the probation officer has said, and that therefore reports should be read aloud. This probably arises from the sense that, since reports may influence the court's decision as to sentence, they should be heard by all present so that justice can be seen to be done. The Matrimonial Proceedings (Magistrates' Courts) Act 1960 indeed requires that reports on the custody of children should be read aloud. But the Court of Criminal Appeal has condemned as undesirable the practice of insisting that the whole report be read out in criminal cases.[1] Though it may be held that press and public might be less critical of decisions in some cases if they knew the contents of the report it is necessary to set against this the interests of the offender and perhaps especially of his family. To have their personal affairs exposed in this way may, in some circumstances, be worse for them than the conviction and sentence itself. It may gravely prejudice, for example, the interests of wife and children, perhaps the chance of a family remaining together or re-establishing itself amongst its neighbours.

3 SUPERVISION OF PROBATIONERS

Like most if not all social workers the probation officer has to work within the confines of his setting. In his case some of the limits are more strictly defined than those of other social workers, since they are imposed by law. Probation itself is a legal concept, the machinery for turning this concept into fact is created by law, and every person who is a probation officer was made such in accordance with the law. Whilst it is true that the police court missionaries were the forerunners of probation officers, it is equally true that by legalizing the practice the law also changed the setting of the social worker and his relationship with the majority of his clients. The missionaries themselves recognized and appreciated this change.

The court social worker, now named the probation officer, became part of a triangular legal relationship, with the court at the apex of the triangle and the probation officer and probationer occupying respectively the other two corners. The court has a duty to the probationer to advise, assist and befriend him through the agency of the probation officer, and the probationer has a duty to the court to keep the terms of the order imposed to ensure his good conduct and to be under the supervision of the probation

---

1. *R. v. Smith* (1967), 111 Sol. Jo. 850.

officer. It is important to note that the relationship between the three, court, probation officer and probationer, is really a triangle and not a straight line. In the first place every probationer has a right of access not only to the probation officer but to the court direct, since he can apply for a variation or discharge of his order; he is likewise responsible to the court itself for any breach of the order. Secondly, although the court imposes supervisory duties on the probation officer in regard to the probationer, it does not delegate to the officer its most vital power over him. In the event of the probationer committing an apparent breach of his order the officer's function is to report the circumstances to the court or to a magistrate. Any subsequent action is instigated by the court and the probation officer's duty is confined to giving evidence to the court concerning the breach, followed by any general information about the probationer's conduct which may be requested by the court. The court then deals with the probationer direct. The probation officer, for his part, has duties both to the court, in carrying out its instructions and reporting to it as requested, and to the probationer whom he must advise, assist and befriend.

Although these may appear to be merely theoretical considerations, they are important in that the treatment of the probationer, particularly if an attempt is being made to change his attitudes, can be considerably handicapped unless court, probation officer and offender are clear as to their roles. There is often a strong temptation on the part of each of the three participants in the probation situation to attempt to vary the roles of the others to meet changing circumstances. It is essential therefore that at least the court and the probation officer shall have a firm grasp of the legal provisions with which practice must be harmonized, and a few minutes spent by the court itself in explaining to the offender exactly where he stands can be very valuable in helping to ensure that probation starts on a sound footing.

Similarly, in dealing with matrimonial cases, confusion may arise from any lack of appreciation of the proper roles of court or of probation officer. Clients should not expect the officer to adjudicate between them, which is the function of the court, or to supply legal advice for which they need a solicitor. A magistrates' court cannot ask the officer (except with the consent of the parties) to give evidence about the relationship between the spouses as revealed in attempts at conciliation. In a divorce case the officer should give such evidence only if subpoenaed and expressly directed to do so by the judge. But he should not, even if he thinks it in their interest, stand in the way of his clients if they wish to seek legal remedies to which they may be entitled.

Tensions may be set up within the probation officer by the claims on his loyalty, sometimes apparently conflicting, of courts and probationers respectively. Since both have very real claims, this conflict has to be faced and resolved, and an officer's success in resolving it will greatly influence the quality of the help he can give to his probationers. If he identifies himself solely with authority and the demands of society he can make little contact with a probationer whose problem at the outset is his resistance to those demands. On the other hand, if he identifies himself too much with the feelings of the offender he is unable to help the latter to resolve his differences with society. The ideal is that he should appreciate both and act as a bridge between the two.

In effect the probation officer has to be at the same time an authority figure representing the court to the probationer and a caseworker trying to help him to resolve his problems. This corresponds to his dual responsibility to the court for the good conduct (as defined by the terms of the probation order) of his probationer, and to the probationer to be his friend and counsellor in helping him make the best of himself.

Properly used the probation officer's authority can be a powerful factor in casework with delinquents. By definition the delinquent is a person who has defied or ignored the authority of the law. He may have deep personal needs or be so stunted or crippled emotionally as to make it difficult for him to accept or conform to authority, but nevertheless he will be hindered rather than helped if his probation officer, who represents authority, himself rejects authority in his effort to get on close terms with his client. If he does this, the probation officer in effect identifies himself with his client's rejection of authority and only confirms his belief that authority is outside his scheme of things. On the other hand, if the probation officer can show that he has a warm and sympathetic understanding of his probationer's difficulties regarding authority, yet himself demonstrate his respect for it by a firm insistence on the requirements of the probation order being kept and by showing no hesitation in properly reporting any breach, there is a hope that the probationer may learn by experience that, contrary to his expectation, authority can be good.

The question of reporting breaches of probation to the court does, in fact, cause a good deal of anxiety to many officers, and is a special instance of the conflict which can be aroused where casework has to be carried out in a setting concerned with law enforcement.

The law prescribes that a probation officer shall report to the court or to a magistrate any breach of a probation order. The court or magistrate may then issue process to have the probationer brought before the court to answer the allegation that he has broken a requirement of his order, and if the breach is proved may either punish him for the original offence, thus terminating the order, or fine him and allow the order to continue.

The officer may well feel that, though a probationer has broken a requirement of his order, it is not for his welfare that the order should be terminated, or even that he should be brought back before the court, at the particular stage which he has reached in treatment. This applies particularly where a breach occurs early in the course of probation treatment. In some such instances it may be felt that the offender needs a sharp warning to take his probation more seriously, in others it is possible that, having only just begun to respond to treatment, he may be unduly discouraged by an early failure, or the breach of probation may be an almost inevitable expression of the hostility which often has to be worked through in the opening stages of treatment. Again, it may be a temporary lapse in a period of sustained improvement. This kind of situation is less difficult if the probation officer has made clear to the probationer, when serving the order, the exact nature of his own responsibility to the court. If this is done the probationer knows the situation at the outset and is much less likely to have a sense of rejection or betrayal if the officer does later have to report a breach. Any doubts about the legal aspect in a particular case can be resolved by discussion with the clerk to the justices, and it is common practice to report breaches through him.

The probation officer is normally consulted before the decision is taken as to whether legal action is to follow. Thus, though the actual decision rests with the magistrates, the probation officer has the opportunity to put the position from the casework angle and say what he feels will be for the welfare of his client. If the case is, in fact, brought to court and the probationer found guilty of breaking his probation, the officer reports on his general response to treatment. This will, in turn, be taken into account by the magistrates in deciding whether the probationer should now be punished for the original offence, or simply fined for the breach and allowed to continue on probation.

Nevertheless, there are some cases where a conflict of loyalties within the probation officer is almost inevitable if he has regard both to his responsibilities as a caseworker and his duty to the court. This is perhaps particularly so when the probationer has himself divulged the breach under the influence of the casework relationship, or when the officer recognizes that it has been committed in order to test the strength and reliability of that relationship. The probationer may be misguided in feeling rejected if the officer takes him back before the court in such circumstances, and every effort must be made to reassure him as to the continuing concern felt for his well-being, but if he is a person with little or no previous experience of satisfactory relationships he may well be confirmed in his old attitude of distrust and reject, in his turn, not only the officer concerned but anyone else who attempts to help him on similar lines in the future. Yet, knowing all this, the officer knows also the terms on which the community, through the courts, entrusts him with the responsibility of caring for his probationers at all, and he cannot ignore those terms without undermining the basis on which rests the whole possibility of giving such help to those who have broken the law and who may be regarded as a potential danger to the community.

From the above it will be evident that the possibility of effective casework in the context of the courts depends to a considerable extent on the relationship between the probation officer and the court, as well as on the relationship which he has with his clients. Many difficulties can be overcome if the courts have some understanding of the nature of the work done by the modern probation officer and can fully trust his integrity, judgment and professional skill.

It is thus of the greatest importance that the courts, on their side, should have a clear understanding of the function of the probation officer. By their very nature, courts are conservative in outlook, and it is not surprising that only in recent years has the probation officer been fully accepted as a professional social worker performing an essential task in the administration of justice. The early missionaries were men and women of outstanding personality who, by their personal qualities and the maintenance of high ideals, sometimes in the face of opposition, achieved their own status in the courts. It was, however, a status accorded to the person and not yet to the profession. It is perhaps significant that the recognition of the probation officer's professional status came most readily from professional lawyers in judicial office. In some ways advances in case-work training and the professional approach have widened the gap between the probation officer and the lay magistrates. The latter regard their common sense and practical experience as an important part of their equipment in fulfilling their judicial duties, and may therefore tend to accept the idea, so tenaciously held by public opinion as a whole, that common sense alone will solve all human problems including those of delinquency. On the whole, however, this is counterbalanced by increasingly general awareness of the emotional subtleties which underlie human behaviour and by a very real desire, especially on the part of the many younger magistrates now appointed, to understand as much as possible of the factors influencing their work and the merits of the various methods of treatment available to the courts. This attitude of enquiry and interest is greatly welcomed by the service, as it holds out the hope that the best use will be made of the probation officer's special skills.

The probation officer needs to recognize and appreciate the function of the clerk to the justices, both as the court's legal expert and as being responsible to the magistrates for its organization. In respecting the position of the clerk the officer is entitled to expect a reciprocal respect for his own function as the social worker of the court. Much depends on a good relationship between clerk and probation officers both in consultation outside the court and in procedure within it.

The acceptance of social caseworkers as part of the machinery of the courts for dealing with offenders and others has brought not only increased opportunities but also considerable conflicts. The natural desire of the caseworker to promote the welfare of his client, which in the long run may well be for the welfare of the community also, can in the short run clash with the apparent demands of justice and the protection of the public, which are the primary concerns of the courts. Thus, though the presence of probation officers has enlarged the courts' understanding of those with whom they deal and has extended the possibilities of treatment, it has also reflected and focused underlying confusions and conflicts in the community at large about the proper attitude to, and treatment of, those who break the laws of the society in which they live. These will be discussed more fully in the following chapter.

CHAPTER 9

RELATIONS WITH THE COMMUNITY

1 RELATIONS WITH OTHER SOCIAL SERVICES

IN ITS report on after-care, the Advisory Council on the Treatment of Offenders pronounced that one of the essentials for future development was "a greatly increased understanding of the part to be played by members of the community in the rehabilitation of offenders".[1] The Council was thinking of after-care and it was thinking primarily of the contribution of volunteers, but the principle can be applied more widely to the care of offenders generally and to the contribution of official agencies as well as voluntary organizations and individuals. The attitudes of all these and their various dealings with offenders can go far to influence their success or failure. So can the attitudes and actions of the community as a whole, whether seen as the immediate neighbourhood in which an offender lives and works or as the wider climate of public opinion.

The dependence of the probation officer on the co-operation of other official agencies in helping his various clients has been increasing for years as the numbers and scope of such agencies have multiplied. That it is still increasing has been indicated at various points throughout this book. In a simpler society, and dealing with relatively uncomplicated cases, a probation officer might be able to cope largely unaided. Under complex modern conditions, and dealing with more complicated and obdurate problems, he can seldom do so. A considerable part of his information is derived from other agencies, a considerable part of his work with his clients con-

---

1. *The Organisation of After-care*, Report of the Advisory Council on the Treatment of Offenders, H.M.S.O., 1963, para. 71.

sists in helping bridge, from both sides, the gaps between them and community services that can help them.

Some of these are services, national or local, designed to deal with material needs on a general basis. Examples are the local branches of the Department of Health and Social Security and the housing departments of borough, urban and rural district councils. Those responsible for these services are all tied by definite regulations which control their dealings with individuals and the extent to which they can adapt their policy to special individual needs. Moreover, although they may have some discretion, their function is the administration of a public service on an equitable basis, and it is not part of their duty or training to consider a person's total needs and problems in the way a caseworker may do. Here, therefore, the frank recognition of difference in function and outlook is essential to profitable co-operation. The probation officer must bear in mind that community repercussions have to be taken into account if specially favourable treatment is given in any particular case. This does not mean that he will not try to break down his clients' suspicion of officialdom by doing all he can to help them secure fair treatment and a full consideration of all aspects of their claim, but in so doing he must himself be fully aware of the limitations and attitude of the agency to which application is being made so that he does not increase his clients' frustration by misdirecting their hopes and efforts. Similarly, in dealing with the officials themselves, he may sometimes meet an inadequate grasp of the personal issues involved on the clients' side and a certain resentment at the idea that an offender or marriage failure should be the subject of special personal intervention whilst respectable people have to make their own way, often in the face of great difficulties. Yet it is just because the probation officer's clients are often well below average in their ability to cope with the normal stresses of life, have already put themselves at a disadvantage, and are probably distrustful of authority, that it is so frequently necessary to give them special help in putting their case.

In recent years there has been a feeling amongst some social workers, including some probation officers, that they should not stop at helping their clients to benefit from whatever social provision has been made, but should go on actively to point out the gaps and anomalies they encounter in such provisions, and to agitate, or encourage others to agitate, for improvement. Certainly they are well placed by the nature of their work to identify the spots where the shoe pinches most. Housing shortages and poverty amongst low-paid unskilled workers with large families have caused particular concern. It is all very well to say that the task of the social worker is to help his clients adjust to society, but what if society's demands of them are beyond their capacity to meet, its provision inadequate to enable them to adjust? Some may feel that it is no part of the duty of a social worker employed to help people live within the law to agitate for changes in social policy. Yet there is evidence that juvenile delinquency at least is often part of a whole complex of social ills, amongst which bad housing and poverty are included. If it is part of the probation officer's duty to encourage voluntary effort to help offenders it can also be argued that it is part of his duty to point to deficiencies in general social provision which are beyond the ability of voluntary effort alone to make good.

Probation officers have never been identified with the police. Yet obviously the two services deal successively, often simultaneously, with the same people, and it is essential that they should understand and respect each other's functions. It is from the police that probation officers get much of their preliminary information about people appearing before the courts; police and probation reports have to be co-ordinated to avoid overlapping. Principal probation officers have the duty of notifying the police of changes in the addresses of offenders on parole; police are required to notify the service if such offenders come to their adverse notice. The fact that the police are now working more closely with the children's departments of local authorities in considering what to do about very young offenders should give impetus to fuller consideration and definition of the roles of police and social workers respectively and relations with probation officers also may benefit from a clearer mutual understanding.

It is significant that it was the increase in officially recorded delinquency amongst young people that led directly to the appointment of the Seebohm Committee to report on local authority and allied personal social services.[1] It was thought that preventive work with families was of cardinal importance in combating delinquency

---

1. *Report of the Committee on Local Authority and Allied Personal Social Services* (Cmnd. 3703), 1968, p. 17.

and that to achieve this there must be a concentration of local resources. The Committee held that the social services of local authorities had hitherto been neglected in comparison with those concerned
with health and education. To remedy this it advocated strong new
social service departments "to meet the social needs of individuals,
families and communities". These should incorporate the existing
functions of local authority children's and welfare departments, together with elements from the education, health and housing
departments.

Amongst other things, the new departments would take over and
expand social services for the schools. They would absorb the
guidance functions of child guidance clinics, reception centres,
remand homes and approved schools so as to offer "a flexible range
of day and residential diagnostic, consultative and treatment
facilities", providing counselling not only for children and parents
but also in particularly difficult marital problems. They would be
responsible for the whole range of services for children in trouble
envisaged in the White Paper of that name: advice and supervision;
a spectrum of "community homes", absorbing amongst other things
the approved schools; and new "intermediate measures", some of
which have already been tried in conjunction with probation.
Moreover they would concern themselves actively with "community
involvement", the guidance of voluntary workers and making fuller
use of voluntary organizations.

The Seebohm Committee recognized that these developments
would impinge at many points upon the existing responsibilities of
the probation and after-care service. Indeed, the whole trend of its
arguments in favour of a unified social service department in the
local authorities implies that that service should also be included.
Though it was outside the terms of reference of the Committee to
recommend this, it urged that the government should undertake an
immediate examination of the implications of its other recommendations for the probation and after-care service.

Whether a large social service, controlled by a locally elected
council and responsible for caring for all the casualties of society—
the halt, the blind, the mentally ill, the mentally backward, the aged,
the young—over the whole spectrum of social need, could and would
provide an adequate service for those who have rebelled against and
injured society is open to considerable doubt. A few probation

officers have argued that only by unification can the tendency to separate and stigmatize offenders as different from others, rather than to recognize and provide for their common needs, be counteracted. The majority would hold that it is only by retaining a separate service that their special needs can be adequately met.

Whatever is decided about implementing the proposals of the Seebohm Committee, or of the White Paper on Children in Trouble, changes are unlikely to be carried through very quickly. The need to build up trained staff in the local authorities would itself preclude more than a gradual expansion of their responsibilities. Meanwhile, the probation and after-care service has to continue to work at many points in collaboration with various existing departments of the local authorities, and to recognize the growing interest of many of them in aspects of social work, often reflected in the direct employment of social workers.

Of these, the children's departments already work in a field most closely allied to that of the probation and after-care service. They have a statutory responsibility to develop preventive work designed to reduce the need to receive children into care or to bring them before a court. This includes undertaking casework with families in their own homes and supervising individual children on a voluntary basis, as well as providing material and financial assistance in suitable cases.[1] Thus much of the "voluntary" social work formerly done by probation officers now comes within their scope. Under the Children and Young Persons Bill they will take over responsibility for most young offenders. However, both services will continue to be concerned with young people brought before the courts: both may be consulted about their backgrounds, either may be required to carry out the courts' order as to supervision and, in due course, intermediate treatment. Representatives of the probation and after-care service will be drawn into planning the provision of such treatment. In dealing with adult offenders, too, and even more so with matrimonial difficulties, the probation officer may need to work in partnership with the children's department to secure the welfare of children involved. Fortunately the two services have much in common in their outlook and methods, including their recognition of the importance of basic emotional needs and of

---

1. *Report on the Work of the Children's Department*, 1964–1966, H.M.S.O., 1967.

family life and their emphasis on individual understanding and treatment: this normally facilitates communication and co-operation.

The child guidance and adult psychiatric services are also closely linked with probation work in certain cases. In most areas clinics and hospitals are available to provide reports for the courts and to undertake treatment where this is made a requirement of a probation order. Apart from this, however, the help given may not extend much beyond diagnosis, the psychiatrist's opinion often being that a client is of too low intelligence to respond to psychiatric treatment and must therefore be left to the ministrations of the social worker. Similarly, the child guidance clinic may feel that it should concentrate its valuable but limited resources on cases where parents are prepared to co-operate fully in treatment, so that it is just those families in which, parents being initially unco-operative, the need is greatest that are likely to be left to the unaided efforts of the probation officer. Nevertheless, the diagnostic services of both types of clinic can be most valuable, both in probation and matrimonial cases, whether as suggesting new lines of attack on a deeply-rooted problem or as giving some reassurance to an officer faced with a particularly heavy responsibility.

Another local authority service with which the probation officer must maintain contact is education, including the local education department, the headmasters of schools and the school welfare service. He is required to obtain reports from headmasters on those under his supervision, and if these can be discussed directly they can throw a great deal of light upon a youth's personality, problems and potentialities. The school may be a crucial place for the identification and early treatment of delinquency. A main root of mischief in very dull young people may lie in their extreme backwardness and lack of any satisfying achievement at school and their whole outlook can often be greatly improved if arrangements can be made through the headmaster or education authority for their admission to special schools. Truanting, also, is sometimes linked with backwardness and delinquency, and here again co-operation is necessary with the school and school attendance officer. Again, there is the restlessness and boredom that often attend the last year at school, probably helping to make it the peak year for delinquency. In some places teachers are being trained as school counsellors, with special responsibilities for educational, vocational and personal counselling. The Seebohm Committee has emphasized the primary need for all teachers to gain further knowledge of social factors affecting their pupils and for experiments in the appointment of liaison officers in schools to keep in touch with outside social agencies. Certainly not all schools would accept that treatment, as distinct from education, is a proper part of their function. Some think of the offender or the maladjusted as an obstacle to teaching, to be removed elsewhere. Some, on the other hand, are increasingly concerned to help such children within the school.

Youth employment services are usually provided by the local education authority. Their co-operation can be of great importance in placing young people leaving school or changing their jobs. Regular and satisfying work may be an important factor in the rehabilitation of an offender, and efforts devoted to saving a young person from drifting irresponsibly from job to job are well worth while. Both the youth employment officers and welfare officers or employers at work will help in this, especially if they can be given some idea of the special problems in a particular case. With adults, where the offence which results in a probation order may have also resulted in the loss of a job, or where a man or woman has to start afresh after a period of imprisonment, satisfactory work is equally vital and often harder to get, whether it is to be obtained by the client's own approach to the employment exchange or an employer, or by an approach made by the probation officer with the client's consent. In the latter case, the need for frankness on the part of the probation officer in dealing with both parties comes to the fore, and in spite of the obvious difficulties, can often bring a very good response.[1] Where an offender is employed with full knowledge of his past he is free from the continual fear of being found out and dismissed, free too to respond to the special trust which has been placed in him. Normally, however, there is a lot to be said for encouraging a client to find his own job, since he is more likely to remain in it if he has obtained it by his own efforts. In that case it may be felt that it is the responsibility of the employer himself to make adequate enquiries before he engages anybody, though in

---

1. On the question of confidentiality in this connection, see above, p. 97.

discussing the matter with the client beforehand the probation officer may well point out to him the advantages already mentioned of making a clean breast of things from the start, particularly where a position of trust is involved.

In the leisure field, especially when dealing with young people, the probation officer may seek the co-operation of local leaders of religious and social organizations who may be willing to take an individual interest in particular boys or girls and offer them more constructive interests and relationships than they have hitherto found for themselves. But attendance at a club or membership of an organization which is obviously imposed to keep a person out of mischief is unlikely either to last or to help, and few probation officers nowadays would put membership of clubs high amongst methods of treatment. Many modern young people, partly because of a generalized distrust of authority, are unable to relate at all to clubs in the old sense. At the same time experiments are developing in new approaches to the needs of the unattached and delinquent, especially in the city areas where so many offenders live. In rejecting the old-fashioned club as a means of helping the new-fashioned delinquent the probation officer needs to be alive to new attempts at helping him to develop social skills, to use social opportunities, to cope with the problems of using his leisure and relating to his contemporaries.[1]

Ideally, in both probation and matrimonial cases, the churches and chapels should be able to help greatly by providing an accepting and welcoming community within which personal problems can be faced and met on the basis that, being all equally sinners, no one is entitled to pass judgment and all are called to help. Where the people concerned are already members of such a community this support may indeed be forthcoming, and will be of the utmost value. But here again the facts of dissociation and distrust of authority must be recognized. In the great majority of cases the probation officer's clients are outside the circle of church or chapel, the language, outlook and people are strange to them, and the vital personal relationship which could make help from this source acceptable does not exist. Once an offence has been committed or a marriage is breaking down, it is not often possible with profit, and without an

---

1. See, for example, G. W. Goetschius and M. J. Tash, *Working with unattached youth*, 1967.

appearance of patronage, to introduce Sunday school or church merely as a curative agent, though the individual interest and support of a friend or relative who cares for the person concerned for his own sake may go far in imparting or restoring faith. As in the youth service, exceptions may be found in cases where churches or other groups have gone out of their way to try to understand and find new ways of helping particular kinds of offender, perhaps alcoholics or drug addicts or homeless ex-prisoners.

The probation officer may also find valuable help from other voluntary organizations, such as the National Association for the Care and Resettlement of Offenders, Alcoholics Anonymous, the Moral Welfare Association, the Women's Royal Voluntary Service, the Marriage Guidance Council, the Family Service Units and the National Society for the Prevention of Cruelty to Children. The degree and fruitfulness of co-operation with these voluntary bodies varies widely with the qualifications, personalities and outlook of the officials and helpers concerned in particular areas. Sometimes mutual distrust between trained and untrained workers, the professional and the amateur, undermines the possibility of joint consultation and action, though training and qualification are not confined to the official side any more than genuine personal interest and warmth of feeling are the sole prerogatives of those working for voluntary bodies or in a voluntary capacity. In many cases cordial relationships are established, each service appreciating the possibilities as well as the limitations of the others. The growing emphasis throughout both statutory and voluntary social services on improved standards of training and a wider general outlook should further break down barriers and extend the sense of common purpose amongst social workers in the future.

A pilot study made some years ago showed that few probation officers attached much importance to the use of other agencies in the treatment of probationers. Those who did were amongst those who also emphasized the value of home visiting. This was interpreted as reflecting a general orientation amongst these officers, often the older ones, towards "situational treatment", treatment concerned with influencing the roles of the offender in the various social groups of which he is a member "by actively treating him in and through his social environment".[1] It was suggested that the

1. *Probation Research, A Preliminary Report,* H.M.S.O., 1968, pp. 16 and 17.

emphasis in modern casework training upon the individual relationship between probation officer and probationer might have led younger and more highly trained officers to concentrate mainly upon that, to the neglect of the situational treatment which might be more appropriate for some types of offender.

If this is so, there are now solid reasons for thinking again. One of the factors underlying the recommendations of the Seebohm Committee and the plans advanced in the White Paper on Children in Trouble has been the conviction that personal social services are at present insufficiently co-ordinated, that they are unable to look at or deal with people as a whole and as part of their social setting. However these plans and proposals develop, probation officers will have to work in close co-operation for the future with those who control most of the resources for diagnosis and residential care or treatment. Again, the new responsibilities for prison welfare and after-care bring with them the need to reconsider the role of situational treatment. It may suffice to deal with a probationer of relatively normal personality and social background by individual interviews designed to enable him to cope better with his own problems. But it is unlikely to be enough in helping many offenders coming out of penal institutions, and it is certainly not enough for those who are inadequate to sustain an independent existence and are unlikely to change much or quickly. It is partly for these reasons that at this end of the scale the need of voluntary help, of community involvement, has been so much stressed. Here too the probation officer must work with others as well as with the individual.

In considering the rehabilitation of the offender in his local community, account must be taken of the attitude of those with whom he actually lives and works; of the natural, normal relationships which are likely to influence him more deeply and permanently than the impact of any of the social services, though the probation officer and other social workers have their part to play in helping him to form and develop them. It has been said that the probation officer's task is one of reconciliation between the offender and society, but reconciliation requires the good will of both parties, the major responsibility lying with the stronger and more mature. The reception the offender or deserting spouse gets on returning to his home and job or starting in a new one can make all the difference in strengthening or destroying his desire to make a success of things.

At this human, practical level—the level of the landlady who will take in a difficult girl, the employer who will give a chance to a man with a bad record, the church which will stand by a member who has disgraced it, the parents who continue to love, without illusions, a delinquent youth—reconciliation can be achieved or frustrated.

Increasing attention is being devoted to the part played by the local community in influencing the attitudes and standards of families and individuals who grow up and live within it. This is particularly relevant to problems of crime and delinquency from the point of view both of diagnosis and of treatment. Sometimes it may decide whether or not an offender can be dealt with at home at all. In any case it emphasizes the need to understand and help the client in relation to his own social setting, holding in balance the external and internal factors in his problem.

2 CONFLICTING PRINCIPLES?

The attitude of the community and the state towards offenders has changed greatly during the past hundred years. From extremes of rejection and attempted deterrence we have moved to a position where, on the whole, we accept responsibility, if not for the fact that we have offenders amongst us, at least for doing something to help them recover or find their position as responsible members of the community. Many factors have contributed to this change of attitude. First, there has been the full achievement of political liberty and responsibility for the individual citizen combined with a reasonably stable and law-abiding social order and acceptance by the state of a large measure of responsibility for the welfare of all. Secondly, there has been the far-reaching acceptance of our duty towards those amongst us who are handicapped and the desire to give them the opportunity of leading full and normal lives as far as possible in spite of their disabilities. Thirdly, there has been the growth of our knowledge, in economic and social spheres, of the extent to which the individual is dependent on his environment, so that society as a whole is, in some sense, responsible when its members go wrong, and therefore also responsible for helping them to recover. Fourthly, there has been increasing psychological knowledge, which has brought some additional insight into the relevance of mental illness, deficiency and maladjustment to delinquency and its treatment. Alongside all these has been the sheer growth in the number of offenders coming before the courts. There is no way to eliminate them from society. Comparatively few can be kept in confinement for any length of time. It is to the interest of all of us to restore them as quickly and fully as possible to normal life.

We are far from having solved every problem. Acceptance of social responsibility for the offender is not by any means general, and our advances in knowledge have in some ways increased our realization of the difficulty of helping him. Moreover, the very development of the factors which have made advance possible has brought us face to face with new problems.

For example, our emphasis on the right of the individual to justice has been one of the main elements in the development of individual liberty. Now, though in considering the offender as well as the offence, and treatment as well as punishment, we are coming nearer to the ideal of justice in one sense, in another we may be departing from it, since widely differing forms of treatment or punishment may follow the same action. Yet we still hold that it is the illegal action that makes the offender liable for punishment or treatment in the first place. There seems, therefore, to be a conflict between the ideas of liberty and justice on one side and of welfare and treatment on the other, the more difficult to solve because they are principles which also complement and serve each other.

Again, there is the possibility of conflict between our growing recognition of the forces which, to some extent at least, determine the attitudes and behaviour of the individual and our belief in the existence of human responsibility, which again is basic to the idea of justice. The problem of free will is as old as human thought and has recurred in many forms, religious and philosophical. In our day it is raised by some of the deductions which can be made from psychiatric observation. To some it may appear that the offender against the law and, for that matter, the law-abiding citizen, is merely the helpless product of his heredity, environment and emotional development, amenable perhaps to psychological adjustment through new personal relationships, but without any real power of choice and therefore without real responsibility. Perhaps we should rather recognize that increased awareness of the springs of human behaviour, in so far as it gives us a better understanding of ourselves, enlarges rather than diminishes our responsibility, since such awareness can make self-control and self-direction more possible. On this basis we may also recognize that the seriously immature, maladjusted, neurotic or psychotic have, in fact, a diminished responsibility in the measure that their disabilities limit their understanding of reality and their freedom of choice. For such people treatment, far from representing a surrender to their present irresponsibility, is a means to a fuller recognition and acceptance of the realities in themselves and their situation and so to the possibility of more responsible behaviour in the future. Certainly it is no service to them to deny that they have some measure of responsibility, even though responsibility must carry with it the possibility of blame, for to deny their responsibility is to deny their dignity as human beings and indeed to deny the very basis of personal relationships within society.

There may be satisfactory theoretical answers to these problems, or they may be amongst those paradoxes which it is dangerous to try to solve in theoretical terms, but which find their reconciliation in the process of living. In that context probation has perhaps something of value to offer towards their solution, in that it is a method of treatment which is used with the consent of the offender himself and implies acceptance of responsibility by him as well as by the community; a method also which concerns itself less with the rights and wrongs of the past than with the possibilities of growth and change in the future.

From the point of view of the community, the first aim must be to promote the welfare of its members as a whole, and whatever special provision is contemplated for offenders or others must be considered in this context. The issue must not, however, be oversimplified: the welfare of the community has many facets, each claiming consideration in any policy which may be framed. Thus, while in dealing with offenders the first aspect which comes to mind is that of public security and protection, this object must be weighed in the balance with economic and financial considerations and also with spiritual and moral values such as liberty and the intrinsic worth of the individual.

Even the best means of promoting the protection of the community is not as obvious as might appear at first. There was, and still is in many quarters, a tendency to assume that severity of punishment in itself will proportionately deter actual and potential offenders, but this is by no means supported by experience. Again, greater certainty of detection and punishment has been put forward as a more potent deterrent, and that may often be the case, but it does not apply to some of the most difficult and persistent offenders, whose response to punishment is abnormal and who may subconsciously be seeking rejection and punishment for its own sake. Scientific research into basic factors in crime and its treatment is still in its infancy, and pending more definite knowledge any experiments in prevention and treatment must necessarily be tentative. It may be argued that non-punitive or non-institutional methods of dealing with offenders, like discharge, probation or fine, even if they hold the best hope of reforming the majority of actual offenders, have less deterrent effect than punishment on potential offenders. Apart from the fact that, in the present state of our knowledge, this cannot be proved either way, it must be remembered that probation treatment, though not designed as a punishment, places an onerous responsibility on probationers which potential offenders may well wish to avoid. Whilst the need of deterrence and of vindicating the dignity of the law may carry special weight in certain cases, as where there is a betrayal of trust by a professional man or a public servant, the consequences of exposure to such people are so serious in themselves that they alone might be expected to deter others. In any case, the importance to the community of deterrence has to be held in the balance against the value of the individual and his claim to justice: expediency in this direction, if carried too far, can have sinister implications.

From the economic and financial points of view there are still protests about expenditure on improved facilities for the treatment of offenders, and a reluctance to consider increased provision of staff and equipment. These services have to compete not only with the economic demands of more appealing or more obviously productive services, but also with the remains of the idea that the needs of offenders must have only the last claim on community resources. Though there has been much progress in recent years, and the ideal of seeking the reformation of offenders is now largely accepted, there is still an inevitable feeling that where public money is to be spent it should be devoted primarily to promoting the welfare of the law-abiding rather than attempting to help law-breakers. Yet offenders, if they continue as such, are a perpetual drain on the resources of the community, both in the damage they do and the work they fail to do, as well as in the cost of imprisonment or other treatment to which they may be subjected. Moreover, the criminal or anti-social parent may well pass on his attitude to his children, thus perpetuating the problem in the next generation. Any effective treatment may thus well justify its cost from the economic view-point alone. Treatment on probation, where appropriate, has the further recommendation that, instead of removing the offender from the community and making his maintenance, and probably that of his family, an added liability, it encourages him to settle down to work and accept his responsibilities.

It may further need to be emphasized that the contribution of probation towards the eventual recovery of offenders is not limited to those cases where it is classed in the short term as "successful". As indicated earlier, the process of diagnosis where a person is placed under supervision continues during much of the period of treatment and, if failure on the part of the probationer obliges the court to consider some other method, the knowledge of the offender's needs and probable response gathered during the probation period can be a valuable guide in its decision as to the best alternative treatment. Similarly, it is recognized that in some cases treatment must perforce be a long-term process, and recent emphasis has been on the importance of ensuring that, where this is necessary, it should also be a coherent process. In this probation may be seen as a first step in a process of rehabilitation which may also necessarily include a period of institutional treatment and which may well be carried on during after-care.

The ultimate basis, however, of the claim that offenders should be given the chance of constructive personal help, whether in the community or in an institution, is faith in the value of the individual person. Even were the chances of reformation less than they appear, or the financial cost to society higher, it would remain true that the opportunity of recovery rather than punishment alone should be held out to those who offend, and this in the interests not only of the of-fenders themselves but of the standards and values of our society as a whole. In so far as recognition of the intrinsic worth of the indi-vidual is fundamental to our beliefs, progress in acceptance of responsibility even towards those who may appear not merely use-less but hostile to the community will continue.

This is not to advocate a sentimental approach to crime or to offenders.   More than most others, probation officers come into contact not merely with offences but with the immature, defective and distorted attitudes and personalities which lie behind them, and they would be the last to underestimate the difficulties of recovery and reformation. But insistence on the harsh treatment of criminals for its own sake is just as much an emotional and sentimental reaction to crime as an attempt to gloss over offences or remove all responsibility from offenders.   The criterion is not whether a particular approach is severe or gentle but whether it does in fact help towards recovery and, if not, just where and why it fails. It is from this point of view that the probation and after-care service faces its responsibilities to the courts, the penal institutions, the community and those placed in its charge and continually seeks to examine, revise and improve its methods of working.

In all this, the ambivalent attitude of the community has still to be taken into account. The acceptance of probation, prison welfare and after-care as public services is striking evidence of the extent to which the idea of help rather than punishment alone is now recognized as a means towards restoration. But this acceptance is still tempered by the suspicions and reservations already indicated, based as they are on old conceptions of the nature of responsibility, justice and retribution, as well as by that desire for a scapegoat which in time of war forces a nation to regard the enemy as wholly evil and itself as wholly right.

The probation and after-care service, bound up as it is with the work of the courts, whose primary function is the protection of society, is necessarily kept aware of this dilemma. It is implied in the probation order itself which, whilst giving the chance of help instead of punishment, holds in reserve the right to punish if the offender breaks the conditions laid down. It is implicit in parole. Society accepts a certain risk and responsibility in allowing the offender to go free, but probation officer and offender also accept a risk and responsibility, and in the event of failure it is the offender who is likely to suffer most.

But, necessary as the conceptions of responsibility and justice may be both to the individual and to the organization and welfare of the community, their significance needs constant re-examination in the light of advancing knowledge. It may be felt that we have advanced far beyond our ancestors' reliance on divine intervention to relieve them of the burden of deciding guilt or innocence, or their disregard of intent in assessing responsibility, or their set scales of retribution without reference to circumstances. Yet in recent years increasing knowledge has undermined many of our assumptions about the rational nature of behaviour, and we are being led to realize, once again, that we are very ignorant of the true nature and degree of human responsibility itself, very limited in our ability to assess, amidst all the complex contributory factors, the individual responsibility in any particular case. Lacking any assurance of this, we lack also a really firm foundation for justice or retribution, other than that of the apparent interests of the community. So far as condemnation of the individual himself is concerned we are brought back at last to the saying of Christ: "Judge not".

The special emphasis of the probation and after-care service from the first has been on reformation through a relationship of acceptance and help. The probation officer's approach, whether predominantly religious or psychological or both, will tend to make him look beyond the surface appearance and the instinctive emotional response to an offence, stressing understanding rather than condemnation as the road to recovery. His training and experience will take him past the merely commonsense viewpoint to consider the significance of a multiplicity of internal and external factors in any individual case and to accept with patience the slow task of encouraging the growth or recovery of an immature or distorted personality.

How far the service can go in following out this understanding in treatment depends largely on the support it receives from the community. In the past its progress has been made possible by the trust and esteem of the courts and, as it has become better known, of the wider community. As it ventures further into work with more difficult offenders, more obdurate problems, it will need this trust and co-operation even more.

3   COMMUNITY INVOLVEMENT

Not only in probation but in many fields of social work the widening conception of social service has brought professionals up against the need to think again about the relationship of the social services, both in the provision of institutional care and in casework outside, with the community at large.

The main pattern in the nineteenth century was the provision of institutions in which the unfortunate could be given refuge from a society in which they could not survive unaided; or, alternatively, of institutions to which society could consign those it could not absorb or tolerate. During the twentieth century, and especially since the second world war, this has increasingly been seen as inadequate. The caseworker has developed largely as an expression of a concern to help people to survive without such removal. He has been held to act for the community in providing support and guidance. In so far as he has seemed to succeed in care and in control he has been seen as an alternative to the institution.

Increasing pressure upon institutions, their increasing expense, increasing difficulty of finding staff, increasing appreciation of their limitations and their damaging aspects, have combined with growing prestige of social work in the community to produce in many sectors a further move to avoid admissions and speed up discharges as much as possible.

This has inevitably added to the responsibilities not only of social workers in the open but of the other members of the community called upon to live with the disabled, the difficult, the anti-social in their midst. Deprived children placed in foster-homes, the mentally ill returning to their families, the probationer or ex-prisoner in lodgings, can all impose considerable strain upon those with whom they live and upon the local communities in which their homes are set. Unless they can not merely be tolerated but accepted and actively helped, their own state may become worse than ever whilst a disillusioned community turns back to the barren expedient of isolation.

For some this may be essential on medical or social grounds: to insist that they be forced to live in the open is merely to invite breakdown for them and a rejection on the part of others that may well extend far beyond the individuals who have aroused it. It is easy for example to identify all offenders with a few who are a real menace to others or to themselves. There is undoubtedly need to distinguish between those who can be helped in the open and those who cannot. And there is a very great need to consider what provision can be made for the latter. Hostels of various kinds and some form of special community have been suggested. These too depend in the last resort, however, on a measure of active good will and tolerance from the community at large.

The question remains whether caseworkers can any longer hope to meet the needs of the many clients who require neither an institution nor a specially protected environment, but who cannot or will not cope unaided with the demands of social life. The break-up of stable communities, the scattering of family groups, have removed the kinds of support and control that many such people could rely upon in the past. The sheer numbers involved are beyond the power of professional social workers to deal with adequately. And in any case, it is realized more and more that it is not skilled individual help alone that is needed but enduring community support.

Hence thought is turning to a third way of attacking the problem of social failure. The community can no longer hope to deal with all its misfits by putting them in institutions, but nor can it hope to hand them over to social workers and forget them. It must itself learn to accept a measure of responsibility for them. The social worker has, in the nature of things, always had to depend upon certain members of the public to join in the rehabilitation of the disabled or the offender. The family, the landlady, the employer, have played a key role in many a recovery. They have often done so, however, in face of much opposition from neighbours or from fellow-tenants and employees, opposition that is frequently most virulent during the difficult early stages. What applies to individuals has also applied to the establishment of hostels, whether for the mentally ill, the maladjusted child, or the former criminal. The social worker may thus have the dual task of supporting and encouraging those prepared to give active help and of trying to influence the local community towards acceptance and co-operation. In casework there has been a movement from doing things for the client to doing things with him or encouraging him to do them for himself. Perhaps the time is coming for a similar movement in relations with the community, a movement away from a situation in which the social worker (or the institution) takes charge of misfits on behalf of society towards a situation in which he helps society to take charge of them for itself.

All this may prove too idealistic. There are many difficulties. As has been observed in discussing voluntary work, it is inviting disillusion to overrate the willingness of the public to consume its own smoke or absorb its own misfits. There are risks in trying to go too fast in obliging it to do so: a serious offence by a prisoner on parole or by a child absconding from a school or home can jeopardize the chances of acceptance of many other offenders and institutions. There are risks even in trying to go too fast in arousing good will and the desire to help: if volunteers find themselves with inadequate support or not enough to do they may not only become disillusioned but spread their disillusionment to others. There are fears that volunteers may become a second-class casework service, seen as an alternative to adequate professional staff. There are doubts as to who should be responsible for arousing and directing community interest: is this a proper task for probation officers, or indeed for caseworkers, or should it be left to others? If it is for probation officers to tackle do they not require additional training?

The Seebohm Committee suggested that, in broad terms, community development should be one of the duties of local authority social service departments.[1] But in the specific matters of finding, training and guiding volunteers who can help prisoners, and of cooperating with those willing to establish and run hostels for them, the probation and after-care service is already involved. In so far as it can succeed in these more limited objectives it will be helping to modify feelings about offenders by virtue of the very fact that some members of the community will become interested in them as individuals. In the future as in the past, the best contribution of the service may lie in concentrating upon the needs of individual offenders and their families, influencing public opinion, as it has already influenced the courts, and even the penal institutions, by its own persistent emphasis upon the offender as a person, a person who is still part of the community even if he offends against it.

---

1. *Report of the Committee on Local Authority and Allied Personal Social Services* (Cmnd. 3703), 1968, pp. 147–154.

CHAPTER 10

ADMINISTRATION

1 THE ADMINISTRATORS

PROBATION is a local service, but not a local authority one. It is the responsibility of probation and after-care committees, consisting mainly of magistrates, with principal probation officers as advisers and administrators. The central authority is the Home Office through its Probation and After-Care Division.

The probation and after-care committee appointed for each area in England and Wales is composed of justices from the constituent petty sessional divisions, together with members of the public who are not justices but who are co-opted for their knowledge or experience, especially in matters affecting the comparatively new responsibilities of the committees in after-care of prisoners and others. The duties of committees are defined in the Fifth Schedule of the Criminal Justice Act 1948 and the Probation Rules. They are responsible for the adequate staffing of the probation and after-care services in their areas, for paying probation officers and other staff and providing them with adequate accommodation and equipment, and for making various payments connected with the treatment of offenders on probation or subject to after-care. They assign officers to courts and arrange for secondment of those going into prison welfare posts. They are also responsible for the organization of after-care, including the task of involving members of the public in the rehabilitation of offenders.

In the last few years, Home Office control over the details of expenditure by probation and after-care committees has been relaxed. Also the duty of inspecting the work of new entrants to the service at the end of their first year and deciding whether they are suitable for confirmation as probation officers has been handed over from the Home Office to the committees, except in cases where an officer was appointed without preliminary training.

The growing responsibilities and broadening scope of the committees have been paralleled by their drawing together in the Central Council of Probation and After-Care Committees, which discusses and makes recommendations on common problems, and which gathers the views of committees on the development of the service and makes them known.

To enable them to carry on their work, committees draw their funds from the local authorities, which in turn claim 50 per cent from the Treasury, less $1\frac{1}{2}$ per cent contribution towards the cost of probation training. On a number of matters, such as the provision of clerical assistance, accommodation and equipment, probation and after-care committees are required to reach agreement with the local authority before incurring expenditure. Committees have, however, complete freedom in the provision of professional staff, the cost of which is the major item in their budgets.

Since the great majority of committee members are themselves magistrates and concerned with problems facing the courts, they have first-hand knowledge of many of the difficulties facing the service which they administer. Furthermore, since they are drawn from all the petty sessional divisions in the area, there should be available within the committee informed opinion on problems peculiar to any particular district. The value of these close ties was particularly stressed by the Morison Committee. The probation and after-care committee will invariably have the clerk of the peace in a combined area, or the clerk of the justices in a single area, as their secretary and so will be well advised on the relevant law and procedure.

There are also, however, links with the local authority. Some magistrates are likely to be members of both bodies. Moreover, except in London and one or two other places, the clerk of the peace and secretary of the probation and after-care committee in a county is also clerk of the county council. This provides an important link with the local authorities who make the largest contribution to the committees' funds. In addition, the treasurer of the probation and after-care committee is always the treasurer of one of the contributing local authorities.

Probation is a professional service and the committee obviously cannot operate properly without professional advice from within the service itself. In some other social services it has been appreciated from the beginning that professional leadership and advice are essential, and appropriate provision has been made at the outset, but in probation the function of organization has been added slowly to an existing service. Lack of earlier realization of the need for it has had an influence in the uneven development of the service in different areas, though that may be regarded as to some extent inevitable in bodies which have been built up gradually to meet local needs. The lack may also to some extent explain why the high esteem in which magistrates hold the probation officer was slow to translate itself into modern equipment, good working conditions and up-to-date facilities.

Now the practice of appointing principal probation officers is well established and there are over seventy of them in England and Wales. They, too, have come together for consultation, in the Conference of Principal Probation Officers. From being an informal organization for the exchange of views this has developed into a more formal body with regular lines of communication between principals themselves and between the conferences and the Home Office. There are also links with the Central Council of Probation Committees.

Full meetings of the conference are held three or four times each year and a three-day residential meeting is arranged each September. Members of the administration and inspectorate of the Probation and After-Care Department of the Home Office attend the residential meeting, the programme and organization of which is arranged by the Department every third year. In addition, principal officers meet in regional groups arranged to provide ease of access for occasional day meetings. The scope of the principal probation officers' conference has increased over the years as the range of responsibilities carried by principals has widened and the concept of leadership in an expanding modern social service has been understood and developed, a process in which the conference has played an essential part.

In some areas the principal probation officer is assisted by a deputy or one or more assistant principals. There are also senior probation officers, part of whose duty is the administration of local offices but whose primary task is increasingly seen as casework supervision and consultation. Sometimes a senior has some specialized responsibility over a wider area, such as training or the organization of after-care.

Finally, there are the responsibilities of the Home Office, through its Probation and After-Care Department. It has been seen that these date back even further than the probation committees. The Departmental Committees of 1936 and 1962 both emphasized that the advantages of local control should be balanced by "a strong and energetic central authority" to foster the contribution of the service to such national concerns as the prevention of crime and the well-being of the community as a whole. The Advisory Council for Probation and After-Care and its two Committees concerned with Recruitment and Training and with After-Care and Parole, are designed to help in this. They are drawn from a wide range of people with different kinds of interest in the service: legal, academic, medical, social. The chairman is a university Vice-Chancellor, formerly a member of the Morison Committee. The Council is concerned both with the administration and staffing of the service and its development. It is represented on the Advisory Council on the Penal System, which is responsible for considering issues relating to the system as a whole, and on the Advisory Council on Child Care, and it maintains contact with the Council for Training in Social Work.

The primary responsibilities of the Home Office lie in inspection and training. It also has to approve major expenditure on buildings, and to approve establishment as well as appointments of senior staff. The Morison Committee suggested, in addition, that it could better meet its duty to reflect the legitimate national interest in the service, to safeguard its efficiency and to justify the substantial Exchequer grant, if it had the power to control the establishment of probation officers in each area. This would mean that the scarce supply of newly-trained officers could be directed to the most needy areas. It was strongly opposed by many people on the ground that it would hamper more progressive authorities in their attempts to improve or maintain their standards. Behind this lies one of the issues that will have to be decided in the future.

2 THE FUTURE

The decision, over forty years ago, that the probation service should continue to be an essentially local one, controlled by a body of local magistrates, was of great importance. It emphasized on one hand its dependence upon the local community, on the other its link with the courts. So far these principles have proved strong enough to resist suggestions that the service should become either a "national" one, directly controlled by a central government department or some central judicial authority, or a local government service similar to the education or children's department of a local authority.

It is argued that the service should remain local because of the vital importance of maintaining interest and responsibility for work which depends so much upon the understanding and co-operation of the local community. It is also pointed out that local needs and resources differ and that local responsibility allows initiative, experiment and advances more varied and more venturesome than would be possible for a centralized body. The obverse, of course, is the fact that if some areas can forge ahead others can lag badly behind: perhaps through lack of interest, but perhaps through financial stringency and sheer pressure of adverse factors. Thus it is unfortunately often the areas with most crime that have the fewest trained probation officers, the lowest proportionate use of pre-sentence enquiries and probation, the largest caseloads, the lowest success rates.[1] In these areas some of the largest prisons are situated, and to them return a high proportion of those released from prison. One remedy might be special subsidies for the work of the service in such areas, or "environmental allowances" for officers employed in them, like those suggested for education in similar conditions. But it is argued by some that the only really effective way to attain the uniformly high level proper to a service of the courts would be a change to a wholly centralized service, which could distribute resources or staff where they seemed to be most needed on a national basis.

On the other hand some of the most recent moves seem to have been in the opposite direction. The duties of confirming new officers and approving much routine expenditure have been transferred from Home Office to probation and after-care committees. And in the general re-organization of after-care not only have the new responsibilities for voluntary after-care been established on a

---

1. See on this *Trends and Regional Comparisons in Probation*, Home Office Research Unit Report, H.M.S.O., 1966.

local basis, but in statutory after-care the Central After-Care Association has been disbanded, leaving local probation and after-care committees directly responsible. Moreover, local probation services, rather than a national body, have been given the task of providing welfare officers for the prisons.

No less important than the emphasis upon local responsibility, however, has been the emphasis upon the link between the service, the magistrates and the courts. It is this that has produced the most strenuous resistance to suggestions that probation officers should be employed directly by the local authorities or become part of any new comprehensive social service department set up within them. It is asserted that the probation and after-care service, as part of the administration of justice, must be independent of local politics, and indeed of control by the executive: it must share the degree of "judicial independence" necessary to preserve the liberty of the subject, and there must never be any suspicion that, in the opinions it offers the courts or the way it deals with offenders, it is subject to political pressures.

Alongside this is the feeling that magistrates and probation officers are engaged in a common task, and that magistrates, more than any local authority committee, understand the needs of offenders and the work of officers. It is feared, moreover, that a local authority committee charged with a whole range of responsibilities for meeting the social needs of children, the aged, the handicapped, would feel unable to give much priority to those who had offended against society. Magistrates, who are directly involved in the duty of controlling and perhaps punishing them, have a direct interest in seeing that everything possible is done also to rehabilitate them.

A suggestion has been made that, even if the administration of the service passed to some other body, the link between magistrates and probation officers could be maintained at the personal level through a modified version of the present case committees. They might set the pace in the courts' use of the probation officers and keep officers aware of the magistrates' expectations. This would not, however, give them the direct say in the key areas of staffing and equipment which is at present the prerogative of the probation and after-care committees.

Yet the position is becoming uneasy. The cost of the probation

and after-care service is met half by the central government, half
by the local authorities. As the latter expand their own social
services, and especially if they unite them in single, powerful and
expensive departments, they may increasingly question the need for
a separate local body with statutory responsibilities for social work.
The expanding duties of the probation and after-care service, the
build-up of its numbers, new training responsibilities, new involvement with voluntary effort in the community, must all add to its
costs. And some have argued that a separate social service for
offenders merely perpetuates the idea that they are quite different
from other people instead of emphasizing the fact that they share
common needs with many others.

   That they share common needs has never been denied and where
other services provide for such needs probation officers are expected
to encourage their clients to make use of them. Yet they have also
special needs in virtue of the fact that most of them are offenders
and have been adjudged such by the courts. Those in penal institutions or under statutory supervision, whether on probation or
under statutory after-care, are, besides, in a special relationship to
the rest of the community in that their liberty has been curtailed
and a deliberate effort is being made to prevent them from committing further offences against it.

   A third trend in the administration of the probation and after-
care service may be traced in recent moves towards regional
responsibility, a compromise between the local and the national,
a bringing together of those from various spheres specifically concerned with the treatment of offenders. In 1967 eight Regional
Group Consultative Committees were formed to consider the need
for and distribution of after-care hostels in their areas. They comprise representatives of probation and after-care committees and
principal probation officers, together with members of the prison
service, the National Association for the Care and Rehabilitation
of Offenders and the Probation Department of the Home Office.
Another straw in the same wind may be the setting up of four
Regional Planning Committees, covering amongst them the whole
of England and Wales, now working with four specially appointed
Regional Training Officers. In addition there have been the
regional meetings of principal probation officers already mentioned
and *ad hoc* meetings between principal probation officers and prison

governors on a regional basis to discuss prison welfare and after-care. It is at a regional level, too, that the service is likely to have a say in any local authority plans for "intermediate treatment" facilities for children and young people in trouble in the future. Yet other possibilities that have been suggested are experiments linked with research which might be carried out within regions, and appointment of psychiatrists or others on a consultative basis to help the service in its task of reporting to the courts. It has been felt, too, that more intimate and continuous contacts could be maintained with Home Office inspectors on a regional rather than a national basis.[1] Steps towards this can be seen in plans to strengthen the Home Office inspectorate in Manchester and in the possibility of a similar inspectorate in Birmingham.

Regionalization is now being discussed in many spheres: it is accepted as the policy for penal institutions; it has been partially implemented in the regional crime squads alongside the older local police forces; it has been suggested as a means of bringing together the branches of the National Health Service. It can offer the advantages of scale, logic and economy in the distribution of resources, whilst retaining some element of local control. On the other hand some fear that, if regional units took over all administrative and planning functions, they would be too large and remote to retain local interest and enthusiasm. Many probation officers, also, would resist the suggestion of identification, as distinct from co-operation, with penal institutions: the prospect of a continued link with the courts would be more welcome.

3 PRESENT TASKS

The ultimate success of probation depends upon the officer in the field who has personal contact with the client. This is true not only of probation, but of all services in which human contact and relationships are vitally concerned—the teacher in the school, the doctor in the hospital, the visiting officer in the Children's Department, all have a vital personal responsibility though it may be sponsored by the headmaster, the medical superintendent or the children's officer.

The first problem facing the administrator in the probation field

1. See *The Place of the Probation and After-Care Service in Judicial Administration*, Principal Probation Officers' Conference, 1968.

is therefore that of staff. What is the correct staff quota? What is a reasonable work-load? These questions are particularly pertinent at the present day, as duties accumulate and experiments multiply. But they are still not adequately answered. They are questions which may be evaded by the affirmation that there is no single formula by which they can be answered. This is the truth, but not the whole truth. There are many variable factors such as type of area, court commitments, number and nature of penal institutions, transport facilities, allied social work, office organization. Last, but by no means least, there is the individual officer concerned, a factor involving complex considerations of temperament, health, speed of operation, training, skill and calibre. Training is advancing; knowledge of the techniques of social casework by which the probation officer works is constantly widening; there are experiments in new techniques like social groupwork; there are new requirements in the involvement of the community; the level at which officers can work is constantly improving and the professional standards of the service have risen. The implications in regard to time are obvious.

In fact, it seems doubtful whether provisions in the practical field have kept pace with the training schemes and in many cases students trained to work at a skilled level find that the pressure of everyday tasks precludes the use of their skills to full advantage. There seems little doubt that work-loads have remained too high and it must be a first consideration in any area to assess in relation to all relevant factors a correct staff establishment and then to fill it with appropriately trained and suitable people.

Probation and after-care, however, is not the only expanding service. Demand for the kind of people and the kind of preparation needed for probation officers is likely to become even keener as the drive to improve local authority services expands. As more and more needs are recognized it becomes increasingly necessary to use these scarce resources economically. In a few areas experiments are being made in using ancillary officers to carry out the more routine or administrative duties of probation officers. In some areas there may be clerical staff already carrying considerable responsibility for receiving callers when the officers are absent at court or visiting. A few find in this kind of experience a stepping-stone to training as probation officers. Obviously it is necessary to guard against dilution of standards. It is necessary also to bear in mind that the performance of apparently routine duties and practical chores can sometimes have great significance in the relationship between probation officer and client. But there is room for imaginative consideration of what can properly be delegated, both by officers in the field and by seniors and principals, to other staff. A double benefit may be found: in enabling officers to devote more time and energy to skilled tasks, and in attracting and retaining staff of good quality to work with them.

It is also manifestly poor economy and poor organization to have a professional staff poorly equipped.[1] It must obviously be a minimum requirement for every probation officer to have to himself a reasonable room—simply but pleasantly furnished—and to be supported by adequate clerical assistance and good organization. Care must be taken that the public are well received and provided with waiting accommodation which will relieve rather than accentuate the tension and despondency which they so often feel. Even where these conditions are to be found in main offices, they are often wanting in subsidiary interviewing rooms. In large areas it is necessary to staff such rooms for a limited time each week in order to interview clients living a long way from the main office, and it should be remembered that a gloomy schoolroom or a dingy church hall are not the best settings in which to cope with an anxious person's problems.

The provision of these material necessities may sometimes be difficult, particularly in city areas where competition for accommodation and for the services of skilled secretarial staff is particularly acute. The problem can be even more difficult in overcrowded prisons, where responsibility for providing office and interviewing rooms, and for clerical assistance, lies with the prison authorities, though responsibility for supervision of the welfare officer's professional work lies with the principal probation officer.

Nevertheless, the provision of material resources is the easiest part of administration: personal issues present much more difficult problems. Those in charge must know their staff very well in their strengths and their weaknesses, they must try to be aware of personal

---

1. See on this the United Nations publication (ST/TAA/SER/C11) *European Seminar on Probation.*

difficulties, they must ensure adequate leave and leisure time and be genuinely concerned all the time for well-being and welfare.

A clear definition and acceptance of the roles of all members of the service is essential at this stage in its development. This is a matter which seems to have occasioned not a little difficulty, partly because of the gradual and experimental way in which the various grades have developed and of some doubt and reluctance, both in leaders and led, in accepting the proper tasks of leadership. Some have even seen it as a threat to the professional integrity and responsibility of the individual officer. Yet the true function of leadership is to create the conditions in which the caseworker can exploit to the full his personal skill: rather than presenting a threat it should offer understanding and support.

The probation officer, fully occupied in the practice of his profession, should be supported by the senior officer, with his responsibility for local organization and the all-important task of casework consultation. The focus of administration is in the principal officer, who holds the general responsibility for ensuring that the work is adequately covered as part of his duties as executive officer to the probation and after-care committee. Good organization has little or no place for dictatorial methods, but issues must be faced realistically. The principal probation officer, in accepting his position, must accept the consequences of leadership. In discharging his duty he must make himself aware of what is going on, and he must be prepared to take decisions and accept responsibility for them. He must not shrink from forthright action and must be prepared to make his views clear when circumstances demand it.

The decision-taking function of the principal officer is seen very clearly in his responsibility to decide at what points and in what circumstances to recommend that a person released from prison, borstal or detention centre to the care of a probation officer who is a member of his staff should be recalled. This kind of provision goes a long way to ensure that recommendations for recall are made only after mature and disinterested consideration, and that there is evenness of treatment, at least throughout each area.

The subject of casework supervision is discussed elsewhere in relation to staff development, so comment here is limited to considering how it may be woven into the pattern of the service from the administrative point of view. As already stated, supervision in no way detracts from the personal responsibility of the officer, but on the contrary should help him to exercise this more fully. It should help him also to come to terms with the fact that, though he has responsibility for his own cases, his complete freedom of action is to some extent modified because he operates in a setting where the law makes certain inescapable demands upon both the client and the caseworker. The advent of parole has further emphasized this, and it is significant that it has been linked with explicit instructions as to reporting on the offender to senior and principal officers.

Supervisory duties in the wide sense include four main functions: those of administration, teaching, consultation and evaluation.

The administrative function involves the general oversight of the work; through this function the supervisor helps the officer to be aware of the kind of responsibility he has assumed in accepting the position of probation officer at all. The supervisor, with the fund of knowledge gathered from contact with other colleagues and with his understanding of the capabilities of each officer, is able to help the individual so to plan his work that the best possible use is made of available time. He is also able to observe areas of special pressure and should make adjustments so that they are spread as widely as possible and not concentrated upon one officer.

The teaching function includes the direct transmission of knowledge and information, the aim being to reduce anxiety by readiness to give information quickly when it is required and, on a more long-term basis, to help officers keep in touch with new developments and experiments and to act as a clearing-house for ideas.

In the role of consultant the supervisor helps his colleague to draw upon the knowledge which he already possesses, stimulates him to think for himself about the available data and make full use of it in interpreting the situation, to evolve a treatment plan and to envisage ways of putting the plan into effect. An important aspect of consultation is to help the officer to be aware of his own feelings, if and when they are interfering with any part of his work. It is no part of the supervisor's function to treat the officer, but he does give help in handling emotional reactions if they affect the officer's attitude towards a client.

Finally, since professional status implies the constant effort to develop skill and understanding, part of the supervisor's task is to help in the evaluation of the standard which the officer is achieving.

The duty of supervision rests largely with the senior probation officer. This is indeed the senior's primary function and full acceptance of the responsibility involved requires that his own fieldwork responsibilities should be substantially reduced, although it is desirable that he should retain some first-hand care of cases. The Morison Committee were unwilling to accept any single formula for assessing the proportion of senior posts but present trends suggest that the optimum size of a team of officers supervised by one senior is about five.

Even in the smaller areas the principal probation officer, with his wider general responsibility and his paramount need to maintain close contact with all the staff in his area, is ill-advised to limit himself by personal involvement in continuing casework, though some casework supervision is a valuable method both of keeping in touch with the work itself and of maintaining direct contact with officers. Given this personal contact he can not only interpret the policy of the committee to the staff, but also interpret the ideas of the staff to the committee. It is a sterile organization which does not provide for a two-way flow of ideals and ideas from the newest recruit to the highest authority and back. The personal relationship between the principal probation officer and all members of his staff, made possible in most areas by the comparative smallness of the administrative unit, can be of great value in promoting the development of the local service. The principal has also much to contribute in other ways: staff meetings, discussion groups, visits, refresher courses and staff libraries all require careful planning if the maximum benefit is to be derived from them and officers are to be given real help in meeting the mental and emotional demands of their work.

Provision for in-service training must be made in the general plan for the service in an area and not left as something to be tacked on to the already crowded programmes of overworked officers. Furthermore, although it is manifestly the duty of the principal probation officer to sponsor these activities and to ensure that they are provided for in the local organization, this does not mean that he should himself be the centre of all activities. His staff will include people with a diversity of interests and experience, of varying skills and strengths, some rich in practical knowledge, others with new con-

cepts and ideas brought from the centres of training; good planning
entails making use of them all.

This subject cannot be left without reference to the part the service
has to play in the training of students. In this sphere, though probation and after-care committees have no statutory responsibility,
they have a very strong moral obligation, for obviously the training
authority must look to the service for help in preparing its own future
practitioners. This is a matter for the closest co-operation between
the Training Section of the Probation and After-Care Department
at the Home Office and the local probation services, since a considerable part of probation students' training consists of work in
the field under the supervision of experienced officers. Local
organization needs to be geared to meet its responsibilities in that
direction. The pattern of training has changed rapidly, emphasis
shifting from prolonged visits of observation where the student
watched the officer at work and learned what he could, to supervised work undertaken by the student himself. This has become
possible as the calibre of officers available as tutors has improved,
but practical training is not a matter for the tutor officer alone.
Training involves the whole team. It is necessary to think out quite
clearly, in co-operation with the training authority, what facilities
can be offered locally and in what way the area can make the best
contribution. Careful preparation must follow, in which all must
be included; it should be remembered throughout that this is something the department as a whole is undertaking and not the rather
precious concern of one or two people. Ideally, students should have
properly equipped rooms of their own and this may be possible in
some larger offices. At the least they need to be properly integrated
into the office system if they are to make the maximum use of their
training and for this to be done careful advance planning is necessary.

Consideration must also be given to the part played by the Home
Office in the general organization of the service. The Department
has close links with the appointment of staff and the work actually
done. Committees are required to send notice of every appointment
of professional probation staff to the Secretary of State. Most of
those who enter the service after a course of training will have been
selected for that purpose through the Home Office procedure.
Those who enter without preliminary training are subject to inspec-

tion and confirmation by the Home Office, though it is usual to delay this for a year, and senior appointments also require Home Office approval. Inspection is secured by the stipulation that probation officers shall keep case records of all their statutory duties in a form approved by the Secretary of State, and that these records shall be open to inspection by or on behalf of the Secretary of State.

From time to time a full inspection of a probation area is undertaken, when the work of the whole department comes under careful scrutiny. During these visits by inspectors discussion with appropriate persons on wider issues is possible and the inspectors have always made themselves available for discussion on matters of common concern. The main task of probation inspectors is to enable the Secretary of State to satisfy himself that reasonable standards of efficiency are being maintained, in itself an important and constructive function. Indeed, the advance of the service over the years has owed much to the work of inspectors with committees as well as with officers themselves. Improved working conditions in the material sense should allow more time for the consideration and encouragement of schemes to promote better work and develop new ideas. But though it is stressed that inspectors' visits are concerned with the dissemination of ideas and constructive suggestions as well as with scrutiny, and though special efforts have been made to bring understanding and stimulus to new fields like prison welfare, in practice the number of inspectors available rarely allows of visits made expressly for the purpose of general liaison. The majority of visits are, therefore, concerned also with inspection, and this can engender a tension unfavourable to the reception and discussion of new ideas.

Here again the idea of regionalization may have something to contribute. With the exception of a regional office in Manchester serving the north-west, the inspectorate is centralized in London. This, combined with a chronic shortage of inspectors over many years, inhibits close partnership between the Home Office and the service in the field. Even principal probation officers lack the frequent formal and informal meetings with inspectors necessary to develop a good working relationship. To the field officer the inspector is a remote figure, whose impact on the service as he knows it is imperceptible. When the inspectorate is brought up to strength, there is a strong case for dispersing inspectors into regional offices, more accessible to surrounding probation areas and able to partici- pate more fully in their activities. This would tie up with the moves already made towards regional consultation and co-operation.

4   THE GRASS-ROOTS

Coming right down to the grass-roots, for all that may be done to guide, support or inspire him, much still depends on the ability of each individual officer to organize his own work, to stand the tension between the ideal and the possible, and to determine priorities.

One of the attractive features of probation work is the degree of discretion and responsibility allowed to the individual officer not only in his casework but in organizing his duties to suit his own personality and methods. The proportion and relative pressure of the factors which have to be taken into account in this organization vary greatly from one area to another. Where staff is adequate the alternation of different duties provides both a wide basis of experience and a stimulating variety of work; where loads are excessively high, however, duties which should be complementary may well become competing. This danger is to some extent inherent in the large measure of responsibility and individuality accorded to probation officers, and it is not suggested that they are alone amongst social workers in finding that their setting has its special difficulties as well as its special privileges. The development of supervision should help to overcome the danger of excessive isolation and pressure at any particular point, but the need for really adequate staffing in the service as a whole remains.

A probation officer's duties fall broadly into four classes: super- vision of offenders and others who have appeared before courts, including supervision of those released from institutions subject to statutory after-care or parole; help to those coming for voluntary after-care; social enquiries of various kinds to assist the courts in deciding upon sentence or other action; and matrimonial concilia- tion. These four groups together account for the bulk of probation officer's work: their special problems have already been considered separately, but all make continuous claims on his time and energy. In addition he has responsibilities for keeping in touch with the homes of young people in approved probation hostels or homes; for helping prisoners' families where they desire it; for co-operating with prison welfare officers; perhaps for visiting prisoners or borstal boys in preparation for after-care. He may also need to consider working with volunteers in particular cases and be prepared to give them adequate support.

Apart from the duties imposed directly or indirectly by the courts, many officers do a good deal of voluntary work with clients who never come before the courts at all. Much matrimonial work may come under this head. But there are also a great many casual callers who come to the probation office because it is available and often because of the very fact that it is linked with the courts. This should be less so if local authority services, including Family Advice Centres, continue to develop. But in 1967 probation officers still recorded around thirty-five thousand requests connected with advice on difficult children, voluntary supervision, unmarried mothers and affiliation enquiries, neighbours' quarrels and financial assistance, as well as over eighty thousand miscellaneous cases coming to their attention. The Morison Committee, whilst holding that statutory duties must be given priority, considered that it would be "neither practical nor desirable to end the probation officer's voluntary work", as much of it could help to prevent offences and it met needs for which alternative agencies were not available. Statutory duties, however, have now increased, especially in enquiries for courts and voluntary after-care. Moreover, the National Association of Probation Officers has stressed the implication of the White Paper on Children in Trouble that the primary responsibility for preventive work affecting children and young people should be placed upon the local authority.

It is obvious that the statutory duties in themselves are so varied that their demands may well conflict. Supervision normally requires set times for interviews, when the probationer can regularly rely on seeing the probation officer and on having enough time set aside to talk to him. If there is to be contact with home or family as well evening visiting will often be essential. And evening interviews or visits by appointment are frequently necessary in matrimonial work. Court attendance demands that a probation officer be available to the court on particular days. But court enquiries, which may involve more than one visit to the accused and his family, often have to be fitted in quickly so as to ensure that a report is available in time. Offenders leaving penal institutions subject to after-care often need help very urgently and make frequent and heavy demands on time during their first few weeks of freedom: there is a special sense of urgency with them, a feeling that much may be at stake, and a need to be quickly available. After-care on a more casual voluntary basis is an unknown quantity: how much time should be given to those who come asking for material aid, how far should the officer look below the surface and try to persuade them to accept help of other kinds over a longer period? And requests for action or enquiries from prison welfare officers, for all the pressure of anxiety behind them, have also to be fitted into a jigsaw of other commitments.

Specialization is one of the solutions suggested to reduce this competition and complexity and to ensure that officers are available to meet particular kinds of demand. In some areas one officer may specialize in reports, at least for the higher courts. Some have specialized for a time in matrimonial work. Others, especially in the large cities, have specialized in after-care, or even in particular branches of it. Prison welfare itself is almost always a full-time specialist job. Specialization not only reduces the variety of competing demands on time: it also enables an officer to concentrate upon one kind of role in relation to his clients, to appreciate its implications and develop it more thoroughly. But it is not practicable in scattered areas, and its advantages must be balanced against the possibly harassing, and often depressing, effects of concentration on a comparatively narrow range. Much of the interest of probation work, and the skill of probation officers, depends on the width of their contacts and the variety of their duties, from the very fact that they see clients and their families in different capacities and from different points of view. On the one hand it is clearly difficult to adapt to different roles, on the other the very effort of doing so should help to prevent stagnation or a stereotyped approach. The best solution is probably the one usually adopted: where officers specialize, they do so only for a few years, returning then to the more general field of probation and after-care work. This should help to prevent specialized parts of the service becoming cut off from the rest and regarded as the responsibility only of a few. It should also encourage the dissemination of specialized knowledge and understanding through the service as a whole.

The practical demands of a probation officer's work cannot be looked at apart from its satisfactions. Most fundamental, perhaps, is the sense of doing something to meet a need in others of which those drawn to the service are particularly aware and to which, for emotional, religious and humanitarian reasons, they respond very deeply. Closely linked with this is the intense interest of the work, in the great variety of people of both sexes and all ages coming within the probation officer's province, and the challenge of their differing personalities and problems. Again, there is the stimulus of continuous learning, for this is not a field in which either knowledge or skill can ever be absolute, since it is as wide and deep as human nature and the possibility of exploring it is limited only by the officer's own powers of perception. It is also a field in which can be used both mental and emotional faculties, learning and experience, such wisdom and such personality as each has been given. Working conditions may be arduous, but they are also varied, involving office, court and outside work in swift alternation, and the fact that men and women are employed on an equal footing makes possible a sharing of ideas and outlook which can be most helpful to both.

Probation officers in the cities, for all their frequently grim surroundings, face some of the most intensive work and some of the most interesting problems. It is here that crime is most concentrated, the problems of the environment most complex, the need probably greatest. Here also there are the greatest possibilities of experiment in teamwork, in specialization, perhaps in research. Country work, at the other extreme, offers perhaps more direct individual responsibility, more personal contact with a range of courts and magistrates, as well as the pleasures and hazards of getting around a large area at all times of the year. Isolation is much less than it was since the senior ranks of the service have developed and inservice training has begun to be thought of not merely as an occasional course every few years but as a regular programme. And since newer universities have been sited in country areas and cast their nets very widely for help with their students, it has become possible for officers in the country as well as in the cities to work in partnership with them in training the social workers, and especially the probation officers, of the future.

Both in quantity and quality, the services expected of probation officers have increased and continue to do so. Great efforts are being made to equip them to meet these demands in the sphere of quality by means of training and supervision, though so far quantity has not always been able to keep pace. There is, however, a great eagerness to learn and to advance, and this is possible on the basis of full co-operation between all grades and branches of the service.

CHAPTER II

THE MAKING OF PROBATION OFFICERS

I IS TRAINING NECESSARY?

THE earliest probation officers were born, possibly bred, but not specifically trained for the work they had to do. Their lessons were those of daily experience. The value of their influence upon the offender was compared to "the skilled help of a doctor to a person suffering from disease", but there was no recognition that they, like the doctor, might need considerable preliminary learning if they were to identify what was wrong in particular cases, to know the range of possible remedies, to conduct a course of treatment. It was enough that they should combine "excellence of character" with "strength of personal influence". Coming as they did "from a different level of society" they would be in a position to reach down, as it were, and "give a helping hand to lift offenders out of the groove that leads to serious crime".[1]

Today there is less assurance, perhaps more humility. The probation officer, it is agreed, needs very much more than a kind heart and a "way with people", or even stability, maturity, insight, self-reliance, resilience. He needs especially "an ability to communicate easily with people from all classes, patience, tolerance and, most fundamental of all, a genuine interest in people and a capacity really to like and understand them". The official recruiting pamphlet goes on: "In case this list of desirable qualities suggests that the service is staffed only by candidates for canonization, it must be added that unless a probation officer is human, with warm-blooded

---

1. *Report of the Departmental Committee on the Probation of Offenders Act* 1907 (Cd. 5001), 1909.

feelings (and passions)—and weaknesses—of his own, he cannot hope to be a success."[1]

The qualities required have certainly been re-interpreted, though perhaps not fundamentally changed. Excellence of character must be defined in terms not merely of moral rectitude, but of self-understanding, of freedom from rigidity and of concern for others. Strength of personal influence must not be the product of self-centredness or inflexibility: there must be scope for recognition and control of the motives underlying its use. Any social or educational advantages need to be balanced by a willingness to understand ways of living, thinking and feeling in other sections of society. At no point of personality, influence or background can effortless superiority be assumed. At every point the help of others is needed if the probation officer is to attain an understanding of himself, of society and of those in his charge sufficient to avoid unthinking harm and to enable him to feel his way forward into appropriate ways of helping many different kinds of people.

It is sometimes suggested that the picture of the probation officer as essentially a person of good character is at odds with the more modern picture of a trained social worker using professional skills. The antithesis appears false. Morality itself implies that those who take on the responsibility for helping others should acquire as much knowledge, understanding and skill as they can to enable them to do it well. Technical proficiency, on the other hand, cannot replace the concern for others which must motivate its use.

2 WHAT NEEDS TO BE TAUGHT?

What does the potential probation officer need to begin to learn during his professional training?

Because he will work in the setting of the law, and especially the criminal law, he must know about the courts, the machinery of law enforcement and the penal system. Because within that setting he functions as a social worker he must know the social services and how to use them. Because his concern is with people in difficulties of behaviour and relationships he must know about normal and abnormal human development, about the dynamics of individuals and of groups. Because he works with and through personal re-

---

1. *The Probation and After-Care Service as a Career*, H.M.S.O., 1968.

lationships he must understand something of his own prejudices, limitations, biases, as well as those of others. Because society, as well as the individual and his family, is involved in the causes, consequences and treatment of delinquency or marital problems, he must know something of the ways of living and thinking in social groups other than his own, as well as something of the wider forces shaping society as a whole. Because social and moral values underlie his work he must know the basis of his own. Because the test of scientific investigation is increasingly being applied to social and penal practice he should know something of its nature, its possibilities and its interpretation.

An understanding of his position and duties in relation to the courts and other aspects of law enforcement is essential to the probation officer even on the narrowest definition of his role, "if only", as was observed many years ago, "to avoid the danger of intervening in directions which might obstruct the administration of justice".[1] The need is all the greater now that he is being called upon to take a more active part in assisting that administration, at all stages from pre-trial enquiries to reports that may lead to revocation of parole. He must know the scope and limits of his functions not only in relation to courts and police but also in relation to the responsibilities of penal institutions, of his own senior officers and of volunteers who may help to care for those in his charge. He must be aware of the law and of administrative arrangements affecting all aspects of his duties, in civil as well as criminal cases.

All this is not just a matter of book-learning, or of facts to be picked up haphazardly as he goes along. He has to come to terms with the emotions aroused by working in this particular setting, especially with partisan feelings that tempt him to identify uncritically with applicant, with offender or with court. He has to learn, for example, to resist the temptation to become either advocate or judge in making his reports. He has to cope with his feelings when the court takes some action other than what he thinks best for an offender. He has to balance his concern for those under his care against his responsibilities for the protection of society through the court or other agencies. The problem is not the same for all students.

1. *Report of the Departmental Committee on Social Services in Courts of Summary Jurisdiction*, 1936.

Some identify most naturally with the court, the welfare of the community, the need on occasion to punish. They may require to develop a counterbalancing sensitivity to the rights of the individual, to genuine injustice, when it occurs, to the possibility that punishment may be used to satisfy the punisher rather than for any good it may do either to a particular offender or to the community at large. Others identify most naturally with the offender, tending to reject authority and control. For them, the need is to learn to accept authority realistically, to recognize its functions both in protecting the rights of others and often in helping the offender himself. This is important in many branches of social work. In probation it is essential.[1]

At a more mundane level, most new entrants will need training in the preparation of reports for the courts and in the keeping of records. A recognition of the court's needs in sentencing, an ability to select what is relevant, an appreciation of the kind of language and length most likely to secure attention and ensure understanding, are all essential tools in making reports. So is skill in maintaining records of supervision and other work that will serve the several purposes of enabling the officer himself and those who may supervise him to see how a case is developing, of recording essential facts for quick reference, of enabling others to take up, if need be, where he leaves off.

The role of the probation officer as a social worker entails a knowledge, at the very least, of social conditions and of the social services. He must know what is feasible in employment, in education, in leisure opportunities, in medical, psychiatric or financial help, and in housing. He must know what other social services, voluntary or statutory, have to offer. He must know how to contact them in a particular locality, how to act as a two-way bridge between the offender or other client and those who might join in helping him. It is less and less possible for any one person to give all kinds of help, more and more necessary for each to see himself as part of a team and to contribute towards making such teams a reality.

As in the courts, so in social work the potential officer must not only learn facts and procedures but come to terms with the roles of

---

1. See F. Jarvis and W. B. Utting, *Aspects of Training*, Probation Papers No. 2, 1965.

others, whether in different services, or in different grades of his own. As administrative units grow larger and more complex it is increasingly important to understand something of the problems and principles of administration, of communication and accountability. Much unnecessary strain and conflict can be produced by false expectations, by a misplaced sense of responsibility, by never having faced the need to cut one's coat according to one's cloth. Again a balance has to be struck between encouraging unrealistic hopes in oneself and others and using realism as an excuse for not striving to bring genuine evils to the notice of those who control resources and may be able to remedy them.

The suggestion that it is enough to meet material needs, and that deeper probing into the problems of the individual is an impertinence, would be rejected by social workers in most spheres. It is certainly seldom true in dealing with offenders or with matrimonial conflicts.

Probation training takes full account of the need to understand the dynamics of personality, normal or abnormal. More than thirty years ago, it was observed that, since so many of those coming before the courts, as offenders or for other reasons, were "unstable in character or of borderline mentality", probation officers needed to be acquainted with "psychological method", with the work done in child guidance clinics and the out-patient departments of mental hospitals. This would enable them to identify, refer and co-operate in the treatment of those needing psychiatric help. But it would also have a wider value: it could assist the officer "to exercise in the most effective way his own personal influence without weakening in any way the personality of those he is trying to help".[1] Emphasis on this latter aspect has been growing ever since.

The twin themes of the development of human personality and the use of the casework relationship have become central to the training of modern social workers, including probation officers. At each stage of his own growth, in the family, at school and amongst those of his own age, at work or at college, perhaps in marriage and parenthood, the potential probation officer will himself have had to try to come to terms with relationships, difficulties, frustrations and

---

1. *Report from the Committee on Social Services in Courts of Summary Jurisdiction*, 1936.

satisfactions. The nature of these, the ways he has found of coping with them, his successes or failures, will have influenced all his expectations of life and of others. To interpret them fruitfully, to be able to use them without assuming that his own pattern is the only one, he needs both theoretical and personal help.

The study of human growth and development, the need to record, evaluate and discuss his own reactions to his clients during training, should combine to deepen his insight into his own attitudes and assumptions and to widen his understanding of those of other people. This part of his education, like his early contact with courts and penal institutions, is particularly challenging. He must draw upon his own experience to understand and test the various concepts put forward; he must question his established feelings and ideas; sometimes he must find them wanting. He may have to come to terms with elements of which he had previously been unaware in his attitudes towards offenders. Yet the very fact that the process of insight and adjustment sparked off by experience of courts and of casework can be so painful makes the experience of particular value. Much of his work as a probation officer will be concerned with helping others to face unpleasant realities, about authority and about themselves, and to modify harmful attitudes.

It has been well said that the nature and quality of support given to a probation officer by those who teach him will do much to set the tone of his own relationships with those he subsequently supervises or tries to help. Yet just as his scope will be greatly restricted if he tries uncritically to impose his own pattern of life and experience on those with very different backgrounds and personalities, so his ability to help through relationships will be impaired if he assumes that the aspect of teaching or supervision which most helped him will necessarily be of most value to his probationers or other clients. For example, the personalities, the intelligence and the future role of those preparing to be probation officers often justify concentration upon developing their insight into their own motivations and defences. For many of their clients this may be impracticable, inadvisable or unnecessary, or it may need to be achieved by much less direct means. What is important is that it should not be regarded as the best or only way of approaching all cases. The underlying human experience of coping with difficulty, learning, adaptation, is common ground to the probation officer and his clients:

the ways of meeting it must match the varieties of people's needs and capacities.[1]

For the probation officer, and the person singled out as an offender, the one-to-one relationship central to much casework is likely to remain very important. The development of prison welfare and after-care increases rather than diminishes the officer's need to understand mental abnormality. At the same time, however, it is increasingly realized that the psychiatric model upon which so much of earlier casework theory and teaching has been based, is inapplicable to much of the work of the probation officer. He will be hindered rather than helped if he comes to interpret the casework relationship as a sort of confidential cocoon into which he can withdraw with his client. He needs, to balance it, a wider knowledge of social influences and obligations.

Catalogues of the tools at the disposal of the social worker almost always include, alongside a knowledge of individual development, a knowledge of society. In practice the balance has hitherto been heavily weighted on the side of the individual, or at least of the individual as a member of a family. Psychology, psychiatry, psychoanalysis, have forged ahead in their studies of topics which appear of immediate relevance to those who have the practical tasks of dealing with individual offenders and others in social difficulties. They can offer theories about attitude and behaviour change, techniques of interviewing and of using relationships. The topics studied by sociologists have often seemed comparatively remote, their findings too general to be applied and tested. But what they have to say about classes and sub-cultures, about varying methods of child-rearing, about the significance of social roles and institutions, can give another dimension to the way social workers look at their clients, and the ways they may try to help them. In particular, the new emphasis on the treatment of offenders in groups links up with sociological studies of penal institutions and adolescent delinquent gangs, whilst calls for "community involvement" to help offenders and others in trouble, stem partly from studies of delinquency areas.

It has been said that in the past probation officers and other social workers have been too undiscriminating in applying the assumptions

---

1. See, for example, Margaret A. G. Brown, "A Review of Casework Methods", in E. Younghusband (ed.) *New Developments in Casework*, 1966.

and methods of psychiatry to their own work. There may be some cause to fear an equally indiscriminate application of sociological theories. But in neither case does the need to discriminate imply that it is better not to know, or to experiment. It is of great importance that those who intend to become probation officers should understand more of social structure, social attitudes and the effects of social change. Without such understanding they cannot assess adequately the meaning of events to their clients, the assumptions, behaviour and responses to be expected of them, the possibilities open to them.

A special area of knowledge to which this is very applicable concerns the understanding of institutions, and especially of penal institutions. In the past the main emphasis within the probation service has been on the need to keep people out of penal institutions whenever possible. Whilst this still holds good, the range of caring has now been enlarged to include not only those who have passed through institutions and have to come to terms again with the outside world but those who are actually serving sentences. Many officers will, in the future, spend part of their careers as prison welfare officers. All will be involved in helping courts in their choice of treatment, custodial or non-custodial, in keeping in touch with families of men in prison, in joining with welfare officers in planning after-care. All will therefore need to know something of the nature of closed institutions and their impact upon those within them, whether as inmates or as staff. Perhaps the courses held at the Wakefield Staff College for the training of probation officers for prison welfare work are an indication of the sort of thing that might be possible. These three-week courses have allowed a short residential placement to be integrated with lectures on the sociology and administration of prisons, all with considerable group discussion led jointly by a tutor from the Prison Staff College and another from the probation service. In whatever way and at whatever stage it is arranged, however, there is great need to recognize theoretical teaching and practical experience of work in prisons as an important and integral part of the training of probation officers.

Similarly at least some knowledge is becoming necessary of the newer approaches in social work. The Seebohm Committee has suggested an experiment in training students not only in casework but also in groupwork and community work, since "all these methods are needed to respond appropriately to social problems which involve individual, family, group and community aspects".[1] Whether it will ever be feasible to encompass all these in one course of training may well be doubtful, but at least it is necessary to be aware of the principles of these methods of working. If they do not use them themselves, probation officers come into contact with those who do and their clients, especially in after-care, may increasingly have been affected by them. Even if no more than an introduction can be contemplated during pre-entry training, it can arouse interest and pave the way to the development of more specialized skill later.

Another direction in which, though specialist skill may only be for the few, some general knowledge of methods and objectives is becoming important for all is research itself. It has been suggested that even a few officers qualified in research could make a very great contribution to the progress of the service at this time of change and experiment. For the majority what is needed is some understanding of the kind of problem research can most usefully tackle, the differences in the objectives and methods of research workers and social workers, the relevance of research to work with offenders.

Values and moral standards are implicit in the principles of social work and in much of the criminal law. In the days of the police court missionary it seemed unnecessary to analyse or question them. It could be taken for granted that they were generally accepted in theory, if not always in practice. There was no hesitation in referring to them or in laying them down. Paradoxically, now that their existence and application is subject to constant questioning, there is far more diffidence about bringing them out and examining their foundations. There is a fear of being accused of rigidity, of "imposing" something, of departing from the doctrines of acceptance and self-determination. Yet if a probation officer does not learn to make explicit his own moral values, at least to himself, he is in as much danger of confusing himself and others, and of being betrayed into evasions and manipulations, as if he remains blind, say, to his own attitude to authority, itself a moral issue. Whenever it is said that a change of attitude is needed, a moral and value judgment is being made, and there must be some idea of the directions in which change is to be sought. Especially in dealing with offenders, it is

---

1. *Report of the Committee on Local Authority and allied Personal Social Services* (Cmnd. 3703), 1968, p. 172.

increasingly acknowledged that the task is often that of social education, of helping people to form or re-examine their values.

Social workers, probation officers included, are well aware that attitudes and behaviour are products of feeling as well as of reason, but it does not follow that reason can be ignored.

> "Social workers must have done their own thinking about what a moral problem is like; and they must hold strongly enough that morality is part and parcel of any normal human life to believe that others will need to see some of their problems as moral problems too. This does not mean that one forces one's solution on them; but it does mean being prepared to throw one's intellectual moral resources as well as one's sympathetic ones into the situation."[1]

Whether this part of an officer's education is best attempted through a systematic course of seminars or as problems arise in the course of casework is debatable. The former may prove too restricted or too remote, the latter too haphazard. What is certain is that the whole complex of modern doubts about behaviour in all aspects of life, together with the common criticism that social workers simply try to impose their own middle class norms upon people living in very different settings, make it more important than ever that consideration of the basis of morality, in its broadest sense, should form part of the education of a probation officer.

Three further, more general, points should perhaps be made. First, in all aspects of training there is an even greater need than in the past to help students to grasp principles rather than merely adopt set positions or techniques: to introduce them to expanding concepts, to promote flexibility rather than conformity, in short to educate. A rapidly changing society and rapidly changing functions and approaches make this essential.[2] Second, it is apparent that the education of a probation officer cannot be purely academic. Some things, like the content of the law, the facts of social administration, can be learned from books or lectures, though even they will gain reality and relevance only as they are seen in action. Most of the rest must necessarily be learned in practice as well as in

---

1. D. Emmett, "Ethics and the Social Worker", in E. Younghusband (ed.), *Social Work and Social Values*, 1967.
2. See on this, for example, P. Parsloe, *The Work of the Probation and After-Care Officer*, 1967.

theory, absorbed as a matter of feeling as well as of intellect. Work alongside serving probation officers is thus to be seen as an equal partner with academic teaching in the preparation of probation students. Third, pre-entry training is emphatically a preparation, a beginning, not a completed process. Supervision of new officers and staff development within the service must be accepted as necessary to maintain the impetus, to enable officers to develop their own full potential, and to keep pace with change and experiment.

3   TRAINING AND RECRUITMENT

In 1963, following the report of the Morison Committee, the strength of the probation service rose for the first time above two thousand. It has been estimated that, to meet its expanding duties, it should be raised to three and a half thousand by 1970, though it is not now expected that this target will be reached before 1971. Even on that basis, the number of entrants completing training each year has fallen short of the three hundred and fifty needed annually, and recruitment has been maintained only by allowing the appointment each year of a substantial number of officers without preliminary training.

Entry without training is possible because no minimum qualification for appointment as a probation officer has yet been laid down, apart from the requirement that the new entrant be at least twenty-two years old. The local Probation and After-Care Committees, naturally prefer trained applicants. But if they are hard-pressed they may have the choice of leaving their existing officers overloaded or appointing people who are still untrained. Direct entrants, however, cannot be left without help and training once they are in the service. To a great extent they must depend for this on the efforts of their colleagues, who may well be overburdened with high case-loads already. It is, indeed, the areas where the pressure of work is greatest that are likeliest to have to resort to the appointment of the untrained. Various devices have been adopted to provide more formal training for them, often in conjunction with the extra-mural departments of universities. But these all depend on day-release and longer periods of concentrated training, and usually upon a smaller than normal caseload during the first months or years. If time and effort has thus to be devoted to their training in any case it is hard to see why it should have to continue to be given on this comparatively makeshift basis.

For many years the National Association of Probation Officers has urged that the Home Secretary should prescribe that an approved course of training should be a necessary qualification for appointment. Hitherto the answer has always been that this cannot be done until an adequate supply of trained entrants can be guaranteed. Training facilities have, indeed, been greatly expanded, but so far neither training nor recruitment has kept up with the increase in crime and the widening duties of the service. This has been a difficulty shared both with other social services and with others involved at all stages in the enforcement of the criminal law, from the police and the courts to the prisons. Indeed in some ways the probation service has done better than most. Some two-thirds of its number have had a course of professional training before entry, which compares very well with other large social services in this country. But these services, too, are now rapidly expanding, both in numbers and qualifications, and the case for adequate training for all probation officers becomes more urgent as their duties grow more complex and demanding.

It is not that there is any lack of candidates for training. In 1967 the Home Office received over thirty thousand enquiries, nearly five thousand applications. Because many different kinds of people, from very varied backgrounds, have proved capable of profiting from probation training and have become effective probation officers, invitations to apply for training have always been phrased in very general terms. Though a good basic education is needed, rigid educational or other limitations are avoided and the age at which candidates may be considered ranges from nineteen into the late forties. This has inevitably disadvantages as well as advantages. Many enquirers are quite unsuitable: in 1967, for example, considerably less than one in ten of all applicants was offered training.

The thorough and searching nature of the selection procedure reflects both the wideness of the field and the extremely personal and responsible nature of the job. On both counts it is necessary to provide a series of sieves and for applications to be thoroughly scrutinized. Many enquirers are seen in the first instance by principal and senior probation officers in their own areas before they make formal application to the Home Office to be considered for training. Applications proper are sifted, in the first instance, by the Home Office Probation and After-Care Department. The next stage is an interview with a probation inspector. The most likely candidates are then seen by a selection board, consisting of members of the Recruitment and Training Committee of the Advisory Council and principal probation officers. This method of selection gives considerable weight to the judgment of those in day-to-day touch with the work of probation officers, who are likely to view applicants not only as potential students but as potential colleagues. Certain universities, however, run special courses for graduates, covering both social studies and professional training for the probation and after-care service. They have now taken over responsibility for the selection of these particular students. They normally include either a probation officer or a tutor with recent experience in probation on their selection panels. Nevertheless, some anxiety is felt as to whether they are in a position to take as good account of the needs of the service as the Recruitment and Training Committee panels.

Who are, in fact, selected? It has been suggested that the ideal age for entry lies in the late twenties and early thirties, when people have had time to gain experience of life and to attain the necessary maturity. There is also an important place for those who join in their forties, after other careers in this country or abroad. These two groups between them account for four out of five new entrants and bring a very great variety of experience into the service. Recruitment of younger people, who can bring or acquire appropriate university qualifications, is also important. The Morison Committee stressed, in particular, the need to bring in a number of good graduates who could contribute to the leadership and development of the service.

Recruitment of graduates, especially from arts faculties, has been encouraged of late by designating certain graduate probation officers to maintain liaison with universities in their own areas. The number with university qualifications completing training in 1968 was around ninety, as against less than seventy the year before. The movement of graduates out of the service, however, exceeds in some years the movement in. This does not mean that their training and experience are necessarily wasted, as many go into teaching, research, or other social services, where a practical understanding of the roles of the probation and after-care service and of its insights into the treatment of offenders can be invaluable. But it does mean that there is need to maintain recruitment at a fairly high level. It means, too, that opportunities for graduates should match those in other fields if enough are to remain to contribute directly to the service as they grow in experience.

It has been suggested that graduates may be deterred by the fact that their degrees as such earn them no special recognition, except entry at a higher point on the incremental scale. However, the service is not as undiscriminating as it may appear. Good senior officers take into account the capabilities of individuals when allocating work. Furthermore, if the graduate's training enables him to "practise and to grow in a manner not open to the untrained" then he will probably achieve a greater measure of responsibility sooner than the less well qualified.[1] The range of possibilities is opening up. Not only administration, but training, consultation and specialist skills of various kinds are likely to be increasingly recognized.

Another set of obstacles, which may particularly deter the younger and more academic entrant, is the present climate of opinion: the questioning of moral standards, the confusion endemic in an uncertainly "permissive" society, the doubts about the uses and misuses of social control, the imposition of values and behaviour by one social group upon another, the motives for accepting any role which implies authority. In fact it is these very things that comprise one of the central challenges with which the service is trying to come to grips. In moving into the difficult fields of prison welfare and after-care, in facing larger responsibilities for advising the courts, it is taking up again its old role as a pioneer in difficult places, it needs more than ever minds that can discriminate, research, initiate, rather than follow safe and established patterns. People coming into the service from other careers can bring with them fresh kinds of expertise, fresh ways of looking at things. Graduates can bring habits of questioning and of systematic thought. Paradoxically, it is only if some of those who continually challenge the functions of control will accept responsibility for a practical share in working out its legitimate place that it can be kept in

---

1. See E. Younghusband, "Looking Backwards and Forwards", *Case Conference*, July 1965.

balance with freedom. In the day to day problems of the service these things pass from the realm of abstraction to that of practical concern.

4 THE ORGANIZATION OF TRAINING

This is obviously a complex problem. The range of knowledge required, the range of students to be taught, the fact that both practical and academic kinds of learning are involved, all conspire to make it so. Moreover, the necessity of swift expansion over the past few years has led to many expedients and experiments. In 1958, when this book was first published, there were three clearly marked possibilities. A younger student might take a social science diploma at a university and then the specialized Home Office course. An older one would take the Home Office course alone. And a student who already had social science qualifications might take a "generic" course in social work with students entering other fields and thus by-pass the specialized Home Office training.

These alternatives still exist, and may perhaps be regarded as broadly typical. But all sorts of variations have been added. Though the Home Office course centred in London still remains the main-stay, something like half of all new entrants passing through it, there has been a steady growth in courses run by universities, either specifically for probation students or for them and other social work students jointly, and there has been a great deal of decentralization, with courses developing in the provinces.[1] Some of these are for mature entrants as well as younger people taking full academic courses.

This proliferation of courses has developed partly to meet varying needs, partly to draw in all available resources in the urgent task of expanding training. Inevitably some aspects of it need further examination. For example, is the one-year initial training given to the bulk of mature entrants adequate and can they afford to give up jobs to take it? Does the theoretical content of courses take enough account of the basic things probation officers need to know? Can they give enough attention to the wider principles underlying social work and social arrangements for dealing with crime, or

---

1. For details of courses available see *The Probation and After-Care Service as a Career*, H.M.S.O., 1968, obtainable from the Probation and After-Care Department of the Home Office.

must they concentrate more narrowly on matters of immediate and specific use in the work of a probation officer? Do they satisfactorily relate the two halves of learning, theoretical and practical, satisfactorily link the tutors responsible for theoretical teaching with those supervising practical work? Who should be responsible for organizing the training of probation officers: the Home Office, the universities or some new Training Board? Should professional training remain, as in most cases at present, a thing apart, or should it be combined with the training of other social workers or of others employed in the legal or penal fields?

At a time of change like the present it is impossible to give hard and fast answers to these questions. Obviously the development of the probation and after-care service is not the only factor that will affect the answers: the expansion of other social services, changes in higher education, competing pressures upon national resources and manpower, will all have their influence. Yet it may be worth while to look at these questions in turn and consider the way things might go.

First, the length of training for mature entrants. It was accepted thirty years ago that ideally a broad academic grounding in the principles of social work should precede specialized training. But a basic university social studies course normally requires at least two years for a non-graduate, at least one for a graduate. And the probation and after-care service has always depended, and is likely to continue to depend, upon a steady and substantial entry of people beyond the normal age for university education. Whilst some of these might welcome and benefit from the full academic course, others have family and financial commitments which make it difficult for them to contemplate two or three years' return to the rank of students.

The Morison Committee considered some of the arguments for believing that one year is not long enough and recommended that "from the earliest possible date every probation officer should receive not less than two years' training before appointment". It drew attention to the growing responsibilities of the probation service, to the rapid advances in the sciences of human behaviour, and to the fact that increased knowledge and professional competence would be demanded of probation officers in the years ahead. It concluded that "a serious situation would arise if the training which probation officers received were at any time insufficient in length or quality to bear the weight of new demands and new knowledge . . . this is the overriding consideration which should be borne in mind when training, whether basic, refresher or advanced is being planned".[1]

The situation has not stood still since then.   The range and complexity of duties, of methods and of knowledge have further increased.   The tendency in other branches of social work, and amongst social workers as a developing professional body, is for two years to be regarded as a minimum for basic training.

The major official objection to extension to two years is that it would impede recruitment, especially of older entrants, at a time when it is urgent to expand the service.[2]   For many such people, however, the system of paying maintenance grants rather than salaries during training was a major obstacle, and the National Association of Probation Officers pressed hard for it to be altered. Amongst other things, it was thought to encourage people to seek appointment without training.   It is hoped that the recent decision to pay salaries during training will make it easier for mature entrants with family and other responsibilities to enter the service through a regular training course.   It is hoped also that it will make it more feasible for them to spend two years rather than one in training whenever desirable.

Naturally there is also the fact that two years' training costs more than one and that the demand for fuller preparation coincides with the demand for larger numbers.   This is part of larger controversies about what share of national expenditure should be devoted to higher education generally and to the education of social workers in particular.   There is at least a strong argument that, since probation officers are being moved increasingly into some of the most crucial of modern social problems, they are entitled to the most thorough preparation to meet them, not only for their own sakes but for society's.

Another obstacle to a two-year course for mature entrants is that it could normally involve more prolonged separation from their families.   This has been reduced to some extent, however, in the

1. *Report of the Departmental Committee on the Probation Service*, 1962.
2. *Report on the Work of the Probation and After-Care Department*, 1962–1965, 1966.

regional courses, where both theoretical and practical work are taken within range of a large provincial centre and where the catchment area from which students are drawn is smaller and more localized than that of the central London course. The further development of regional courses could thus reduce still more the objection to a two-year initial training.

A fourth objection to a two-year course for mature entrants, however, is more fundamental. It is the suggestion that for many mature people it seems unnatural to revert to student status for a prolonged period and that they can profit more by postponing part of their learning till they are on the job. Many of them have experience of life and of previous employment which can be of great use to the service, but it does not come easily to them to embark on extended academic learning. One view is that just because of this they need longer to get going and therefore more than a year for their preliminary training. It is argued, too, that some will find it more worth while to make the break and embark on a new career if they are to be given a thorough preparation at the outset.

Against this, however, it is argued that what most of them need is not a two-year course at the outset of their careers but what has been called "phased training": one year to begin with, then a series of shorter periods after appointment to enable them to integrate their growing experience with more advanced theoretical learning than could have been accessible to them earlier.[1] There is some attraction in this idea from the educational point of view. It may perhaps be compared with the pattern of learning for a doctor, in which the initial period of intensive education is followed by supervised experience and further learning on the wards, then perhaps by general practice, with more advanced training later for those who are to become consultants. But the idea of phased training in itself implies that one year alone can no longer be regarded as enough. If it is to succeed, new entrants should have caseloads of no more than about thirty-five in their first year, and later phases of training would have to be carried out systematically, either on the basis of regular day release or of block periods. It would be necessary for the officer, his colleagues and his seniors to recognize that his role and his work during his first year or so should be

---

1. *Report on the Work of the Probation and After-Care Department*, 1961–1965, para. 142.

determined by his need for training as well as the needs of the department. Because of the administrative problems and the difficulties of dove-tailing the initial and subsequent training, this kind of expedient would have to be justified in educational terms rather than in terms of economy of effort or resources.

Next comes the question of the theoretical content of courses. The central one-year Home Office course includes classes and seminars dealing with cultural influences on behaviour, the family and the social services and criminology. The most important subjects, however, apart from law and probation practice, are human growth and development, psychiatric aspects of delinquency and social casework. It is hard to compare this with the contents of the various university-based courses, as resources and priorities vary in different places and so does what is actually taught under any particular heading. It does seem, however, that the Home Office course has remained strongly weighted towards psychiatric factors and the one-to-one relationship as the essential basis of treatment. The other courses, starting later, pay perhaps more attention to the social influences upon individuals, families and communities. In this respect they may adapt more easily to new ways of working and thinking, to the concern with treating people as part of their families and social groups.

Another controversy hinges on the question of whether, in the limited time available for training, the main emphasis should be upon generic elements—the kind of thing all social workers need to understand—or on the more specialized demands of the probation and after-care service as such. There is no doubt that at the moment probation training, like the service, is being pulled hard in both directions. As the functions of all social services change and widen it is more necessary than ever to develop mutual knowledge and co-operation between them, to recognize and emphasize what is common to them all. But as the specific responsibilities of probation officers penetrate further into the administration of justice and the penal system it also becomes more essential than ever to impart specialist knowledge of these fields and to consider specifically how the general principles of social work relate to the whole range of settings, from matrimonial conciliation or divorce court welfare to prisons and after-care. There is not only the problem of time and teaching resources. There is also the problem of what students can absorb, especially if they are older people who lack advanced academic training. "The capacity to transfer knowledge from one field to another, to see general applications, is generally conceded to be related to intellectual capacity. How far can we assume that, at basic level, all social workers can be trained to grasp the general applicability of certain concepts rather than their specific application to certain situations?"[1]

Even if the solution of "phased training" is adopted, it is still necessary to decide what should be attempted at what stage. Is it best to concentrate in pre-service training primarily upon giving students a preliminary grounding in principles generic to social work and the penal and legal systems, leaving them to learn later about their specific applications? Or is it the specific knowledge that is most urgently needed to launch them safely on their careers as probation officers, leaving the general principles to be discussed more fully later, when they have enough experience behind them to test their validity and understand their significance? Also, are there particular areas of the work that can safely be omitted, or touched upon only lightly, during preliminary training? Can teaching about prison welfare, for example, safely be left until later, as a specialist job for experienced officers, or should it rather be included in any basic course so that officers may appreciate from the start that it is an integral part of the service? The answers will no doubt always be compromises but they need to be reasoned compromises, and they presuppose that what is omitted from preliminary training will receive adequate attention later on in supervision and staff development.

To complicate the situation further, it has been argued that it is not only with social workers that probation officers should share generic knowledge and at least part of their training. As their role as social advisers to the courts, civil as well as criminal, becomes more important, it has been suggested that some at least of them might be linked up with lawyers as part of a total court service. As they proceed further into prison welfare and parole it has been suggested they should join with others concerned in dealing with offenders in studying the whole range of what the Americans call "corrections".

In practical terms it seems likely that the core of the probation

---

1. Olive Stevenson, "Specialisation within a unified social work service", in *Case Conference*, Vol. 15, No. 5, September, 1968.

officer's training will always be social work. However closely he may come to be affiliated with courts and the penal system, his distinctive contribution to them is that of the social worker. Given that grounding, he should have much both to offer and to learn from those who work with offenders in other ways.

As has been pointed out, the very nature of probation training implies that practical experience must be given equal place alongside theoretical instruction. The role of the probation officers in the field who supervise students should therefore be one of partnership with tutors. Unless the two are adequately linked it will be hard for students to integrate the two kinds of learning. To achieve this there are at least two prerequisites. There must be enough probation officers qualified to supervise students in the field, and there must be continuous understanding between them and the tutors responsible for theoretical studies.

To the first of these the Home Office has contributed by regular training courses to prepare officers to undertake training and, since 1964, by the institution of senior probation officers with special training responsibilities. There are now sixteen of these, based strategically over the country, taking groups of about six students at a time. In some areas, other probation officers with responsibilities for training have been able to attend group meetings, perhaps with a psychiatrist, or extra-mural courses arranged at universities. It must be recognized, however, that probation training is a commitment of the whole service. Most officers who supervise students do so in addition to their normal duties and with no special recognition in seniority or pay; to make it possible for them to do it other officers may have to accept extra burdens. In any case the local service to which a student comes will, consciously or unconsciously, contribute much to his picture of the service and of what is expected of him.

As regards the second requisite, continuity of contact between field supervisors and theoretical tutors, the position of the central Home Office course is different from that of any of the university-linked courses, including those similarly designed to give one-year's training to mature students. The difference arises partly from the fact that the central course, taking such large numbers of probation students, must seek practical work placements for them all over the country, often at a great distance from London. The course is accordingly divided into three main blocks: a short practical work placement of about three months, normally outside London; a continuous theoretical course in London lasting another three months, and a longer second practical work placement lasting between four and five months, again usually in the provinces. In contrast with this, the university courses, taking fewer probation students and in most cases able to find placements for their students in their own areas, are able to run the theoretical and practical parts of training more or less concurrently. The pattern is two or three days a week on theory, two or three on practice. The tutors on these courses are better placed than those on the central course to keep in touch with local supervisors throughout.

Though the contrasted pattern of block placements and concurrent theory and practice may be seen partly as a function of the availability of nearby practical work supervisors, there are also differing opinions as to which is, in fact, the most helpful for students. Though the "concurrent" system is academically fashionable at present, and though it would seem, theoretically at least, to give better opportunities for students to take material from either the practical or academic side and discuss it directly with their tutor or supervisor on the other side, it is by no means certain that this does produce better results.[1] The following discussion of the block placement system illustrates both the role of practical work supervisors and the sequence of teaching in the training of the majority of probation officers who enter the service by way of the central course at present.

During the initial period at a probation office, the supervisor has the complex task of offering the new student his first developing relationship with a serving officer, of acting both as theoretical and practical teacher. He must help the student begin to look in a new way at human behaviour and at the professional response to need in social casework. It used to be considered that at this stage teaching could not go much beyond observation and discussion. Now it is felt, at least by some training officers, that some direct experience of casework is necessary if the student is to derive full benefit from his subsequent theoretical learning, and that therefore

---

1. For a discussion of the unproven assumptions and ambiguities in arguments about the methods of teaching theory and practice, see Noel Timms, "The Block Placement in Training for Social Work", *Case Conference*, February 1963.

he should himself begin to supervise two or three relatively normal cases almost from the outset. Certainly it is now clearly appreciated that this first placement is of great importance in influencing the attitude of a student to the remainder of his course. It is by no means a simple job, either intellectually or personally, for his supervisor.

The second and longer period of practical training, following the theoretical course, involves helping the student to begin to apply his fresh learning, so far usually undigested, to the actualities of the job. It is at this stage that he has a chance to make casework a part of his personal experience, so that it becomes really alive and meaningful to him. A variety of cases will be assigned to him, increasing in number and complexity as he becomes more skilled. The fact that he has now his own cases stimulates his desire to learn, his resourcefulness and his imagination. It confronts him with live problems, to the solution of which he can make a contribution whilst he learns. At the same time it brings him up against the stresses of working under pressure and the difficulties of maintaining the necessary degree of objectivity whilst emotionally involved in a live situation. He will be required to keep detailed records of his interviews, trying to describe his clients' feelings and his own as well as the other facts of the situation. The very process of getting these things on paper can contribute to his insight into what is taking place, an insight which will be supplemented by regular discussions with his supervisor. Partly this joint consideration will be directed to helping him to recognize his own strengths and weaknesses, partly it will be concerned with helping him to discover the relevance and usefulness of what he has learned in the theoretical part of the course. At the same time it enables the supervisor to make sure that obligations to the client and community are being met. Through it, also, the student can develop skill in selecting the essential features of an interview, so that when he subsequently has a much larger number of cases as a probation officer he will know what needs to be noted in regular case records. He will similarly have to learn, by experience as well as discussion, his own role in preparing reports for the courts, what they should include and how they should be presented. And now that he is playing an active part and becoming increasingly responsible for his work, he will need further help in coming to terms with his relations to the courts, and others involved in the administration of justice, in seeing these as a very real part of his work, not merely tiresome interruptions.[1]

It will be seen that the block system of training imposes heavy demands upon the fieldwork supervisors at both stages. At the same time, links with the theoretical course are comparatively tenuous and the student himself has no continuous contact with the tutor who is responsible for him during his period of academic learning: he may not see him before he goes to take this in London.

This difficulty has not been wholly overcome by the appointment, already referred to, of training seniors to supervise groups of students during their second placements. Such groups, however, have certain things to offer in their own right, as well as certain special difficulties. They contribute to the whole problem of linking theory and practice by reducing the isolation of students during their practical work. Group interaction can facilitate teaching. Groups may include trainees not only from the central course but from the provincial ones, doing practical work at one or more offices, and they may also include, for example, non-probation students, intending to enter child care or some other field, who are spending a period at a local probation office. And training seniors are able to specialize in this very important and exacting work. There is some agreement that, ideally, students should have experience of both individual and group placements during training.

Practical work under the system of concurrent theory and practice has the same objectives as under the block placement system. Here, however, the same group of students will meet together throughout; continuity and support will be provided by a single tutor keeping in contact with successive practical work supervisors. On the one-year regional courses, for example, tutors, supervisors and staff can meet before each course begins and continue to meet monthly whilst it continues; and some supervisors teach probation practice at the university to the students they will be supervising in the field. Cases can be followed up over a long period and it is less easy for students to reject, as academic and unreal, those parts of the course, such as theories of human growth and behaviour, which may threaten long-held and emotionally powerful assumptions. On the other hand, they may feel confused about their own

---

1. On all this, see F. Jarvis and W. B. Utting, *Aspects of Training*, Probation Papers No. 2, 1965.

roles, find it a strain to switch continually from one kind of work to the other, or to identify themselves satisfactorily either as students or as professionals. For older, less academic, students particularly, there may be advantages in the block system with its more clear-cut role at each stage, its closer identification in turn with study and with the work of a probation office.

5   RESPONSIBILITY FOR TRAINING

The question of responsibility for organizing training has become increasingly controversial over the past decade. The credit for having initiated the modern system of professional training for probation officers lies with the Home Office. It initiated the first experiment in pre-service training in 1930; it developed the first regular professional course; ever since the war it has been expanding this in the wake of constantly increasing demands on the service. Yet the Home Office has never been alone in its responsibility for preparing probation officers. In early days the Police Court Mission and the University of London played a part, through extension courses for serving officers. The first experiment, on which subsequent official courses were based, involved the co-operation of probation offices on one hand and universities on the other. The National Association of Probation Officers has traditionally provided study conferences for serving officers, and has shown increasing concern about the whole framework of training. Now, though the Home Office course still takes the biggest single share, and though the Home Office retains ultimate responsibility for the selection and training of the great majority, it no longer has the monopoly in this and its position is no longer unchallenged.

It can be claimed that in the past the Home Office has been responsible for raising the general level of training in the service as high as it is. It can be claimed that it has provided a legitimate way in for older students who might never have been able to qualify for university entrance. It can be claimed that, since the majority of all officers have passed through its courses, with or without a prior university course, it has avoided a sharp division in the service on the basis of academic background. It has been claimed that, since the Probation and After-Care Department is part of the Home Office, it can co-ordinate courses for probation officers with those for child-care officers on the one hand, prison officials on the other.

It has been claimed that, as the government department ultimately responsible for the effective manning of the probation service, the Home Office must control selection and the level of training. It can be claimed that because the probation and after-care inspectorate is in constant touch with the work of the service it knows, better than any purely academic body, what qualities are to be looked for in new entrants, what should be the priorities in training.

Against this has been set, in the first place, the argument that Home Office control of training in general, and the central course in particular, have all the defects of their qualities. The fact that they were first in the field, the enthusiasm with which they adopted what were then new ideas, may militate against openness to change. So may a tendency to inbreeding, a lack of direct contact with other branches of social work. The continuity of direct Home Office responsibility through selection and training to inspection and maintenance of standards can also be seen as a liability as well as an asset. It has been argued that the dual role of inspectors, as educators during training and as assessors of competence and of suitability for promotion later, arouses undue anxiety amongst students, suspicion amongst serving officers: a tutor who is a member of a university, independent of the government department which may later have a decisive voice in an officer's prospects, is felt to be much less inhibiting.[1] Most fundamental of all is the contention that a government department, seen as necessarily hierarchical and conservative and organized on the basis of administrative checks and balances, cannot be, or at least remain for long, a satisfactory educational body, open to change, encouraging freedom of thought, criticism and experiment.

Various alternatives to the present system have been put forward, some seen as long-term, others as short-term solutions.

The National Association of Probation Officers has accepted the view that the existence of three major councils concerned with professional training—one providing for probation and after-care, one for child-care and one (the Council for Training in Social Work) mainly for those in the health and welfare departments of local authorities, is wasteful of resources and prevents satisfactory planning of social work training as a whole. The Association has

---

1. *N.A.P.O. Policy Statement*, para. 17. See also on this, however, *Report of the Departmental Committee on the Probation Service*, 1962, para. 297.

therefore favoured the establishment of a new Social Work Training Council, independent of any government department and financed from public funds, on the lines of the present Council for Training in Social Work. This Council would include representatives of the professional social work organizations and of the other interests concerned, and would accept a responsibility for developing social work training of all kinds in conjunction with the universities and other places of higher education. In the field of non-graduate training the Council would award a qualification, similar to the present Certificate in Social Work, but applicable to non-graduate training of the required standard for all forms of social work.[1] A similar line has been taken by the Seebohm Committee, which emphasizes that even though the probation and after-care service as such may remain separate from the unified local authority social service departments proposed, it should be included in the new integration of training.[2]

It may, however, be a long time before an integrated advisory and training council can be developed, even if it then proves to be an appropriate body to take over probation training. Accordingly, at least for the present, the National Association of Probation Officers has proposed a training council for probation rather more like the Central Council in Child Care, which sponsors but does not organize its own courses. With this would be combined the further development of provincial courses or other provincial training facilities, so that pressure could be taken off the central course and so that it would gradually lose its key position in training. It is hoped also that such a development of other facilities would allow a gradual change to a two-year training for all entrants.

Already direct Home Office control has relaxed. Universities have been playing an increasing part, not only at the preliminary social science stage but in professional training also. There are more opportunities for probation officers to learn alongside other social workers. Changes in the social services as a whole are tending towards greater unity. It is important for probation officers, their clients and the community that training for the service should not be cut off from the mainstream.

On the other hand, too narrow a definition of social work itself, too exclusive a view of social work training, could narrow and dis-

---

1. *N.A.P.O. Policy Statement*, paras. 1, 18, 19.
2. *Report of the Committee on Local Authority and allied Personal Social Surveys*, 1968.

tort the outlook of probation officers, as of other social workers. All social workers need some understanding of the legitimate functions of control. It would be bad for probation and after-care to cut itself off from the rest of social work, but it would be bad also for other social workers to cut themselves off from those who have to deal with delinquency and crime. The penal system is a part of society, and those involved in it are as much in need of the help of social workers as any.

It is partly because of a feeling that social work training and social work concepts at present can fail to cover adequately the whole range of the probation officer's responsibilities that there have been suggestions from time to time of some kind of training institution either concerned with probation alone or linking it with others specializing in the treatment of offenders, including the wardens of homes and hostels and some institutional staff. The idea of a residential Probation College with a whole-time director and staff was rejected by the Morison Committee on the ground that it could not be justified at that stage of development, though it might merit further consideration in some form later. Developments since then in the size and duties of the service might yet mean that this scheme could be revived, perhaps in an extended form.

6 IN-SERVICE TRAINING AND STAFF DEVELOPMENT

Finally, and closely related to the problem of expanding training to keep up with new demands, there is the question of continued learning after appointment: of keeping serving officers abreast of new knowledge, of encouraging experiment and initiative, of what has been called "staff development". It is very evident that all that a probation officer needs to know cannot be taught during his initial training. This is not merely a question of the limited time available. It is only as he grows professionally that he will know in which directions he can most profitably advance and perhaps specialize. For another thing, knowledge and methods are themselves in a continuing state of development; and the environment, both social and administrative, in a continual state of change.

There is an obvious distinction between an officer's first period in the service, while he is still acquiring basic skills and strengthening his precarious grasp on new ideas, and his subsequent years of development in experience and competence. The mutual expectations of officer and senior will gradually change as he moves from one stage to another.

The first thing he has to face is the move from being a student to being a fully responsible officer, from a caseload selected and planned to meet his needs in learning, to the expectation that he take his full share in the work of the service and face the full pressures of demands from all directions to which a probation officer is normally exposed. At this crisis the new officer often regresses, apparently disowning for a time much of what he has learned, ambivalent about his dependence on the senior and uncertain in his expectations of himself and his colleagues. Most seniors try to carry on regular supervision at this stage: but the focus is no longer solely on individual learning. Periodic evaluation and reports are made to the principal who, either personally or through his deputy or assistant, also maintains contact with the new officer.

The first year of work culminates in an inspection by the principal or his deputy, with a view to confirmation of appointment. Until 1968 these inspections were carried out by the Home Office and there is little experience yet of the new system. It has the merit of freeing Home Office inspectors to develop their work with more experienced officers and to help the service with its growing administrative and organizational problems. It has also the merit of involving probation officers more directly in responsibility for their own professional standards: "It will not be easy always to reconcile satisfactorily the need to support and encourage with the duty to inspect and, in effect, on occasion recommend dismissal".[1] This is in part the dilemma of a supervisor or senior at any time, and much will depend on the professional competence and detachment of the inspecting principal.

There is no sharp division between work before and after confirmation. For the senior the term "experienced officer" may include those with a few or many years' experience, of very varied personalities, some with little training or skill and others better equipped in both these respects than himself. His responsibility is still, however, both to give continuing support and encouragement

---

1. *Probation*, Vol. 14, No. 1, March 1968.

in professional development and to ensure the maintenance of reasonable standards of competence. This is partly because it cannot be assumed by any public service that all its staff are equally reliable and partly because the way in which new duties, such as parole, are organized emphasizes the collective responsibility of the service. The senior is required to make a written report annually to the principal concerning the progress and competence of each officer and the principal then sees each officer to make an evaluation of his professional development.

The difficulty of seniors in carrying out their dual function is reflected in differing views about the balance between individual responsibility and control and in the uncertain use of key words such as supervision, consultation, inspection, scrutiny, to describe the meeting between the senior and the officer. Seniors tend to see their work with inexperienced staff as supervision, in which the initiative rests with the senior. With experienced staff the term "consultation" is more frequently used, emphasizing the initiative of the officer and perhaps expressing something of the senior's own diffidence. The first edition of this book in 1958 talked about case-work supervision as possibly the best method of meeting the need for continuous learning but referred to it as "still a tentative development in the Service".[1] With the increasing number of new officers who have had a good experience of supervision in training and expect it to continue on the job, and with the loss of older officers whose experience has been different, it seems likely that any uneasiness will continue to be reduced. The enabling and the inspecting aspects are complementary in good supervision.

In many offices there are regular meetings of the office group, though these vary greatly in frequency. They may focus on a specific topic, perhaps producing a paper on it, or they may appear more haphazard, allowing individual members to bring what they wish. Many groups will concentrate upon particular cases, looking at one client and his family in terms of diagnosis, treatment, casework methods, the officer's involvement. Others study specific subjects such as school phobia, addiction, the use of authority, particular offences or personality types, matrimonial cases, after-care. Some groups draw in officers from neighbouring areas who have common

---

1. J. King (ed.), *The Probation Service*, 1958, pp. 138 and 141.

needs, such as those still awaiting confirmation. Some officers meet with social workers from other agencies, perhaps child care officers or psychiatric social workers, sometimes with a psychiatrist or other case worker as leader or consultant. Many officers, however, attach considerable importance to the basic grouping of the senior and his team: here difficulties of unevenness of experience and need may be outweighed by the advantages of an ongoing service of diagnosis and review of treatment methods, by the unity and mutual support generated within the working unit, and by the opportunity for the unit in this way to develop a corporate identity, with a distinctive contribution as a part of the local community.

In addition to these activities, which are mainly office-based, there is considerable use of outside bodies for special seminars, courses and for various forms of advanced training. A recent survey by the National Association of Probation Officers found that almost all of the thirty-three probation areas which replied to the question-naire were using local universities, colleges of technology or further education; half had access to psychiatric hospital staff, the Institute for the Scientific Treatment of Delinquency or the British Association for Social Psychiatry; slightly less than a third made use of the Family Discussion Bureau; and the Howard League and the Workers' Educational Association were used by two areas.[1]

The Home Office arranges certain short residential courses on a national basis. They include refresher courses, usually held at a university but with a probation inspector taking part, courses for tutor and senior officers, an advanced course in matrimonial con-ciliation work run by the Family Discussion Bureau. A few principal and senior officers join others concerned in the administration of justice and the penal system on the Senior Course held every two years at the Institute of Criminology, Cambridge. A very small number of officers are seconded annually for longer advanced training courses run by other bodies, such as the Tavistock Clinic and the London School of Economics. Probation committees are now responsible for meeting the cost of this advanced training but, though many adopt a liberal policy, the number of probation applicants has dropped sharply since this responsibility passed from the Home Office to them in 1965. It seems important that the service

---

1. *N.A.P.O. Policy Statement*, para. 11, 3, 4.

should not lose the opportunity that these courses offer, and that it should be geared to make full use of the skills acquired by those who take them. There is a growing need, as administration becomes more complex, for training in administration also to be made available for caseworkers moving into higher administrative positions.

The newer developments in the work of the service also call for specific kinds of in-service training. Seminars in groupwork have been mentioned elsewhere. The use of volunteers and the problems of voluntary after-care are other such topics. So is prison welfare. Some of these are subjects which may rightly be treated only in outline in pre-service training. All will have been omitted altogether from the preliminary training of the great majority of those already in the service. They therefore need special attention at a later stage. Lectures, visits to institutions, exchanges and discussions have been arranged to help officers in their new after-care responsibilities. For those entering prison welfare there are three-week courses at Wakefield, designed to give a broad understanding of penal institutions and how they function. It has been suggested that for the future a short course should be taken before an officer enters prison work, to prepare him for the impact of a prison, to give him a working knowledge of its hierarchy and structure as well as of the duties of the welfare department. After a year's experience, he should take a fuller course like that at Wakefield, which would qualify him amongst other things to act as a casework consultant and take an active part in prison service staff training.

Variations between areas appear in all aspects of training, as in working conditions. The value of courses depends largely on whether they are part of a planned programme of professional development or are isolated events never followed up. This applies whether they are designed to give training on a specific subject, like prison welfare, or have a wider purpose in developing casework skills or in giving an opportunity for re-appraisal after a number of years of work.

The most active areas in staff development are not necessarily the cities. Some large rural areas have made careful arrangements to overcome the dangers of fragmentation. There may be one- or two-day staff meetings, held perhaps twice a year, with residential conferences every two years, drawing together officers from the whole county and both preceded and followed by periods of work in individual groups and areas. This enables use to be made of outside resources, like universities and experts in other fields, whose contribution can be clearly focused. It is sometimes easier to carry through this kind of continuous programme in rural areas than in the larger urban areas, where sheer numbers present acute problems of organization. But whereas some areas have argued that the pressure is so great that it would be impossible to provide in-service training, others have held that just because of this continued training is essential.

The need for more coherent policies of in-service training and staff development is now acknowledged. During 1969 four regional training officers have been appointed, based on Bristol, Leeds, London and Nottingham, to co-ordinate and develop the training of serving probation officers in England and Wales. They are responsible to regional training committees, consisting of magistrates and principal probation officers representing the interests of all the probation and after-care areas in the region. It is envisaged that they will co-operate with existing educational establishments in their regions, especially university extra-mural departments, and that they will establish links with other social work services embarking upon related training. The officers will keep in close contact with the Home Office in preparing training plans for their regions. Their primary tasks are to strengthen the provisions for officers during their first year of service, to plan regional training for experienced senior probation officers, and to plan regional courses to meet the needs of basic grade officers. These arrangements should help officers to keep abreast of developing duties and new knowledge.

Whatever may be said about the making of probation officers at this time—and it must be apparent that many different things are being said—it cannot be complained that any aspect is static. There is movement everywhere, inside and outside of the service, and it is clear that there must be yet more movement. Whatever the direction ultimately taken, it must have full regard to the purposes of the probation officer's work. It must equip people to live with the problems of those who are at odds with society.

Training at all stages costs money and calls for the investment of scarce resources. But demands for the sorts of people who make good probation officers are increasing on all sides. The harder it is to raise numbers the more vital it is to improve quality. Those who do come into the service must be used as fully as possible at all stages of their careers, not only directly but as consultants and guides for new entrants, for volunteers, perhaps for ancillary workers and prison staff who become involved in welfare. The recent bold moves to keep more people out of prison and to release more prisoners earlier depend at many points upon the skill and judgment of probation officers. It cannot be assumed that treatment and supervision in the open can be adequately provided at negligible cost. The education of probation officers, though it may well be more expensive than in the past, is an investment in the future of the whole system of criminal justice, perhaps of civil justice as well.

CHAPTER 12

RESEARCH

THIS subject is inevitably technical. Yet it is of great importance, both to probation officers and to magistrates. It has a special importance also for probation and after-care committees, who will, it is hoped, increasingly consider the need for participation in research in assessing the appropriate establishment of probation officers in their areas. The Inner London and the Liverpool Services, for example, have already made provision for two officers to undertake research into the needs of homeless offenders. If the extent of new responsibilities is to be adequately assessed, if new ventures in treatment are to be tested, this kind of investigation will be increasingly necessary.

The United Kingdom spends a higher proportion of its national income than most countries upon research in the penological field. And the work of the probation and after-care service has in recent years come in for a very fair share of attention. Even so, the proportion of resources devoted to research of this kind falls far short of what an industrial concern would consider essential. There is a very real interest in penal reform, and sweeping legislative changes are being made. It is acknowledged that these need to be complemented by continuing research into their working and their effects.

For all this, caution is necessary in interpreting the findings of research, particularly, perhaps, research into the effectiveness of treatment.

Obvious though it may seem, it is still often forgotten in public discussion of results that the success rate of a particular measure, in terms of subsequent behaviour, depends upon the sort of offender for whom it is chiefly used, not merely (probably not mainly) on the treatment itself. Thus, for example, measures applied to offenders with long criminal records or with serious personal or social problems are, in the nature of things, likely to be followed by a higher proportion of reconvictions than measures reserved mainly for first offenders or those thought unlikely to offend again. Only when different forms of treatment are compared in their application to groups of offenders presenting the same risk of reconviction at the outset can we come anywhere near conclusions as to which are most effective in preventing further crime.

It is sometimes said that the prevention of crime alone is an inadequate criterion of the results of a measure like probation which has also wider objectives in the way of social rehabilitation. The possibility of finding other appropriate criteria has been under investigation, but so far the indications seem to be that a relapse into crime is likely to be as good an indication as any of the failure of rehabilitation in other directions. On the other hand, it must always be borne in mind that the rehabilitation of a persistent offender is not likely to be achieved quickly or easily. With some people a number of failures may be inevitable on the way to success: with them even a reduction in the frequency or seriousness of offences committed may be a sign that some impression is being made.

Another fact that should perhaps be emphasized is that research in this field is still in its infancy. It is still developing its tools, it is barely beginning to repeat studies made at one place and time to see how far generalizations from them elsewhere can be justified. It is becoming increasingly clear that studies of the effects of particular measures upon an undifferentiated group of offenders are of little help. There are indications that (as might be expected) people with different kinds of personality, different degrees of maturity, respond differently to different kinds of approach. There are very great difficulties, however, in dividing offenders into "types" relevant to their response to treatment. There are still greater difficulties in thus dividing kinds of treatment. Hence progress in this sort of research is likely to be only gradual. Apparently positive results may give clues as to useful directions for experiment, but should not lead to hasty or sweeping changes in policy. Apparently negative results should not cause undue discouragement. At this stage they are as likely to stem from the shortcomings of research tools and methods as from the shortcomings of the treatment.

Though too much should not be expected too quickly, research is a most wholesome antidote to complacency, its development a most necessary basis for further advance.

During its formative years the modern probation and after-care service has gained much from the application of insights and skills derived from clinical experience in allied fields. The influence of the analytical schools of psychology on the development of social casework theory helped to provide the basic diagnostic and treatment tools which have become an integral part of the probation officer's skills. But the last decade has seen a growing recognition within the service of the need to examine and learn directly from its own experience. This has perhaps been stimulated by the comments of the Streatfeild Committee on reports to courts and by the assumption of new responsibilities in, for example, after-care, the use of volunteers and prison welfare.

Coincident with this development has been the recent growth in criminological research in this country, and the establishment of the Home Office Research Unit and the Cambridge Institute of Criminology. These centres (and some University Departments of Social Science) have not only sought the help of the probation and after-care service in research projects, but have given probation officers themselves the opportunity to learn something about research methods and to begin to consider how their accumulated experience could be examined systematically and objectively. Thus inside the service probation officers have begun to look more critically at their methods and to recognize the relevance of research as a means of obtaining the knowledge to cope with increasingly diverse and complex duties.

Common interest has drawn the research worker and the probation officer together, but differences in outlook can still hamper effective partnership. The research worker, of necessity, sees the offender in relatively objective terms as a member of a category or type, while the probation officer sees him in the context of a subjective relationship as a unique individual. Similarly, each may be handicapped by his perception of the other. The research worker sometimes seems prone to undervalue the probation officer's diagnostic and treatment skills, not through any lack of respect for him, but because he must rely so often upon clinical insights which lack objective evidence or reliable means of measurement. The probation officer, for his part, sometimes feels that the research worker lacks a sense of practical urgency; he is prone to expect either far too much or too little from research findings. Superimposed on these misunderstandings lies the problem of communication, especially for the probation officer, who finds many research papers difficult to follow and is easily discouraged by what may seem to be an excess of tables and statistics.

To talk of research and its implications in general terms may not be very helpful. Accordingly, the bulk of this chapter is devoted to examples of what is being done in this country, and in one or two instances in the United States, with a direct bearing upon the work of the probation officers. This illustrates something of the variety of aspects being studied and the variety of ways of approaching them. It also shows how far probation officers have been directly involved both in planning and execution.

Real as difficulties of co-operation are, there is a growing sense of partnership and understanding between the research worker and the probation officer, each acknowledging his need of the other if projects are to be competently carried out yet related to practical realities. A major contribution to this co-operative spirit has come from the Probation Research Project, started in 1962 by the Home Office Research Unit. From the outset, staff on the project went into the field to meet probation officers, to canvass their opinions about what sorts of research they thought were needed, to enlist their co-operation in a joint enterprise and, most important, to establish mutual respect and confidence at a personal level. In the reverse direction, the secondment of probation officers to the project has ensured that the practitioner's viewpoint has been represented at every stage of the work.

Although the Probation Research Project was by no means the first research related to the probation officer's work, it may be useful to discuss it before some other research in this field. Most of the findings of the project have still to be published, including those from the National Study of Probation which forms its central theme, but four reports dealing with various parts of the total programme of research have so far appeared.[1]

The first of these gives a general outline of the research programme, taking as its starting point the wide variety of types of

---

1. For a general discussion of the Project, see also *Report on the Work of the Probation and After-Care Department*, 1962–1965, H.M.S.O., 1966.

offender put on probation, and the equally wide variety of types of treatment used by probation officers. It describes the general purpose of the project as being "to study differences in outcome for different types of offenders who have been dealt with in various ways whilst on probation". It also records the findings of the pilot project, carried out in Middlesex during 1962, to provide general knowledge and experience of probation for the research workers, to enlist the active collaboration of Middlesex probation officers in the planning of the National Study of Probation, and to make a preliminary study of treatment. Its findings are, of course, very tentative, but they include a comparison of the attitudes of officers of different ages, experience, sex and training to various factors in the assessment and treatment of probationers, and the results of a study of the records of a sample of adult and juvenile probationers. These findings have been used in the development of the treatment typology used in the National Study.[1]

The second published report describes a study designed to provide a broad statistical background to the National Study. It examines trends in the work of the probation service and its staffing between 1950 and 1961. These figures showed that, although the total numbers on probation continued to rise during the decade a declining proportion of all offenders were being put on probation, except in the higher courts. They showed, too, the tendency for probation to constitute a somewhat smaller part of the probation officers' total caseload as his other duties expanded. Comparisons between different parts of England and Wales during 1961 revealed that in regions where the number of indictable offences known to the police was high (London and the North), probation was used proportionately less. It also revealed that those regions which had a higher proportion of staff who were untrained before appointment and higher caseloads (the North, the Midlands and Wales) had a lower "success rate". All these differences, of course, may relate to the different characteristics of the regions and their different social problems.[2]

---

1. Steven Folkard, Kate Lyon, Margaret M. Carver and Erica O'Leary, *Probation Research: A Preliminary Report: Part I, General Outline of Research; Part II, Study of Middlesex Probation Area (S.O.M.P.A.)*, H.M.S.O., 1966.

2. Hugh Barr and Erica O'Leary, *Trends and Regional Comparisons in Probation (England and Wales)*, H.M.S.O., 1966; see also McClintock and Avison, *Crime in England and Wales*, 1968.

The third report resulted from the research team's interest in treatment innovations and collates the opinions of seventy-five probation officers with experience of group work.[1] It includes an extensive critical discussion of the value and limitations of this kind of treatment, as used so far by probation officers in this country. The potential value of such assessments of developing areas of treatment is considerable. Again this is to be regarded as a preliminary report, needing to be followed up by more intensive study.

The fourth report gives the result obtained when male probationers aged seventeen to twenty-one were tested with the Jesness Inventory, an American psychological test which attempts to assess personality problems of delinquents.[2] This also was preparatory to the National Study.

The National Study of Probation itself involves a programme of work lasting some eight years. Probation officers have been interviewed in eighteen cities and towns, and in eight of these—Liverpool, Manchester, Sheffield, Leeds, Birmingham, Coventry, Glasgow and parts of London—a more detailed study has also been made of male offenders aged seventeen to twenty-one years who were put on probation during 1964. In seven of the cities most probationers were allocated to officers on a geographical basis, as is the usual practice, but in Sheffield an experiment in matching probation officer and probationer was conducted. The general purpose of the research in both the experimental and the non-experimental situations has been to discover whether certain specified forms of treatment are more effective than others in dealing with different types of offender.

The framework used for classifying the probationers' problems took account of the inter-relationship of personal problems, whether of inadequacy or disturbance, and social problems, whether cultural influences or situational stresses. Similarly, probation treatment was classified according to the relative emphasis given, firstly, to helping the probationer solve or mitigate his problems (support) as compared with regulating his behaviour (control); secondly, to treatment focused primarily on the individual probationer (individual treat-

---

1. Hugh Barr, *A Survey of Group Work in the Probation Service*, H.M.S.O., 1966. On some of the findings, see above, pp. 162–167.
2. Martin Davies, *The Use of the Jesness Inventory on a sample of British Probationers*, H.M.S.O., 1967.

ment) as compared with treatment focused primarily on his social environment (situational treatment). These dimensions of treatment were combined to give four main categories: individual support, individual control, situational support and situational control. It was not assumed that these categories would be mutually exclusive, and it was recognized that a probation officer might use more than one approach in dealing with a particular case, or change his approach during the course of time.

Using information based on probation officers' opinions, records have been completed on the assessment and treatment of some seven hundred probationers. Using reconviction figures and other criteria, it is hoped that the analysis of the study may throw some light on the effectiveness of the different types of treatment for various types of probationer.

Anyone familiar with probation practice will recognize the difficulties in reducing the complexity of assessment and treatment to a relatively simple conceptual form, and thus the ambitious nature of the National Study of Probation. Its publication is awaited with interest, but it would be unwise to expect many clear-cut conclusions from this, the first study of its kind in this country. Even so, it has already proved a valuable aid towards clarifying concepts of assessment and treatment.

A number of other supporting studies are in hand within the Research Unit. As a contrast to the broad scale of the main study, detailed research is being carried out by techniques such as process recording to throw light on the way in which certain probation officers and probationers perceive each other and how they interact in interviews. Other enquiries are looking at methods of predicting the risk of reconviction amongst probationers, at stresses in the lives of probationers, and at the working of probation hostels and after-care hostels. It is likely that most of these will be published very shortly.

Although the Probation Research Project was originally designed to last only five years, it has now been put on a permanent footing operating from Manchester as a section of the Home Office Research Unit.[1] This development has been welcomed on behalf of the service

---

1. For a description of future plans for the permanent unit, see A. Watkin, "A report on past and future research", *Bulletin* 1/8 *of the Central Council of Probation and After-Care Committees*, March 1968.

by the National Association of Probation Officers and the Principal
Probation Officers' Conference, both of which are represented on
its steering committee. Through them, probation officers can
influence the sort of studies undertaken and future research policy.

There were three earlier studies which particularly helped to
create interest in probation research. The largest was carried out by
the Cambridge Department of Criminal Science and published in
1958.[1] It was the first study of the reconviction of probationers in
England during and after the termination of their orders. It was
based on information about ten thousand probationers in London
and Middlesex collected in the ordinary routine during the period
1948-1953, which the Cambridge team was asked to analyse. Although the scope of the information on each offender was unfortunately very limited, the findings did show that female probationers
"succeeded" more frequently than male, adults than juveniles, and
first offenders than recidivists.

The other two pioneering studies were respectively by Wilkins[2]
and Grünhut[3]. Wilkins found no significant differences in the
reconviction rates of two small matched samples of probationers
and other offenders (most of whom were sent to prison or borstal);
the study thus raised important questions about the effectiveness of
all these methods of treatment and so partly led to the present
Home Office study, in the early stages of which Wilkins himself
played an important role. Grünhut's study was more descriptive,
being an account of the use by the courts of probation with a condition of medical treatment under s. 4 of the Criminal Justice Act
1948, and an analysis of the characteristics and response of the
offenders in respect of whom such orders were made in England
and Wales in 1953.

An encouraging feature of recent developments has been the
increasing interchange of information with research projects in the
U.S.A. To attempt a synopsis of all American research in the probation field is beyond the scope of this chapter. But one study, the
San Francisco Project which involves a major comparison of types
of supervision given to Federal probationers and parolees may be

---

1. F. H. McClintock, *The Results of Probation*, (English Studies in Criminal
Science), Macmillan, 1958.
2. Wilkins, L. T., "A Small Comparative Study of the Results of Probation",
Brit. Jour. Delinq., 1958, Vol. 8.
3. Grünhut, M., *Probation and Mental Treatment*, Tavistock, 1963.

of particular interest. Four types were defined and each of these was related to the size of caseload thought appropriate for an officer providing such supervision. They were as follows:

"Minimum" (or "crisis") supervision: The only obligation on the offender is to send a written report to the probation officer once a month. Otherwise no action is taken by the probation officer unless the offender specifically seeks help in a crisis. There is no routine contact. (Approximate caseload 350.)

"Intensive" supervision: Offenders are contacted at least once per week. (Caseloads not more than twenty, plus one pre-sentence report per month.)

"Ideal" supervision: Offenders are contacted at least twice per month. (Caseloads not more than forty, plus two pre-sentence reports per month.)

"Normal" supervision: As currently carried out by Federal probation officers in San Francisco.[1] (Approximate caseloads eighty to eighty-five plus three or four pre-sentence reports per month.)

In the first phase of the project all offenders coming to the probation office were allocated at random to one of the three "special" types of treatment. The overall "violation rates" (excluding merely technical violations) after two years were: "Minimum" supervision 22.2 per cent; "Ideal" supervision 22.2 per cent; "Intensive" supervision 20.0 per cent. As the authors say, "These data suggest that the *random* assignment of offenders to caseloads, despite variations in the intensity of supervision, does not modify the outcome".

In the second phase of the project, offenders are classified on a three-point scale for each of four factors, namely, age, previous criminal record, current offence and psychological stability (psychological stability is measured using the socialization scale from the California Psychological Inventory). A "profile" is then built up for each offender from these ratings and he is assigned to a particular type of supervision on the basis of a table which gives the type of supervision thought appropriate for each profile.

Although research techniques and methods of classification differ, as regards both offender and treatment, the San Francisco Project and the Probation Research Project are both attempting a com-

---

1. This study is being carried out by the School of Criminology, University of California, Berkeley. Mimeographed research reports are available on request.

parison of the effectiveness of various types of treatment for various types of offender. Despite the many technical problems involved in such projects, it hoped that they will hold the key to improving the effectiveness of treatment and, therefore, in time, may have important implications for probation practice.[1]

So far, very little research has been done on the probation officer's vital responsibility in forming opinions which may be included in his reports to the courts and influence them in deciding treatment. In a small study in Philadelphia, seventeen probation officers were asked to select the type of information they needed from a list of forty-nine possibilities to enable them to decide whether a particular offender was or was not suitable for probation. This revealed a "lack of consensus among trained officers as to the value of information in decision making", and whilst twelve officers thought that the offender should be put on probation, five did not. These differences were not related to sex, degree of training, or length of experience.[2] Another small-scale study in a Sunderland magistrates' court compared reconviction rates before, and at two periods after, an extension in the use of pre-sentence reports. The author's tentative conclusion was that "the bench improved in its ability to make effective use of reports in sentencing the longer the scheme was in operation".[3] If this should prove to be nationally applicable it would be very encouraging to probation officers. Though it could be misleading to read too much into small-scale research, there is a clear need to examine systematically how decisions are made and how the provision of probation officers' reports, whether or not they include specific opinions on treatment, affect sentencing practice and reconviction rates.

Despite the growing importance of after-care, this also has received little attention from the research worker, with the notable exception of borstal boys. In 1955 Mannheim and Wilkins published their prediction tables which, in statistical terms, gave the probability

---

1. For a fuller review, see R. F. Sparks, *Research on the use and effectiveness of probation, parole and measures of after-care*, Council of Europe, 1968, mimeographed.
2. L. T. Wilkins and Ann Chandler, "A Study of Pre-Sentence Decision Making", *British Journal of Criminology*, Vol. 5, pp. 22–35.
3. R. Hood and I. Taylor, "Second Report of the Study of the Effectiveness of Pre-Sentence Investigations in reducing Recidivism", *British Journal of Criminology*, Vol. 8, 1968.

of a boy with certain characteristics being reconvicted.[1] Such prediction scores can be used as a yardstick to compare an offender's
actual response against that which was to be expected. Although
the Mannheim-Wilkins score became an integral part of the information given to a probation officer when a boy was discharged, its
potential value was never fully realized and, of course, since conditions change so fast, such prediction methods become less accurate
the longer the interval between the original research and their
practical application.

There have been several studies of the effects of changes in the
treatment of boys leaving borstal. In 1966 Roger Hood, using the
records of the Borstal After-Care Association, examined various
aspects of the after-care and after-conduct of homeless borstal boys,
some of whom had been dealt with by a special pre-discharge
planning unit. The results suggested that for this type of boy the
plans made before release had no effect on reconviction rates.[2]
Derek Miller in his description of social relations in Northways, a
hostel for discharged homeless borstal boys, compared their reconviction rates with those of carefully matched borstal boys who had
not been to the hostel. The Northways boys had a substantially
better success rate, but within the limits of the very small number
of boys involved the result was not statistically significant.[3]

A major study of borstal treatment including after-care, is currently being conducted by F. H. McClintock and A. E. Bottoms
of the Cambridge Institute of Criminology.[4] The main aim of
the project is to compare the effectiveness of two different regimes
in one borstal. This involves a comparison of over six hundred
boys discharged from Dover borstal during the years 1960–1962,
who had been trained under a traditional closed borstal regime,
and three hundred received into the same institution after the
beginning of 1965, who underwent treatment in a modified regime,
which attempted to place greater emphasis on individualization and
on a problem solving approach. This is an example of action

---

1. H. Mannheim and L. T. Wilkins, *Prediction Methods in relation to Borstal Training*, H.M.S.O., 1955.
2. Roger Hood, *Homeless Borstal Boys*, 1966.
3. Derek Miller, *Growth to Freedom*, Tavistock, 1964.
4. Not yet published. For a general description of the project see A. E. Bottoms and F. H. McClintock, "Operational Research in a Borstal Institution", *British Journal of Criminology*, Vol. 8, 1968, pp. 59–61.

research in which the research workers co-operate with the practitioners in modifying treatment methods or the total treatment
situation, and then work closely together to observe the effects of
the changes brought about.

An encouraging recent development has been the initiative of
individual probation officers who have started their own research,
often selecting areas of the probation officer's duties which, so far,
have escaped the attention of the research organizations. Recent
examples of these have been studies on probation hostels, on the
attitudes of prison welfare officers to their work, on the attitudes of
probation officers, magistrates, justices' clerks, police, medical
social workers, marriage guidance counsellors, psychiatric social
workers and social work tutors to the role of the probation officer.[1]
Another probation officer's study has involved getting some four
hundred adult defendants at London courts to complete the
Maudsley Inventory and relating the scores to information about
them and their backgrounds and subsequently to their reconviction
rates.[2] Yet another has made a study of drug addicts.[3]

When published in widely read journals, these studies provide a
stimulus to thought, and the author's intimate knowledge of his
subject compensates for a lack of statistical sophistication. These
studies may also serve as pointers in planning large-scale investigations at a later stage and thus help to extend the total range of
research in the service. A further benefit is that they help to accustom the service to the idea of research, and even officers with no
direct interest in it develop an appreciation of it and its application
to their practical work.

While independent research by probation officers may well increase as more graduates enter the service with a grounding in
social research methods, the day to day pressures of work will
always lead to conflict, unless more can be done to second staff to
research projects and to provide enough help and advice from
experienced research workers. The initiative taken by the Home

1. R. E. Leeves, "What Criterion for Admission to Probation Hostels?", *British Journal of Criminology*, Vol. 7; F. V. Jarvis, "The Prison Welfare Service: a Survey", *Probation*, Vol. 13, No. 1, March 1967 and "Role Conflict in Probation", *New Society*, 12 October 1967.

2. McWilliams: not yet published.

3. Bean: not yet published.

Office Research Unit in both these matters is most welcome and could set a pattern for the future. No formal qualifications in research are required for the short-term Cropwood Fellowships at the Institute of Criminology: though very limited in numbers, they are open to anyone with responsibility and experience of work in law enforcement, the administration of justice or the treatment of offenders, who wishes to undertake or complete a specific piece of research and who can put forward a well conceived plan of study

From the large-scale project to the local enquiry by a probation officer, it is clear that research has now found an established place within the probation and after-care service. But in an age when research is fashionable there is a danger of overestimating what it can achieve. Criminology is a young science still struggling to emerge as an independent discipline and still imprecise in its methods. Current research may be laying foundations for future progress, but is often unspectacular to the onlooker. The notion of a scientific "breakthrough", as in the physical sciences, has little relevance and progress is likely to be slow and often painstaking.

To the probation officer, conditioned by his casework training and experience to expect modest results and to mistrust the dramatic, it should not be difficult to see the parallel in this between his own work and that of the research worker. Even so, the probation officer needs also to learn to recognize the kind of problem or topic which can be formulated as a research question. The research worker, for his part, needs to be honest with the probation officer about his ability, within the limits of current research skills, to tackle a particular question. He must also make clear the possibility that answers will be no more than tentative, and how long it will be before any findings can be expected. The question may arise out of a situation which must be resolved quickly and decisively by administrative action: if research findings are unlikely to be available for five years they may have no practical value, quite apart from the possibility that the nature of the problem will have changed. Sometimes it may be necessary to take difficult administrative decisions now, relying on judgments based on such information as is already available, rather than wait for the more objective or more complete information that research may eventually be able to supply. On the other hand, when changes are introduced, built-

in research from the outset may contribute to review of a new programme after three to five years.

On the other hand, as has been seen, it is wrong to assume that
all research need be long term and the Probation Research Project
has recently undertaken short term surveys, such as an enquiry into
after-care hostels, designed to aid the administrator. In such studies
there is clearly a need for close co-operation and understanding
between administrators and research workers, with provision for
the former to be apprised of findings as they come to light rather
than waiting for the publication of full reports.

A balanced programme of research needs to include some studies
of this short term kind, designed to help with practical and sometimes urgent problems, and also some of a long term kind which
may eventually throw light on more fundamental problems. What
he can learn directly from the former may act as an incentive to
the probation officer to collaborate also in the latter. Research
involves him in additional work, which may be tedious and take
a lot of time: understandably his feelings about it are mixed and
he needs some incentive, some sense that research can help him
with at least a few of his practical problems.

As research increases, so probation officers are more and more
asked to help, sometimes with studies which have very little practical
application, intended primarily as exercises in research method for
social studies students. They should not be so overloaded with
requests of this kind that they feel unable to participate in major
studies that are well planned and staffed by competent research
workers. The Research Advisory Committee of N.A.P.O. exists to
assist research workers who wish to enlist the help of practitioners
and to advise officers regarding any requests made to them. Part
of its function is to encourage the small study and to stimulate
interest in research, but it is appreciated that some restraint is also
needed.

Perhaps the most exciting prospect for the future is the setting
up of projects in which research worker and practitioners together
can develop innovations in treatment method with built-in evaluation. The project at Dover borstal, the recent experiment with
remedial teaching methods at the Rainer Centre for juvenile probationers in Woolwich, and current developments in the field of
voluntary after-care, could form models for such collaboration.

A third party, however, needs to be brought in: the teacher. In marked contrast to the situation in the academic world as a whole, where teaching and research are closely associated, in probation and after-care they have so far remained largely separate. Undoubtedly the teacher has much to offer in the formulation and carrying out of research and much to gain by first-hand knowledge of findings as they become available. A persuasive argument can be advanced for an institute which would combine innovation in treatment method, research, and a major part in pre-service and in-service training, thus acting as a nerve centre for the probation and after-care service. One facet of its work could be to teach probation officers an appreciation of research methods, as an aid to communication with research workers, and as a preparation for playing an active part in projects.

It would be difficult to overstate the potential value of the accumulated information recorded by the service about a broad cross-section of offenders. The files in a probation office may now contain details relating to an offender's childhood, his court appearance with social enquiries about his background, his response on probation and possible subsequent career in borstal or prison, his contact with the welfare officer and his response to after-care or, perhaps, parole. Unfortunately, much of this information is unsystematically collected and does not lend itself readily to research use. It is difficult to devise records which would satisfy the needs of research workers perhaps years hence, but an exhaustive review of data collection, storage and retrieval in the light of modern business and research methods is long overdue. It would also be helpful to cross-reference all information collected on probation officers' files with various indices of offenders recently started by the Home Office.

Other chapters have drawn attention to the rapid changes taking place in the penal system in general, and in the probation and after-care service in particular. It has moved from the periphery of the penal system, dealing usually with the less hardened offenders put on probation, to a central role in the assessment and treatment of a wide range of offenders. The formidable tasks involved in extending and strengthening existing services and in the implementation of new proposals contained in recent legislation makes it certain that the pace of change will quicken rather than slacken. The service must not shrink from the challenge that these changes present, but it is fully aware of the pressures and demands involved and the limits of its resources. In these conditions it is too easy to become preoccupied with day-to-day problems and administrative matters and to forgo the opportunity to think, to look critically at established practices and to evaluate.

It is perhaps significant that the Probation Research Steering Committee which formerly exercised general oversight of research in the probation field, and the Probation Research Communication Committee, which was concerned with keeping the service interested and informed about research developments, have now combined their functions in a single Probation and After-Care Advisory Committee.

Certainly the introduction of research as an integral part of the service is timely. It could produce a focal point for progressive thinking, tempered by critical and relatively objective study.

THE NATIONAL ASSOCIATION OF PROBATION OFFICERS

THE National Association of Probation Officers had, at the end of 1968, well over two thousand full members, seventy per cent of those eligible. It includes probation officers of all ranks. Since 1966, prison welfare officers, as members of the probation and after-care service, have been eligible for full membership of the Association and recently social workers in detention centres and other penal institutions have also been admitted. In addition the Association has a wide associate membership including many magistrates and others with a special interest in the service, and a group of "teaching associates" engaged in the training of probation officers in the academic field.

When it was founded in London in 1912 the Association was primarily a means by which the few and often scattered individual probation officers could keep in touch.[1] Although the first local branch was established in Yorkshire in 1913, it was not until the nineteen-thirties that a regular network of branches was developed all over the country to enable officers to meet and work together in local groups. These branches remained very active, maintaining links not only amongst probation officers but with magistrates and other social workers in their areas. There are now twenty-four in England and Wales. Each formerly sent a representative to the National Executive, but in 1966 they were grouped, for this purpose, into twelve regions, one of which was the then Scottish Branch, subsequently divided into five branches. The branches remain autonomous, however, and carry on their own local activities. Most meet at least once a quarter. Many, in addition, organize open

---

1. On the early history of the Association see L. Le Mesurier (ed.), *A Handbook of Probation*, 1935, and J. King (ed.), *The Probation Service*, 1958 or 1964.

meetings and conferences, either individually or in co-operation with other branches, at which probation officers, magistrates and others can meet in an informal atmosphere and discuss matters of common interest.

The National Executive Committee of the Association consists of the Chairman, two Vice-chairmen and the Honorary Treasurer, all elected annually by national ballot, and the representatives of the regions, each elected by a regional committee. It is the governing body responsible for the direction, organization and policy of the Association as a united body. Regional representatives are not primarily delegates called upon to voice and vote according to the views of their regions. Naturally they seek to know the feelings and opinions of officers in their own areas, and will discuss with them matters coming before the National Executives and decisions it takes. But their role on the Executive is that of representatives in the parliamentary sense: they are required as individuals to make decisions in accordance with the aims and interests of the service and the Association as a whole.

For all its strongly democratic basis the Association has owed much to its leadership. In the earliest days, when probation officers were few and very poorly paid, it depended, quite frankly, on the interest and patronage of influential people from outside. Mr. Sidney Edridge, Clerk to the Justices at Croydon (who is commemorated by the Edridge Benevolent Fund which assists present or retired probation officers and their families if they are in need), was its founder and first chairman. He brought in such people as the Earl of Lytton, Sir William Clarke Hall, Miss Gertrude Tuckwell, and the Earl of Feversham, who had himself been involved in probation work in South Africa and whose contribution was a most notable one, extending over more than thirty years until his death in 1963. All these did much to stimulate interest in the Association and to raise money to support its work. But their eventual aim was to make it independent, self-governing and self-supporting. The first step towards this was taken with the employment of the first full-time Secretary, H. E. Norman. The second was the adoption of the modern democratic constitution in 1941.

Leadership from within the probation service has been given by a series of distinguished chairmen, all well seasoned in the work of the service and the branch and national activities of the Association. Most, but not all, have been principal probation officers; all but one have been men. The direction and emphasis of the Association's endeavours in each period of office has depended greatly upon the leadership, insight and foresight of the chairman; because of that members of the Association have taken a keen interest in elections to this and other national offices.

The office of full-time Secretary has also been of crucial importance. The Association has been particularly fortunate in the two men who have held this position longest: H. E. Norman and Frank Dawtry. It was "Skipper" Norman who virtually created the modern Association, on one hand developing the system of branches which gave so much scope for immediate local activity and, on the other, strengthening links with the Home Office through the strong working relationship he developed with Mr. (later Sir) Sidney Harris. Both Sir Sidney and Mr. Norman were elected Vice-Presidents of the Association after their retirements and their wise counsel remained available to it until their deaths.

Frank Dawtry was General Secretary for nearly twenty years, from 1948 to 1967. He brought with him a wide range of experience and contacts: amongst other things he had been the first welfare officer appointed by the National Association of Discharged Prisoners' Aid Societies to be based inside a prison and he had been Secretary of the National Council for the Abolition of the Death Penalty. His zeal for penal reform, his direct knowledge of work with offenders, his experience of political campaigning, were combined with his personal integrity, industry and deep concern for individuals in the service he gave the Association. He set it high professional standards, he helped to keep it constantly aware of what was going on in wider penal and political fields, he ensured that it spoke on the basis of the fullest available information and with an authoritative and respected voice. His services, too, were recognized in his appointment as a Vice-President when he retired, as well as by the award of the O.B.E. and by an honorary degree from Leeds University. His death within two years of retirement was a great loss to the Association and to many others concerned with the treatment of offenders.

From the outset, two central aims of the Association have been to stimulate and improve the work of probation officers and to foster public understanding of it. As the service became more órganized, professional and full-time, and as the Association itself became a democratic body, there was added to these increasing concern with the conditions of service, salaries and training. The constitution which established the modern organization of the Association in 1941, also set out its aims:—

   (a) To promote and assist in promoting the social welfare of the community by the practice of probation and kindred social services.

   (b) To provide a common ground where members can study, discuss and publish matters relating to the prevention and treatment of delinquency and the other social services of the courts, so that the most effective methods may be adopted to ensure the efficiency of the probation service.

   (c) To promote fellowship and co-operation among probation officers and all who are concerned in the administration of justice and the treatment of delinquents.

   (d) To ensure collective action on matters affecting the probation service; to protect and promote the welfare of probation officers and to improve conditions of service.

The first three of these objectives are in part achieved by the various branch and regional activities already referred to. In addition the Association holds its National Conference in a different part of the country every year. Whilst part of this is devoted to the internal affairs of the Association, the rest is open to associate members and others, and allows for discussion of important topics affecting the future of the service, such as training, or of still wider social and penal issues. Conferences have been addressed by experts from many fields; also by people in leading official positions, including Home Secretaries, the Lord Chief Justice and other judges, the Attorney-General, the Director of Public Prosecutions, the Chairman of the Prison Commissioners.

Another extensive contribution by the Association to promoting improvements in the work of the service and the treatment of offenders has been its evidence to many and various commissions and committees. It has never taken a narrow view of its functions in this direction. Whilst it has obviously had much to say to committees specifically appointed expressly to examine the service and its work, like those that reported in 1922, in 1936 and in 1962, it has also given evidence in many other contexts about matters affecting some particular aspect of its work or its clients or on which it has felt it has relevant experience. For example, the committees reporting on the treatment of young offenders in 1927, on corporal punishment in 1938, on homosexual offences and prostitution in 1957, on the business of the criminal courts in 1961, on children and young persons in 1960 and on local authority social services in 1968, all received evidence from the Association. A comprehensive series of statements was prepared for the abortive Royal Commission on the Penal System and the views of the Association were put before the Advisory Council on the Treatment of Offenders when it made its major enquiry into after-care. Evidence has also been given to independent enquiries, such as that of the Nuffield Foundation into causes of crime, joint B.M.A. and Magistrates' Association enquiries, a Labour Party study group on crime, and a committee established by the National Institute for Social Work Training and the National Council of Social Service on the use of voluntary workers.

Certain recent White Papers have had as much impact on the treatment of offenders and the role of the probation and after-care service as the formal enquiries. *The Adult Offender* foreshadowed the 1967 Criminal Justice Act. *Social Work and the Community* led to the Social Work (Scotland) Act. Both were the subject of detailed comment by the Association which strongly, though unsuccessfully, opposed the decision that probation officers in Scotland should become part of the new local authority social work service. Some of the proposals of the first of the two White Papers concerned with young offenders, *The Child, the Family and the Young Offender*, 1965, were also strongly opposed by the Association, particularly the suggestion that juvenile courts should be replaced by "family councils". This criticism contributed to the considerably modified plans outlined in the second Paper, *Children in Trouble*, 1968, which formed the basis of the Children and Young Persons Bill in 1969.

The Association has not confined itself to commenting in advance upon proposed legislation. It has closely followed the passage of this Bill, as it did with many earlier measures such as the Maintenance Orders Act 1958, the Children Act 1958, the Matrimonial Proceedings (Children) Act 1958, the Criminal Justice Act 1961, the Criminal Justice Administration Act 1962, the Criminal Justice (Scotland) Act 1963, the Children and Young Persons Act 1963, and the Criminal Justice Act 1967. This has involved keeping track of Committee proceedings, proposing amendments and providing information for Members of both Houses of Parliament—a service also extended to Members who have sought the Association's help in preparation for more general debates on penal matters, after-care or mental health. The Association has also been responsible from time to time for arranging parliamentary questions on matters of current concern to the probation and after-care service, and it has attached considerable importance to keeping matters relating to its work before Parliament. Whereas it was possible in 1948 for the House of Lords to conduct a full-day debate on juvenile delinquency without a single reference being made to the service, in 1958 a debate in the Commons was devoted entirely to its work, in 1962 there were two adjournment debates about its problems, and the service has been regularly referred to in recent debates about the penal system and the social services.

In many matters the Association has acted in co-operation with other bodies working in the same or kindred fields in this country, such as the Principal Probation Officers' Conference, the Central Council of Probation and After-Care Committees, the Magistrates' Association, the various associations of social workers, the National Association for Mental Health, the Institute for the Study and Treatment of Delinquency and the National Association for the Care and Resettlement of Offenders. On several occasions joint committees of such bodies and the Association have discussed matters of common concern, or views have been exchanged through deputations. The Association has often been able to call upon the experience of these bodies and similarly, from time to time, to make a contribution through them in a field somewhat wider than that of probation, after-care and the work of the courts, in which the experience of probation officers has nevertheless proved useful.

Alongside this close concern with policy and legislation at home, the Association has developed increasing communication with individuals and associations concerned with the treatment of offenders in other countries, and with international organizations. It has provided a link between probation officers in Britain and in other countries. Many of the Commonwealth countries have probation services which were pioneered by officers from Great Britain, and a number of them are now entirely local in staffing and administration. Their members call upon the Association for information and advice, and in many cases are in membership with the Association. This also applies to some who are working in probation or in kindred fields in America and in many of the European countries. There is a regular exchange of publications, and of information, between the Association and its members abroad. As the whole field of ideas and discussion about the treatment of offenders becomes increasingly international these links grow in importance. It is of interest that some European countries, which formerly thought of probation solely in terms of suspended sentence or of statutory supervision on release from prison, are now adopting it as we understand it here. Undoubtedly there is much that we, in turn, can learn from them and from other countries. To foster exchanges of experience and ideas is an important part of the work of an association concerned with the treatment of offenders.

The Association took an active part in the first United Nations European Seminar on Probation, held in London in 1952. In addition its headquarters and members are consulted by many individual visitors to this country. It has been consulted by the United Nations and U.N.E.S.C.O. on matters relating to probation and similar measures and it was represented at the International Congress on Mental Health in 1948; at the twelfth (and final) International Penal and Penitentiary Congress in the Hague in 1950; at the Conference of Northern European Criminologists in Copenhagen in 1952; at the United Nations Congress on the Prevention of Crime and the Treatment of Offenders in 1955, 1960 and 1965; at the Fifth International Congress on Criminology in London in 1955, and at the World Health Organization Seminar on the Psychiatric Treatment of Crime in Copenhagen in 1958.

To keep the public correctly informed about the work of the service the Association maintains contact with the press and the B.B.C. From its earliest days it has published the journal *Probation* which now appears every four months. Contributions from probation officers and both teachers and practitioners in the treatment of offenders, book reviews, parliamentary notes and a Forum are regular features of the journal, which circulates beyond the membership of the Association to magistrates, probation officers, social workers and universities in all parts of the world. (Since 1965 information about the internal affairs of the Association has been published in a separate monthly bulletin to probation office members.)

The first *Handbook of Probation*, edited by Le Mesurier, was published by the Association in 1935. The two previous editions of this volume, under the title of *The Probation Service*, were also prepared and published on behalf of the Association and written almost entirely by its members; so was *Social Problems of Drug Abuse*, edited by Frank Dawtry. In addition, the Association has published a series of monographs, almost all written by serving probation officers, on matters of professional interest. Their general title is *Probation Papers*: subjects so far covered include aspects of training, after-care, the selection and duties of senior probation officers, case recording and probation hostels.

The interest of the Association in the recruitment and training of probation officers can be seen as stemming both from its concern for the standards of work of the service and from its concern with the conditions of probation officers. It was an early advocate of training and has been a steady but constructive critic of the training methods introduced and maintained by the Home Office. It suggested that special training should be provided for officers supervising students in the field, a need which is now being met. It has supported the development of generic training for social workers, and has helped the service to take its proper place in the expansion of social work training in the universities. A policy statement on training was approved by the annual general meeting in 1968 and has been under discussion with the Home Office. The Association has constantly pressed its view that the service cannot command the standing its work justifies until there is a well established or recognized standard both of recruitment and training. It has urged the Home Office that officers should be appointed only if they have undergone such training. The Association welcomes improvements in the financial arrangements for students—a significant factor in recruitment—and advocates an extension of training courses for mature entrants to two years.[1]

The early conception of probation work as a vocation was long used to justify salaries or fees of a very low order and it was not until the Departmental Committee of 1936 issued its report that any serious attempt was made to provide a reasonable standard of salary for probation officers. Negotiations on salaries up to 1946

---

1. On the Association's view on training see also above, pp. 251 and 265–266.

were conducted directly between the Association and the Home Office, but as almost half the cost of the service is borne by the local authorities within each probation area, the Home Secretary then decided that a negotiating body to recommend terms and conditions of employment for probation officers should be established and should represent all interests. This was eventually set up in 1950. It was made up of representatives of the local authorities, the Home Office and the Magistrates' Association on one side and of representatives of the National Association of Probation Officers on the other. The Association was thus recognized as the sole organization competent to represent probation officers in negotiations about conditions of service. In 1965, following the Report of the Morison Committee, the constitution of the Joint Negotiating Committee was revised, so as to give a more even balance of representation between the employing bodies, now represented through the Central Council of Probation Committees instead of the Magistrates' Association, and the paying authorities. Ironically enough, it was only in 1965 that the salaries and conditions of probation officers in Scotland were brought within the same negotiating machinery as that for England and Wales. The Joint Negotiating Committee now includes eight representatives of local authorities in England and Wales plus seven of the Central Council of Probation and After-Care Committees, one of the Home Office.

The Morison Committee also recommended that the power of the Secretary of State to prescribe the salaries of probation officers should be terminated. But in view of the current economic climate involving close government scrutiny of all proposed salary increases it is difficult to see this power being relinquished in the near future. However, it was agreed that salaries should be reviewed every two years and in 1966 the first comprehensive agreement was concluded. It included a substantial revision of the structure of the salary scale, for the first time recognizing that qualifications and experience should be factors in determining an officer's starting salary. The new pay scale, when fully implemented, brought improvements to all ranks of the service.

Through the Joint Negotiating Committee also, the Association has been able to negotiate improvements in travelling and subsistence allowances for officers and an improved sick-leave scheme.

Moreover, it has gained for its members the right to be represented by their Association, should they so wish, in the unfortunate case of any dispute with an employing committee in which the officer's suitability for office is called into question. A code of conditions of service applying to England and Wales was produced in July 1965 after protracted negotiation and marked a great advance in establishing proper conditions of service for officers and in clarifying the permissive and mandatory powers of employing committees. A revision of the code is now being undertaken.

In all these activities the Association has achieved recognition as a fully representative organization for the probation and after-care service in Great Britain. However, the practice of probation and the other functions of the service place probation officers within a larger group as professional social workers. As the Morison report said, "Today, the probation officer must be seen, essentially, as a professional caseworker, employing, in a specialized field, skill which he holds in common with other social workers". In recent years the various groups of professional social workers have begun to draw closer together, and to develop the concept of a single profession. In 1963 seven of these bodies, including the Association, formed the Standing Conference of Organizations of Social Workers. The Standing Conference, with the later addition of an eighth organization, brought together child care officers, medical and psychiatric social workers, mental welfare officers, family caseworkers, moral welfare workers and other social workers, as well as probation officers.

The Standing Conference was not envisaged as a permanent form of collaboration, but rather as a means to enable the organizations to work together whilst considering what permanent structure might be established to give expression to the growing sense of professional identity of social workers. In 1967 all the organizations considered a paper setting out the alternatives of a federal structure or complete unification. As a result, seven of the organizations decided to go ahead to full unification, but the Association held back, indicating that it was prepared to consider only a federal structure. The decision of the other organizations however obliged the Association to reconsider its position, and at its annual general meeting in 1968, and afterwards in a referendum of its members, a small majority favoured unification, provided they could be satisfied that the constitution of a new organization would satisfactorily protect the interests of the Association's members.

The issue has caused members to question fundamentally the nature of their profession. It is unfortunate that in some debates it should have been implied that the choice before the Association was exclusive identification either with the profession of social work, or with the penal system. One of the greatest contributions of both the Association and the service lies in their involvement in both: if either is lost, much of their value and potential is lost with it. Strong links need to be maintained both with other fields of social work and with others involved in the administration of justice and the treatment of offenders.

A second source of questioning has been the size and the catholic nature of the proposed new body. It is these that seem to promise greater interchange of ideas, and greater influence on public policy. Yet at the same time there is anxiety as to whether such a body could deal as effectively with the special problems connected with the treatment of offenders and the work of the service. The provision of specialist sections within the new organization is intended to mitigate doubts of this kind which, of course, affect other groups of social workers as well as probation officers.

The matter is still open. In the middle of 1969 it was decided that there should be a referendum when members had had an opportunity of considering the draft constitution of the proposed British Association of Social Workers. A two-thirds majority would be required for joining.

In any case it will be a matter of major concern for probation officers that all the central objectives of the Association shall be maintained: the development of the work of the service and of the prevention and treatment of delinquency; co-operation amongst all concerned with the treatment of offenders. Local, central and international links, not only with social workers but with courts, the penal system and penal reform; the collection and sifting of experience and the presentation of evidence; influence upon specialist and public opinion through various channels; parliamentary work; negotiating machinery: all these have contributed to the Association's effectiveness. All of them would need to find equivalents within any new and larger association. They are vital not only to the service but to those it works with and those it serves.

INDEX

A

ACTIVITY GROUPS
nature of, 162
ADMINISTRATION
appointments, 233
casework and, 230
equipment, 229
future developments, 223
inspection of probation area, 234
principal officer, function of, 230
Probation and After-Care Committees, 220
problems, 227
staff, 227
students, training of, 233
supervision, 231
training
in-service, 232
See also TRAINING
training schemes, 228
ADOLESCENCE
delinquency in, 86
drug addiction, 179
insecurity in, 87
teenage culture, 87
ADULT PRISONERS
after-care responsibilities, 16
ADVISORY COUNCIL FOR PRO-
BATION AND AFTER-CARE
Home Office department, 34
AFTER-CARE
administration, 220 et seq.
adult prisoners, 16
approved schools, 16
Borstals, 16
casework in, 119
committees. See PROBATION AND
AFTER-CARE COMMITTEES
compulsory, 121
discharged convicts, 16
ex-prisoners
practical problems of, 125
types of, 123
group work, 160
hostels, 148, 155
listening, principles of, 124
mentally abnormal, 168, 172
parole, 48
penal institutions, 41
prison, 29
voluntary, 24

AFTER-CARE—contd.
prison welfare, 54
re-establishment in society, 23
specialized provision, 57
statutory, 44, 122
voluntary, 53, 122, 140
young offenders, 44
See also PROBATION AND AFTER-CARE
SERVICE
ALCOHOLISM
age factor, 175
Alcoholics Anonymous, 161, 176
drunken offences, 175
hostels, 160
voluntary, 175
meths drinkers, 176
prison system, 176
probation order, use of, 176
Rathcoole, 177
Simon Community, 177
APPLICATIONS
entry into service. See TRAINING
APPROVED SCHOOLS
after-care responsibilities, 16

B

BORSTALS
after-care responsibilities, 16
group work in, 165
study of régimes, 284
supervision notices, 45
BRAIN COMMITTEE
drug addiction, 178
BREACH OF PROBATION ORDER
See PROBATION OFFICER; PROBATION
ORDER

C

CARE AND PROTECTION
children and young persons in need
of, 7
CASEWORK
acceptance of the individual, 91
administration and, 230
after-care, 119
assumptions, basic, 90
case records, 108
clarification, 102

CASEWORK—*contd.*
confidence, 96
contact, ending of, 106
control, 102
courts, in context of, 197
definition, 25
diagnosis, 100
drug addicts, 182
duty and, 97
emotional involvement, 99
environmental aspect, 104, 129
evaluation, 100
fact-finding, 100
flexibility, 101
freedom, 94
generally, 83
help, provision of practical, 105
insight, development of, 102
interview, 107
matrimonial, 131
method, choice and emphasis of, 106
offender, needs of, 112
permissiveness in society, 92
planning of treatment, 100
principles of, 90
prisoners' families, 127
prisons, in, 113
probationers, relationships with, 88
processes of, 100
psychotherapy, contrasted with, 103
relationship, 98
self-awareness in, 92
self-determination, right of, 94
self-responsibility, 96
social enquiries, 110
starting point of, 101
support, 102
tools, 107
transference, 99
treatment
  direction of, 101
  planning of, 100
uniqueness of an individual, 90
values, 92
visits, 108
CENTRAL ASSOCIATION FOR DISCHARGED CONVICTS
after-care of offenders, 16
CHILDREN
child guidance, 205
children's departments, 204
education, 205
school counselling, 206
social enquiry reports, 79
special problems, 87
supervision of, 28
  in matrimonial proceedings, 80
welfare of, 77

CHILDREN AND YOUNG PERSONS ACT 1933
care and protection, 7
CHILDREN'S ACT 1963
supervision provided by, 7
CHURCH ARMY
hostels, 156
CHURCH OF ENGLAND TEMPERANCE SOCIETY
activities of, 3
CHURCHES AND CHAPELS
community relations, 207
COMMITTEES
See PROBATION AND AFTER-CARE COMMITTEES
COMMUNITY RELATIONS
agencies, inter-relationships of, 200
children's departments, 204
churches and chapels, 207
community involvement, 203
development, 219
generally, 200
involvement, 216
leisure, organization of, 207
offender, attitude towards, 210
personal social services, 209
principles and problems, 210
protection, 212
rehabilitation of offender, 209
services, local and national, 201
social provisions, shortcomings of, 201
social service departments proposed, 203
youth employment services, 206
See also SOCIETY
CONDITIONAL DISCHARGE
See DISCHARGE
COURTS
decisions concerning probation, 88
magistrates and probation officers, 225
matrimonial relief, 74
probation officer and, 184
CRIMINAL JUSTICE ACT 1967
parole, introduction of system of, 18
probation and after-care service, 5

D

DAMAGES
offender to pay, 9
DANGEROUS DRUGS ACT 1965
provisions of, 179
DAYTOP LODGE
drug addiction, 182
DELINQUENCY
adolescent, 86

DELINQUENCY—*contd.*
poverty and bad housing, link, with, 23
DEPARTMENTAL COMMITTEE ON THE PROBATION SERVICE 1962
See Morison Committee
DETENTION CENTRES
supervision notices, 45
DISCHARGE
conditional, to replace probation order, 13
DISCHARGED PRISONERS' AID ASSOCIATIONS
after-care, 16
DIVORCE
See Matrimonial Cases
DRUGS
absue, 178
Brain Committee, 178
courts, attitudes of, 180
Dangerous Drugs Act 1965, 179
Daytop Lodge, 182
dependence, 179
emancipation through, 87
penal institutions, 181

E

EDUCATION
local authority service, 205
school counsellors, 206
EMPLOYMENT
youth employment services, 206
EMPLOYMENT EXCHANGES
responsibility for finding work, 20
ENQUIRIES
duty of probation officer to report, 14
See also Reports; Social Enquiry Reports

F

FAMILY
casework with prisoners', 127
probationer's, 86
FAMILY DISCUSSION BUREAU
marital casework 134
work of, 75
FINANCIAL DIFFICULTIES
family, 22
FINE
breach of probation order, for, 13
supervision, reconciled with, 10
supervision order, 18
FREEDOM
individual liberty, 211

G

GANGS
delinquent, 85
GRENDON SYSTEM
psychiatric facilities, 171
GROUP WORK
activity groups, 162
Alcoholics Anonymous, 161, 176
Borstals, in, 165
confidentiality, 164
dangers of, 163
discussion groups, 166
Howard Centre for Penology, 163
permissiveness, 165
probation officers, by, 161
psychiatric experiments, 163
GUARDIANSHIP
probation officer as guardian *ad litem*, 81
social enquiry reports, 79

H

HOME
See Parents
HOME OFFICE
central training course, 260
Children's Branch, 34
Probation and After-Care Department, 34, 222
Probation Division, 34
responsibilities of, 33
HOSTELS
after-care, 148, 155
alcoholism, 160, 175, 177
Church Army, 156
finance, 158
links, 160
mentally abnormal, 174
multi-purpose, 157
offenders over 21, 154
penal institutions, as an alternative to, 147
prison scheme, 155
probation home, compared with, 149
Rathcoole, 177
Regional Group Consultative Committees, 157, 226
residential child care, courses in, 159
Salvation Army, 156
staff, 159
value of, 151
wardens
tasks and duties of, 159
training of, 160
HOWARD CENTRE FOR PENOLOGY
group work courses, 163

I

IMMIGRANTS
  probation officer, relation with, 132
IMPRISONMENT
  supervision, reconciled with, 10
INSPECTION
  probation area, of, 234
INSTITUTION
  requirements of residence in, 12

J

JUVENILE COURT
  conviction, expression abandoned, 7
  supervision orders, 7

K

KILBRANDON REPORT
  generally, 5

L

LEISURE
  organization of, 207
  uses for, 21

M

MARRIAGE
  breaking, 72
  matrimonial conciliation, 72
  See also MATRIMONIAL CASES
MARRIAGE GUIDANCE
    COUNCILS
  work of, 76
MATRIMONIAL CASES
  casework, 131
    principles of clarification, 132
  children, welfare of, 77
  children of marriages breaking up,
    enquiries concerning, 15
  conciliation, 72
  court, direct application to, 73
  courts, relief from, 74
  divorce, welfare work and, 78
  Family Discussion Bureau, 75
  Marriage Guidance Councils, 76
  means, reports on, 81
  Morison Committee, views of, 73
  peace negotiations, 134
  principles of probation officers' work,
    24
  probation officer
    legal aspects and, 74
    role of, 194
  probation officers as conciliators, 15
  reconciliation, possibility of, 133

MATRIMONIAL CASES—contd.
  special needs in, 75
  supervision of children of parties in,
    80
  support, 133
  Tavistock Clinic, 75
  See also MARRIAGE
MENTAL HEALTH
  alcoholism. See ALCOHOLISM
  discharge from prison, 171
  drug addiction. See DRUGS
  Grendon prison hospital, 171
  home leave, 171
  hostels proposed, 174
  medical treatment, 169
  Mental Health Act 1959, 170
  mentally abnormal offenders, 168 et
    seq.
  Morison Committee, views of, 170
  Prison Medical Service, Report on
    the Organization of, 171
  probation officer, role of, 169
  probation requiring treatment, 168
  psychopathic disorder, 172
  recall centres proposed, 174
  restriction order cases, 171
  treatment, requirement of, 12
  Van der Hoeven Clinic, 173
MENTAL HEALTH ACT 1959
  provisions of, 12
MINISTRY OF SOCIAL
    SECURITY
  grant to discharged prisoner, 57
MISSIONARIES
  early activities of, 13
  first probation officers, 26
  police court, 3
    authority of, 23
MORISON COMMITTEE
  casework defined, 25
  hostels, views on, 153
  matrimonial work, views on, 73
  mental treatment, views on, 170
  orders not to be substitutes for proba-
    tion, 19
  probation, case for, 6
  review of probation service, 4
  salaries, views on, 298
  social enquiry reports, 191
  training, views on, 255
  voluntary duties, views on, 236

N

NATIONAL ASSOCIATION FOR
    THE CARE AND RESETTLE-
    MENT OF OFFENDERS
  after-care hostels, 158

NATIONAL ASSOCIATION OF PROBATION OFFICERS
aims, 292
commissions and committees, 293
Executive Committee, 291
functions, 34
international relationships, 295
legislation, comment on proposed, 294
membership, 290
other bodies, co-operation with, 295
Parliamentary questions arranged by, 295
press and radio contacts, 296
publications, 297
salary negotiations, 297
Secretary, 292
Standing Conference, 299
training, views on, 297
NEW BRIDGE
voluntary social help, 140

O

OFFENDERS
acceptance of, 92
Advisory Council on Treatment of Offenders, 17
community, attitude of, 210
enquires. *See* SOCIAL ENQUIRY REPORTS
families of, 70
homeless, 157
hostels for adult, 154
mentally abnormal, 168 *et seq.*
needs of, 112
probation officer, relationship with, 25
probation officer's report, knowledge of, 192
rehabilitation of, 209
reports on, 15
sentimental approach to, 214
treatment, expenditure on, 213
See also YOUNG OFFENDERS
ORDERS
probation, not a substitute for, 19

P

PARENTS
responsibility of, 21
PAROLE
conditions of, 51
dossier, 50
eligibility, 47
introduction of, 18
licence, period of, 52

PAROLE—*contd.*
mentally abnormal, 168
probation service and, 48
duties of, 52
recommendations for, 51
rejection for, 49
release, likely circumstances on, 50
selection of men for, 48
PENAL INSTITUTIONS
drug addicts in, 181
hostels an alternative to, 147
parole. *See* PAROLE
prison welfare, 42
See also PRISON WELFARE
probation officers, links with, 46
probation service and, 41 *et seq.*
social work in, development of, 121
training of probation officers in connection with, 247
young offenders. *See* YOUNG OFFENDERS
See also PRISON WELFARE
PERMISSIVENESS
social acceptance, 92
POLICE
probation officers, relation with, 202
POLICE COURT MISSION
early activities of, 3
PRISON
after-care, 29
voluntary after-care, 24
PRISON WELFARE
after-care, 54, 119
specialized, 57
alcoholism, 176
casework, 113
diagnostic aspect, 115
special difficulties, 118
confidentiality, 118
diagnosis, 116
discussions on regional basis, 226
families of offenders, 70
family, contact with prisoner's, 56
governor, assistant, role of, 64
governor, role of, 61
Grendon prison hospital, 171
homeless men, 57
hostel scheme, 155
initial interview, unhurried, 55, 66
mentally abnormal, 171
Ministry of Social Security, grant from, 57
officers, 54
Influence of, 67
team conception, 63
work of, 59
prisoner, social settings of, 113

PRISON WELFARE—*contd.*
  probation officer
    correspondence with, 55
    duties of, 18
  probation service and, 42
  Reception Centres, 156
  release
    basic needs on, 57
    maintenance of contact after, 58
  research, 69
  Seebohm Committee, 71
  self-responsibility, principle of, 115
  social enquiries, 68
  syndrome of the 'good prisoner', 116
  treatment
    planning of, 117
    teams, 65
  Wakefield, course at, 271
  wives and children of offenders, 70
PRISONERS' WIVES SERVICE
  functions of, 144
PROBATION
  breach of, reporting, 196
  case for, 6
  child guidance, 205
  courts, decisions of, 88
  discharge, distinction from, 8
  files, 288
  financial difficulties, 22
  homes, 152
    hostels, and, 149
  mentally abnormal, 168
  officer. *See* PROBATION OFFICER
  punishment, distinction from, 8
  reports before, 14
  sentimentality, 214
  situational treatment, 208
  suitability for, 283
  training. *See* TRAINING
  treatment of offenders, successful, 214
  work, main features of, 235
  youth employment services, 206
PROBATION AND AFTER-CARE
    COMMITTEES
  case committees, 32
  Central Council of Probation and
    After-Care Committees, 32
  composition, 220
  functions of, 31
  funds, 221
  professional advice, 222
PROBATION AND AFTER-CARE
    SERVICE
  acceptance, principle of, 25
  administration, 220 *et seq.*
  Advisory Council, 34, 223
  after-care, classes of, 16
  alcoholism, 175

PROBATION AND AFTER-CARE
    SERVICE—*contd.*
  applications for entry. *See* TRAINING
    basis, 1 *et seq.*
  care and protection, 7
  casework. *See* CASEWORK
  change in, 35 *et seq.*
  children and young people, 77
  Children and Young Persons Act
    1933, 7
  Children and Young Persons' Bill
    1969, 7
  Children's Act 1963, 7
  committees. *See* PROBATION AND
    AFTER-CARE COMMITTEES
  conditions, 11
  cost of, 226
  Criminal Justice Act 1967, 5
  Departmental Committee on, Report
    of, 4, 6
  drug addiction. *See* DRUGS
  experimental work, 39
  family advice service, as, 16
  financial difficulties, 22
  future directions, 35, 223
  general survey, 35
  group work. *See* GROUP WORK
  historical perspective, 1 *et seq.*
  Home Office, responsibilities of, 33
  immigrants, 132
  institutions, requirement of residence
    in, 12
  intermediate treatment measures, 21
  Kilbrandon Report, 5
  legal basis, 6
  legislation, early, 4
  local nature of, 223
  material resources, 229
  matrimonial casework, 15, 131
  mental treatment, 12, 170
    requirement of, 12
  Morison Committee, 4
  officers. *See* PROBATION OFFICER
  parents, direct approach by, 16
  parole
    duties in relations to release on, 52
    system of, 18, 48
  penal institutions, 41 *et seq.*
  prison welfare, 18, 42
    See also PRISON WELFARE
  prisons, work in, 59
  probation, case for, 6
  Probation of First Offenders Bill,
    1886, 3
  Probation of Offenders Act 1907, 1
  recognizance, 2
  regional responsibility, 226
  regionalization, 43

PROBATION AND AFTER-CARE SERVICE—*contd.*

requirements, 11
research. *See* RESEARCH
residence, requirement of, 12
roots, 1
Scotland, in, 5
social enquiry reports. *See* SOCIAL ENQUIRY REPORTS
staff development, 271
Streatfeild Report 1961, 15
students, training of, 233
Summary Jurisdiction Act 1879, 3
supervision. *See* SUPERVISION
training. *See* TRAINING
volunteers, attitude towards, 142
young offenders, 44

PROBATION OF OFFENDERS ACT 1907

provisions of, 1

PROBATION OFFICER

acceptance, principle of, 25
after-care, statutory, 122
after-care responsibilities, 16
agencies, relation with other official, 200
alcoholism, 175
appointment, 26
attitudes and personality of, 30
authority of, 95, 195
breach of probation, reporting, 196
casework. *See* CASEWORK
character of, 26
children and young people, duties related to welfare of, 77
classes of after-care, 16
community agencies, use of, 162
community repercussions, 201
Conference of Principal Probation Officers, 222
contacts, regular, 95
correspondence with prisoner, 55
courts, work related to, 184
drug addiction. *See* DRUGS
duty of, 97
    classes of, 235
    extraneous, 17
educational attainments of, 27
educational authorities, contact with, 205
enquiries, 14. *See also* SOCIAL ENQUIRY REPORTS
families of offenders, 21, 70
fines supervision orders, 18
generally, 26
group work, 161
guardian *ad litem*, 81
immigrants, relations with, 132

PROBATION OFFICER—*contd.*

legal authority for work of, 23
leisure, organization of, 207
loyalty, claims on, 195
magistrates and, 225
matrimonial cases, 15, 72 *et seq.*
    See also MATRIMONIAL CASES
matrimonial casework, 131, 194
men and women, 28
mental health cases, 169
missionaries, first, 26
National Association, 34
    See also NATIONAL ASSOCIATION OF PROBATION OFFICERS
offender, relationship with, 25
one-to-one relationship with offender, 10
parole, enquiries in relation to, 50
Parole Board functions, 18
part-time, 28, 30
payment of, 27
penal institutions, links with, 46
police, relation with, 202
principal
    activities of, 232
    appointment of, 222
    senior probation officer, and, 32, 33
prison, attitude to régime, 62
prison welfare, 18
prisons, work in, 61
psychiatrist, co-operation with, 169
recruitment, 37
religious conviction, 27
research worker, and. *See* RESEARCH
satisfaction of work, 238
school counselling, 206
situational treatment, 208
social competence of probationer, development of, 21
social enquiry reports, 110
    See also SOCIAL ENQUIRY REPORTS
social worker, as, 15, 20
specialization, 30, 237
statutory duties, 236
teams of, 10
training
    in-service, 232
    See also TRAINING
training schemes, 228
    See also TRAINING
voluntary, 28, 29
voluntary duties, 236
voluntary help, responsibility for, 138
voluntary organizations, help from, 208
women, 28
work
    helping people find, 20

PROBATION OFFICER—*contd.*
work—*contd.*

main features of, 235
young offenders, 44, 46

PROBATION ORDER
alcoholic, 176
breach of, 12
conditional discharge, replacement
by order of, 13
discharge of, 13
explanation given to offender, 8
hostels, 148
implications of, 95
instrument in treatment of offenders,
24
offender, consent of, 7
origin, 2
punishment, considered as by
offender, 9
variation of, 13

PROBATIONER
address, change of, 11
breach of order, 12
childhood, 85
criminality, factors in, 84
discharge of order, right to apply for,
13
family, 86
financial difficulties, 22
generally, 84
hostels for, 148
intermediate treatment measures, 21
interviews with, 107
leisure activities, 21
mental treatment, requirement of, 12
mentally abnormal, 168 *et seq.*
officer, visits from, 11
relationships, ability to form, 88
restrictions upon, 11
social competence, development of,
21
social groups, 85
supervision of, generally, 193
variation of order, right to apply for,
13
visits to, 108
work, record of, 86

PROJECTS
research, 287

PSYCHIATRY
adult psychiatric services, 205
after-care, 172
diagnosis of mentally abnormal, 168
group work experiments, 163
psychiatrist, co-operation with probation officer, 169

R

RATHCOOLE
hostel for alcoholics, 177
RECEPTION CENTRES
ex-prisoners, for, 156
RECOGNIZANCE
device of, 2
REGIONALIZATION
generally, 226
inspectorate, 234
**REPORT OF THE DEPARTMENT-
AL COMMITTEE ON THE
PROBATION SERVICE** 1962
See MORISON COMMITTEE
REPORTS
divorce courts, 79
drug addiction cases, 180
guardianship, 79
history and surroundings of offender,
14
parole dossier, 50
Streatfeild Report 1961, 15
See also SOCIAL ENQUIRY REPORTS
RESEARCH
allied fields, clinical experience in,
276
files, analysis of, 288
Mannheim-Wilkins prediction tables,
283
National Study of Probation, programme of, 279
penological generally, 274
pioneering studies, 281
probation, suitability for, 283
probation officer and research
worker, 276
probation officers, initiated by, 285
Probation Research Project, 277
programmes of, 287
projects, 287
re-conviction rates, 283, 284
San Francisco Project, 281
teacher, 288
RESIDENCE
requirement of, 12

S

SALVATION ARMY
hostels, 156
SAMARITANS
voluntary social service, 136
SCOTLAND
service in, 5
SEEBOHM COMMITTEE
community development, 219
Local Authority and Allied Personal
Social Services, 202

SEEBOHM COMMITTEE—*contd.*
 social service departments, 71
 training suggestions, 247
SIMON COMMUNITY
 alcoholism, 177
 voluntary social service, 136
SOCIAL ENQUIRY REPORTS
 casework in, 110
 children
  in relation to custody of, 79
  of marriages breaking up, concerning, 15
 content and purpose, 189
 diagnosis, 111
 divorce courts, 79
 family, interviews with, 189
 generally, 185
 guardianship, 79
 Home Secretary recommendations,
  188
 interviews, 111
 Morison Committee, views of, 191
 offender, personality of, 190
 offender's knowledge of report, 192
 parole, in relation to, 50
 pre-trial, 186
 prison welfare officer, by, 68
 probation officer as defending
  counsel, 190
 reading aloud in court, 192
 selection, 187
 Streatfeild Report, 188, 191
 timing of, 186
SOCIAL GROUPS
 delinquent gangs, 85
SOCIAL WORKER
 acceptance, principle of, 25
 confidential information and, 98
 emotional involvement, 99
 matrimonial cases, 76
 prisons, in, 59
 probation officer as, 15, 20
 resources of, 93
 society, changing values of, 93
 staff, relation with other institutional,
  63
 Standing Conference, 299
 See also CASEWORK
SOCIETY
 permissiveness, 92
 values, changing, 93
 See also COMMUNITY RELATIONS
STANDING CONFERENCE OF
 ORGANIZATIONS OF
 SOCIAL WORKERS
 formation of, 299

STREATFEILD REPORT 1961
 reports on offenders, 15
 social enquiries, 188
STUDENTS
 training of, 233
 See also TRAINING
SUMMARY JURISDICTION ACT
  1879
 discharge of offenders permitted, 3
SUPERVISION
 administrative function, 231
 after-care, 122
 Borstals, notice from, 45
 breach of probation, 196
 children, of, 28
 Children and Young Persons' Bill
  1969, 7
 children of
  marriages breaking up, 15
  parties to matrimonial proceedings, 80
 Children's Act 1963, 7
 consultation function, 231
 detention centres, notice from, 45
 evaluation function, 231
 fine, reconciled with, 10
 fines supervision orders, 18
 hostels, 148
 imprisonment, reconciled with, 10
 notice of, 45
 orders, 7
 period of, 11
 petty sessional division named, 10
 positive weapon, as, 9
 probation officer
  authority of, 195
  by named, 10
 probationers, 193 *et seq.*
 requirements, failure to comply with
  notice, 45
 San Francisco Project, 281
 senior probation officer, function of,
  232
 supervisor, duties defined, 7
 teaching function, 231
 young offenders, 45

T

TAVISTOCK CLINIC
 work of, 75
TEAMWORK ASSOCIATES
 voluntary social help, 139
TEENAGE CULTURE
 commercial fostering of, 87
TEMPERANCE
 Church of England Temperance
  Society, activities of, 3

TRAINING
actualities, first contact with, 262
applications, scrutiny of, 251
appointments, confirmation of, 268
block placement system, 261
candidates for, 251
concurrent system, 263
courses, theoretical content of, 258
emotional self-control, 242
entry without, 250
generic elements, 258
graduates, entry of, 252
Home Office central course, 260
in-service, 267
legal knowledge, 242
length of, 255
mature entrants, 255
moral values and judgments, 248
National Association of Probation
   Officers, views of, 297
necessity for, 240
organization of, 254
penal institutions, 247
phased, 257
practical experience, 260
principles, general, 249
prison welfare, 271
Probation College, idea of, 267
professional development, reports on,
   269
psychological methods, 244
records, 243
recruitment of graduates, 252
Regional Committees, 272
reports, preparation of, 243
residential courses, short, 270
responsibility for, 264
Seebohm Committee suggestions, 247
seminars, special, 270
social conditions and services, knowledge of, 243
Social Work Training Council
   proposed, 266
society knowledge of, 246
staff development, 271
subjects to be taught, 241
supervision of students, 263
TRANSFERENCE
casework in, 99
drug addiction, 182

V

VAN DER HOEVEN CLINIC
psychotherapy at, 173

VOLUNTARY AFTER-CARE
See AFTER-CARE

VOLUNTARY HELP
failures and discouragements, 147
historical aspects, 136
homeless discharged offenders, provisions for, 156
hostels, 157
married prisoners, work with, 144
New Bridge, 140
organizations, 208
prisoners, long-term relationships
   with, 143
Prisoners' Wives Service, 144
responsibility, 138
Samaritans, 136
Simon Community, 136
Teamwork Associates, 139
volunteer, activities of, 145
volunteers
   exact role of, 137
   range of activities of, 137
   recruitment of, 141
   selection of, 145
Working Party on Voluntary Service
   in After-Care, 140
W.R.V.S., 140

W

WHITE PAPERS
Adult Offender, The, 294
Child, the Family and the Young
   Offender, The, 37, 294
Children in Trouble, 28, 294
Social Work and the Community, 294
WORK
unsatisfactory record of, 86
youth employment services, 206
See also EMPLOYMENT EXCHANGES

Y

YOUNG OFFENDERS
probation officer, work of, 46
statutory after-care, 44
supervision, period of, 45
YOUNG PEOPLE
welfare of, 77
youth employment services, 206

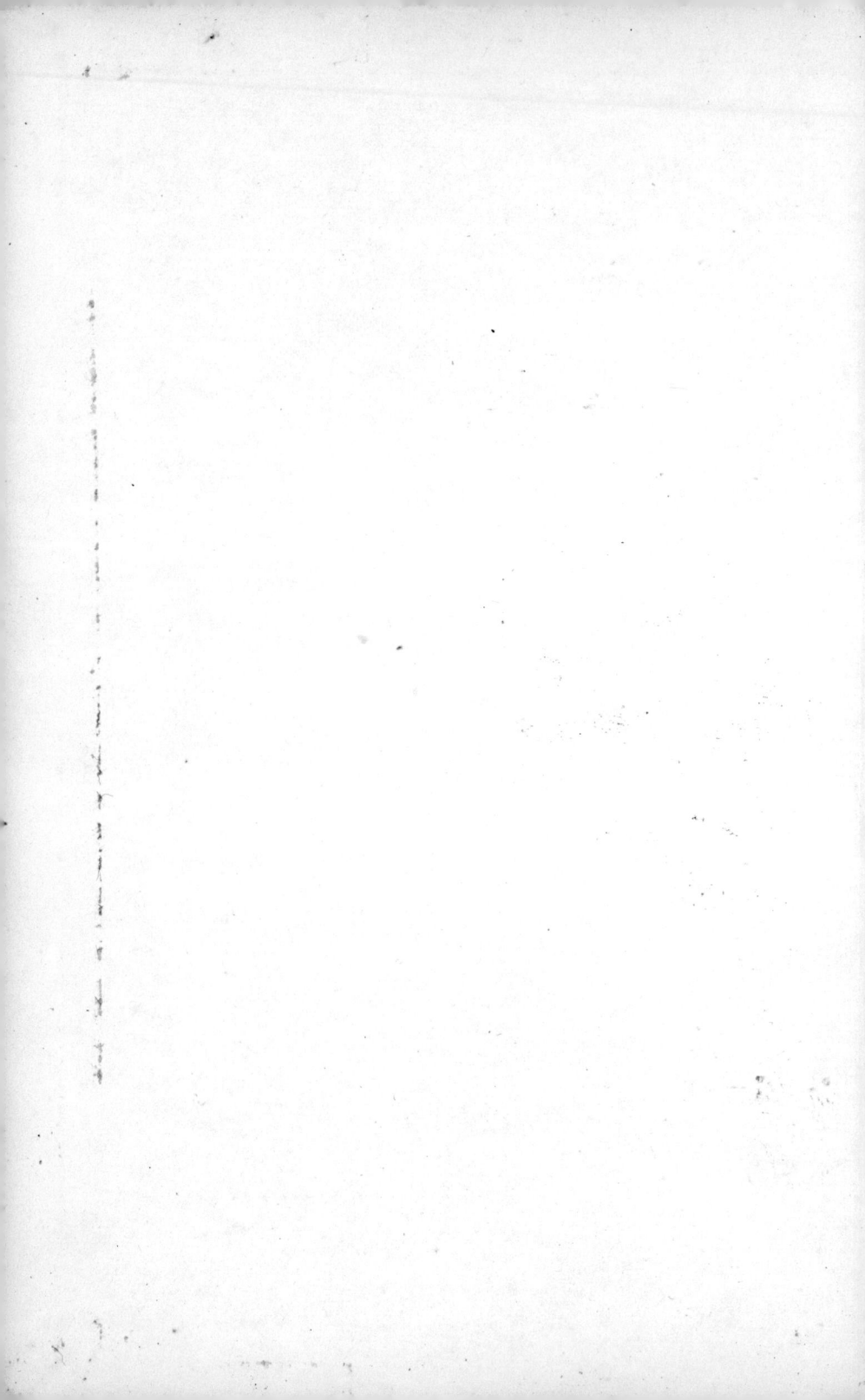